EDWARD HEATH
PRIME MINISTER

Edward Heath

Prime Minister

Margaret Laing

SIDGWICK & JACKSON

LONDON

First published in Great Britain
by Sidgwick and Jackson Limited in 1972
Copyright © 1972 by Margaret Laing

ISBN 0 283 97859 7

Made and printed in Great Britain by
William Clowes & Sons, Limited
London, Beccles and Colchester
for Sidgwick and Jackson Limited
1 Tavistock Chambers, Bloomsbury Way
London WC1A 2SG

Acknowledgements

Among the many people who have helped me in gathering material for this book, I should particularly like to thank the Prime Minister, his father, Mr William Heath, his step-mother, Mrs Mary Heath, and his brother, Mr John Heath.

In the Cabinet, I am indebted to Lord Carrington, Mr James Prior, Mr Peter Walker and Mr William Whitelaw. Sir Michael Fraser and members of the Conservative Research Department provided help and access to records. Among the Prime Minister's own staff, I should particularly like to thank Miss Rosemary Bushe, Mr Douglas Hurd and Mr Michael Wolff.

Others who contributed greatly to my research include: Mr Julian Amery, Mr James Bird, Col. and Mrs George Chadd, Mr Anthony Churchill, Mr Patrick Cosgrave, Mr Cecil Curzon, Mr Edward Denman, Mr Edward Dines, Mr Hugh Fraser, Lord Fulton, Lord Hailes, Mr Ian Harvey, Mr Denis Healey, Major W. Harrington, Mr Philip Kaiser, Mr Anthony Kershaw, Mr Gordon Knight, Miss Moura Lympany, Mr John MacGregor, Mr Michael MacLagan, Mr Peter Masefield, Lord Morris, Mr K. Potten, Mr Reginald Pye, Mr Vincent Quinn, Mrs Jean Raven, Miss Margaret Raven, Mr William Rodgers, Sir Eric Roll, Mr & Mrs Madron Seligman and the *Sunday Times* and *The Times* libraries.

Contents

Illustrations

Plates are by kind courtesy of Madron Seligman, Major W. Harrington, M.B.E., the Keystone Press Agency Ltd, and Popperfoto

1
Alternatives

Towards the middle of June 1970, Edward Richard George Heath woke several days running from his normally heavy sleep with an unaccustomed feeling of gloom. The sensation was most acute during the week before the election on Thursday, 18 June. Some members of the Conservative election team regarded his depression as a dangerous loss of morale but an accurate marker of his low political ebb. Frankly they did not expect him to win.

Yet at the end of that election week he had become the country's least expected Prime Minister since Clement Attlee, with whom he shared that 'extraordinary ordinariness' defined by Harry Boardman of the *Guardian*: 'True there is no colour, no magnetism, but there is great concentration of purpose, a mind with a razor edge, and something of harsh resolution.' He became, too, the most unlikely Conservative Prime Minister since Disraeli, for working-class origins had taken still longer than Jewishness to win acceptance in his party. In the anxious days of the previous week he himself was convinced that twenty years of ambition were coming to an end: within the week, he thought, he would have left politics for good and chosen a new career.

Most members of his own party, of the Opposition, of the Press, of the pollsters, and therefore apparently of the public, agreed with him. Four years earlier he had lost an election by the biggest margin since 1945. Two-thirds of the British electorate since 1884 had been working class; yet in eleven of the thirteen elections since then in which a single party held the majority of seats, the Conservatives had won.[1] Some assumed this was because of a deferential element in the working-class voters to whom Heath's similar background would make little appeal.

As a bachelor Heath was unlike any Prime Minister elected in modern times. Although when he was born no woman had the vote, by 1970 the Conservative Party depended on women not only as the majority of the electorate but also as the sex more faithful to Conservatism. (Men, the minority in the franchise began to show a greater inclination to vote Labour.)

Edward Heath seemed no natural magnet for this female vote. He had never shown any great liking for women as a group, though there were individual exceptions; he saw their role as fundamentally distinct from that of men. Only a month before he had told the National Council of Women that while 'the woman who seeks a career must be able to advance in it with perfect freedom and every hope of promotion', he also thought that 'Equality – in the sense of carrying out the same activity – is obviously nonsense in the context of the home'. More revealingly, he had said four years previously that he would like to see more women in the House of Commons and at all levels 'so long as they are providing what women can and not just duplicating what men can do'. From someone who had himself complained about being categorized as a bachelor, such delineation was at least tactless in terms of wooing his basic vote.

A meeting had been arranged for the Friday following when, with the help of his friends, Edward Heath would try to choose a new career. One of those who had been advised that he would be required to attend the meeting says, 'He was preparing himself for what he ought to do – perhaps go into business and make some money. He could have had any number of jobs in industry.'

Members of the Cabinet agree that, as one of them put it, 'The weekend before, none of us thought we were going to win, and he certainly didn't at that stage.'

High and low alike, the party watched, fascinated, the spectacle of their man fighting for his political life – and fighting it, as the incumbent Prime Minister Harold Wilson was only too glad to point out, very much on his own. A former Minister admits, 'They all

[1] *Studies in British Politics* edited by Richard Rose, Macmillan, 1969.

ratted on him at the General Election – nobody really gave him any support; he fought that election almost single-handed. Macleod had just lost his mother and had to go to the Hebrides; Maudling hardly spoke, and the only person who contributed much at all was Enoch Powell and that was a deliberate embarrassment. If we had lost I have absolutely no doubt whatever in my mind that Ted would have been flung out – I think they would have gone for him at once.'

Those who were in Heath's own team found their admiration and anxiety increasing equally. Since May Heath had been going through his third great period of depression as leader; but as James Prior, the Minister of Agriculture and a close aide, says, 'My admiration for him grew more, seeing him go through the trauma of Enoch, of losing the election, of seeing the whole thing drifting away . . . up against this supremely clever manipulator of public opinion and public relations which is Harold Wilson. But he could command the loyalty of the people who mattered to him, and to whom he mattered.'

And others, too. Lord Hailes had left the Commons thirteen years before. 'My admiration for him increased very much in the election,' he says. 'I did talk to him once or twice on the telephone, and he never showed a flicker, when the polls were against him, of anything of doubt of any kind. It was an exhibition of guts absolutely – a supreme exhibition of guts. One hundred per cent marvellous. One night when it was very high against him he came to a dinner at the Unionist Club. He made a speech exactly the same as usual, but I know that he was troubled, and I think some of the people were just watching to see how he was going to take it.'

A reporter who gave him the news when the polls were worst simply gave him the figures 'against', and was almost dazed with admiration at the way in which Heath steadily asked, 'against them?'

At the Press conference it was the same. When asked on 17 June about a Labour victory he said off-handedly, 'Oh well, I hadn't considered that; all the evidence runs the other way.'

For a man whose career was far more important, both qualitatively, in terms of intensity, and quantitatively, in lack of alternatives, to him than most men, and who, as his agent knows, had also been running a race against time – 'he wanted to be the *youngest* whip, the *youngest* leader', and, presumably, the youngest Conservative Prime Minister since Balfour – the strain must have been almost intolerable. But the fact that a date was set for the end of the agony helped him to combine with his natural pride the qualities he so greatly admired, of dignity and tremendous nerve.

There were those who feared that by refusing to use all the political weapons within his grasp he would throw away even what tiny chance he appeared to have. He refused to retaliate against Enoch Powell's forays and preferred instead to ignore both them and him. 'That's Powellism, just as that was Macarthyism, and there's nothing I can do about it,' he said once; but the subject came up again and again at Shadow Cabinet meetings. Even at his most despondent, when the party machine virtually stopped ticking over, when researchers and secretaries alike sat without working, 'touched by the clammy hand of despair' as one of them put it, he refused to change his intrinsic style. A man who had written a speech for him in more eloquent tones than he generally used was kept behind at the end of one meeting and told, 'It's good, but I can't use it.' The pathos lay in the fact that he understood his own predicament. His memory of the 1966 election was strong. 'In predicting disaster then he had not prevailed over the Labour Party,' says one of his advisers. 'In 1970 he wanted to remain above this – to remain optimistic, and let Reggie and Macleod predict disaster. Then Macleod had to go to the Hebrides. In the end Heath decided that he must go back to his Cassandra role – I was very disappointed the day after Cromer[1] when he didn't: I thought if he didn't dent the euphoria there was nothing else worth saying.'

It took ten days for his team to persuade Heath to resume this 'Cassandra' role, and to say that it was up to Mr Wilson to state whether or not there was a financial crisis.

---

[1] On 1 June 1970 Robin Day interviewed Lord Cromer and Lord Kearton on *Panorama*. Lord Cromer said, 'I think there's no question that any Government that comes into power after this next election is going to find a very much more difficult financial situation than the new Government found in 1964: for instance the very large debts which are still outstanding, the debts which were taken on for balance of payments reasons still stand at just under 4,000 million dollars and this in comparison with the position in 1964 makes for a very adverse start.' Lord Kearton agreed that the situation was more difficult than in 1964.

The double 'crisis meeting' at which he was persuaded to change his mind took place in his Albany chambers. Determined neither to repeat the mistakes of four years before, nor to acquire a reputation for knocking Britain, he had to steer a hairline course. Since it was judged that the Press was, at this point, not interested in policy, there was little alternative to dangling the 'crisis' deterrent before them.

The balance between visible integrity and implied peril could have been upset by the slightest suggestion of dogmatism or exaggeration; but with his tongue as careful as his nerve was steady, Heath countered the question at the routine Press conference on 11 June: 'What about the economic crisis?' with the reply, 'What I was quoting were the words of Lord Kearton and Lord Cromer that the incoming Government would face a very difficult financial situation. I have told you I haven't used the word crisis.'

It was Macmillan, credited by Heath with having the most creative mind he had known in politics, who had once noted that electors tended to vote Left in prosperous days and Right in days of depression. Now the realization that in spite of Labour's balance of payments surplus there were debts of 4,000 million dollars was beginning to spread.

In the last two or three days before the election, those who truly wished Heath victory began to hope, despite the predictions of all but one of the polls, that he just might prevail.

Polling day was Thursday, 18 June.

After midnight, tension in Bexley turned to hope. Down in Broadstairs, the candidate's father, William Heath, and his stepmother Mary had invited a dozen people to come in during the evening: at one in the morning they had a house bursting with fifty visitors.

Edward Heath has a habit of speech that many people find disproportionately irritating: he often says 'we' instead of 'I' – Conservative colleagues say they don't know whether he's referring to his family or his constituency, outside friends say they don't know whether he is referring to Parliament or the crew of his yacht. But it would take a hard heart indeed to find fault with the modesty with which, smiling shyly, he turned round an hour or so later from a television set in the drill hall in Bexleyheath. 'We've won,' he said.

He had. At two thirty he telephoned his father. The same day, instead of choosing a new career, he chose his Cabinet. Four months later at the Party Conference he promised his followers – whose support throughout his career had been no more predictable than that of the whole uncommitted electorate had proved in the summer of 1970 – a 'quiet revolution'.

It had already taken place.

2
The Carpenter and the Lady's Maid

Broadstairs stands where the cliffs of Kent are swept by strong arctic winds. Buildings and faces are outlined sharply in the keen air. The old part of the town is, as Charles Dickens wrote, 'without the slightest pretension to architecture and very picturesque in consequence'. Below lies the harbour, a reminder that two hundred years ago Broadstairs was a fishing offshoot of the village of Thanet, and that the way of life for most of the ninety families was one of the hardest – cod-fishing in Iceland. The newer parts of the town are even less notable architecturally. The yeoman fields of eastern Kent which lie behind are fertile but flat and open, with none of the cosiness the county has closer to London. The people seem practical, pleasant and shrewd, a no-nonsense lot, and one is not surprised to see, among all the reminders of the time Dickens spent working there, a house bearing the plaque 'Charles Dickens did not live here'.

The first one of Edward Heath's family to live near here was his great-great-grandfather, Richard Heath, a coastguard and boatman who was born in Cockington, Devon, in 1797, and later moved to Ramsgate. In 1830 he had a son, George, who became a merchant seaman, then worked at Trinity Light, and ended as the Pierman of Ramsgate. His son, born in 1865, was Stephen Richard, the Prime Minister's grandfather. He became a railway porter, then a carrier and vanman, and in 1886 married the daughter of a Ramsgate greengrocer. She gave birth on 10 October 1888 to William George Heath, carpenter and later master-builder, now in his eighty-fourth year, who was born in Ramsgate but came to Broadstairs as a tiny baby. He says, 'Wherever I've been since, I've always longed to get back to Broadstairs.' William Heath worked until he was seventy-six and only gave up then on doctor's orders, because he injured his back. Now, he is fresh-faced, brisk, and as direct as he was in his teens; he is a combination of tender sentimentality and realism. 'Is your hair natural?' he asked me, having wondered about my blondness for an hour or two; then, surveying my tall laced-up boots, 'What time do you have to get up in the morning to put them on?' ('Parents are getting out of control,' said the Prime Minister when I mentioned this to him.)

He also asked me at our first meeting, not at all rudely, how my book was being financed, and quickly corrected a mistake in my mental arithmetic. All this suggested a man of lively curiosity, close concern with financial detail, exacting attention to appearance and interest in character. As I got to know him better, I realized how important all these aspects of life were to him, and how essentially they had been passed on to his son. William Heath still dresses extremely smartly, in keeping with his country and seaside environment and is hardy enough to wear light clothes even in chilly weather. Allowing for the mellowing of age, it is clear that he has a core of 'niceness' (there is no better word) and sense of humour. Edward Heath once described him objectively as 'a very likeable and good man, and a good craftsman'.[1]

He is married happily to his third wife, Mary, who is younger than Edward Heath. 'Teddy's mother', as William always calls her in affectionate tones, died in 1951.

Mary, who married him in 1964, is only fifty – five years younger than her step-son – but she finds William a match for her. 'He's absolutely determined once his mind is made up,' she says. 'If he says "No", he says it very gently, but that's it and nothing will budge him unless I can produce reasons that will *prove* to him that he's wrong. He won't argue – he will go out for a walk or go into the garden. Ted avoids show-downs like his father – if he's annoyed he

[1] Interview with Kenneth Harris, *Observer Colour Magazine*, 23 January 1966.

will walk to the end of the garden.' (However, a different temper emerges outside the domestic sphere, and many of Edward Heath's colleagues must wish that a walk to the end of the garden would end their problems.)

An incident that revealed both himself and Mary at their best occurred in July 1970, when news came of a threat to kidnap the Prime Minister's father. They were staying with Madron and Nancy-Joan Seligman, friends of Edward's, when the Prime Minister rang Madron to tell him of the threat and added 'Don't tell Daddy'. 'That was silly, as Daddy is adult and knew something was up when the police called,' says Madron. 'When he was told he said, "If they haven't got good colour television I'm not going to be kidnapped," and Mary said, "Nobody would want you, you silly old fool." They laughed it off, but it was nasty.' The Prime Minister could not get away to be with him but rang three times over the weekend to make sure all was well.

William Heath prefers occupation to retirement and gets a little restless now. He is helpless at household tasks of the simplest kind, even on the odd occasion when Mary is ill in bed. But he enjoys listening to *The Archers*, following the champions of snooker, which he used to play at a club once a week and still likes to on Mondays if he is fit enough, and keeping as *au fait* as possible with his son's life.

William Heath knows his own character fairly well, and is, as a kind and fair man, reasonably pleased with it. He largely equates character with fate: 'I've always had that independent streak in me, and stubbornness. I would say no to any offer, however good, if it would place me under an obligation. I could never have borrowed.'

Part of the reason for this is natural pride. Another part depends perhaps on the reasoned faith of a truly egalitarian outlook: William Heath has always rightly thought himself as good as the next man, *whoever that might be*, and has taken pains not to spoil the picture of himself in his own eyes or those of his neighbour. This belief means that he can say with complete self-confidence, and without any feeling of inferiority, 'We're a working-class family and no two ways about it.' It means that he has not tried to alter his tastes or interests to accord with any imaginary picture of what a Prime Minister's father should be like. 'I would rather go to the Cup Final than the Budget speech,' he says with a cheeky smile, well aware of the implications of that remark, and on his eighty-second birthday (after the victory election) nothing his son could say would dissuade him from his first choice of theatre celebration. They all went to see *Charlie Girl*.

If the son has much of the father in him, in terms of character if not tastes and personality, where did the father learn his independence? William was one of a family of six, four boys and two girls, whose father always reminded them that it took a wise man to save money, while any fool could spend it. They were poor perhaps because his father did not take his own advice and in 1900, when he was twelve, William passed his Labour examination at Ramsgate Commercial School (fees: one shilling a week) and left school with no regrets.

His father was evidently something of a Jack-of-all-trades. As well as being a porter and carrier he had been a dairyman and in the early 1900s (perhaps under the influence of his wife, the greengrocer's daughter) had a fruit stall on the beach. William helped him sell the fruit, and meanwhile planned a more ambitious career for himself. Perhaps as a reaction against his father's life he wanted to be master of one trade. He wondered about becoming a cobbler, but finally settled for a carpenter, and at the age of fifteen was apprenticed for half-a-crown (twelve and a half new pence) a week.

It turned out to be more than a career – it was a vocation. 'Woodwork's a marvellous hobby for anyone that's prepared to work at it,' he said recently stroking a walnut table he once made. His work was not delicate carpentry like cabinet-making, but arduous and basic, doing joinery for a builder. He started work at 6 a.m., worked till 8 a.m., when he had breakfast, again from 8.30 a.m. till noon, when there was an hour's break for lunch, and then from 1 p.m. until 5.30 p.m.

When he was eighteen, a fresh incentive was added to his efforts. 'My mother had told me not to think about girls until I was twenty-five', he remembers; but his father after all had married at twenty-one, and at the age of seventeen William himself was already smitten by the girl who was to become his first wife. Her name was Edith.

He was not the only one to be enchanted by her. Twenty years after her death those who knew Edith Heath, *née* Pantony, tend to smile when they speak about her, and it seems unlikely that she made

a serious enemy in her life. 'She was a sensitive woman, very sensitive. If you cried she would cry with you,' says William. Edward
Heath, her elder son, was thirty-four when she died. He still feels her
loss too profoundly to enjoy talking about her; 'I asked him about
her once and he shut me up like a trap,' says one of his closest friends.
Finding it easier perhaps to talk to a comparative stranger he
managed once to define her to Kenneth Harris in terms that from
another man might be detached, but from him were overflowing with
tribute: 'My mother was a fine character with a strong personality,
a high sense of morality and public responsibility . . . she had the
spiritual sense of her Christian faith. Not that she was at all ethereal
about it . . .' With her no doubt there died the tenderest part of his
emotional life, and also probably his main opportunity for emotional
outlet.

Marian Evans, who was married for ten years to the Heaths'
younger son, John, and who has recounted many of her former
mother-in-law's kind ways, believes that the Pantonys were opposed
to the courtship of their daughter by the young apprentice carpenter.
It is true that Edith, having left school at fourteen had had two years
more schooling than he. After joining the domestic staff of a family
called Taylor she became Mrs Taylor's personal maid. Sweet-faced,
fair-haired and gentle in manner, she travelled with them when they
went abroad to Switzerland and Austria 'taking the waters', as
William now remembers. 'She was the belle of the village, although
I didn't know that then,' he adds, which suggests that there may have
been other opinions about her prospects, and how 'well' she might
marry.

However, Edith seems to have resisted family influence, and she
had soon promised to marry William, who was the same age as herself. He is a man who believes in being well equipped for whatever
task is in hand. 'It was nearly eight years before we were married,'
he says. 'Before then I set myself to save a hundred pounds. When
I finished my apprenticeship, at twenty, I was getting fourteen
shillings (70p.) a week.'

By the time they married, at twenty-five, he was earning a comparatively good wage of two pounds a week, and as their rent for
the bottom floor of a small semi-detached house, No. 2 Holmwood
Villas, was six shillings and sixpence (37½p) a week, they had enough

to live on. They had already, with the hundred pounds, bought everything they needed. 'We had everything for comfort – good kitchen utensils, a nice bedroom . . . '

It was in this bedroom that, three years later, on 9 July 1916, their first child, a son and the future Prime Minister of Britain was born. He had three inches of black hair that – as is normal – fell out, and was later replaced by brown. Compared with his two immediate predecessors in the Conservative Party – Harold Macmillan, who was born into an upper-middle class family engaged in publishing, and Alec Douglas-Home, whose family were not only aristocratic but rich – he seems at first sight to have had few advantages. In fact it was to turn out that the very lacks and hardships themselves were in his favour; they nurtured the iron in his temperament and gave it a cutting edge in maturity.

He also had one unseen immediate advantage. Instead of a nanny, he had a mother. Instead of being a small cog in the nursery, he was at the heart of the household, adored by both his parents. William is still marvellous with children, and, in the absence of grand-children of his own, plays with those available through relations and friends. If this sounds, today, an atmosphere so much to be taken for granted that it can almost be dismissed, it is worth com-paring it with the childhood of Harold Macmillan, who was conscious of having a somewhat lonely childhood and felt overshadowed by two older brothers although he had devoted parents and a marvellous nanny. The nursery was 'the true centre of life and the only secure world', as he says in *Winds of Change*.[1] Yet:

> I cannot frankly say that I was as happy as I think children are now . . . I was always anxious lest I might do something wrong or commit some solecism. I was oppressed by some mysterious power which would be sure to get me in the end . . . there was always a feeling of unease. Talleyrand said that anyone who had not known France before the Revolution had never known *la douceur de vivre*. This may have been equally true of the life of some people before the First War. But there was not much *douceur* about the nurseries of the upper-middle classes in my childhood. But perhaps we were

---

[1] *Winds of Change*, Macmillan, 1966.

different. We had, of course, times of great happiness and enjoyment. Yet I always felt that, on the whole, the world was something alarming, and people of all ages would be more likely to be
troublesome than agreeable. Hence I grew up shy and sensitive.
It is only by a long self-training that I have, to some extent,
overcome these inhibitions. I have hardly ever had to make an
important speech without feeling violently sick most of the day
before . . .'

Beneath a stolid exterior, Heath too was to grow up shy and sensitive in some respects, though for very different reasons. But inside or
outside the political arena he apparently never is, and according to
his family never has been, a prey to nerves, in the sense of feeling
foreboding or terror for no accountable reason, or any anxiety *out of
proportion* to the cause of it. Even as a child, according to his father,
he never suffered from nightmares, and, if memories are to be trusted,
was never even afraid of the dark.

This makes him sound very different from the average child. It
suggests that even as a child he was too proud to show fear, or that
he lacked imagination. Good friends remain doubtful today about
the degree of imagination he does possess. Perhaps in view of his
choice of career he was lucky in not having too much. Yet there are
different varieties of imagination as there are of intelligence: it is
fair to define Edward Heath's as 'vision', with all that the word
implies of clarity and purpose, rather than the flexible, if more
understanding, imagination of the introspective.

It is impossible, also, to disentangle temperament from environment, but it seems that he was a physically and mentally robust
child who was given what we now consider to be the best start in life
of all: a stable and happy home. This was no accident. Temperamentally his parents were as different as they were physically – the dark,
dynamic husband and softly spoken wife. But their outlooks har-
monized as well as their strength of will. It was essentially an egalitarian marriage. 'In a marriage, nobody's boss – I don't believe in
that,' says William Heath today. And then, with one of those touches
of brevity that make everything clear, 'We talked things over.'

About one thing however he was determined: 'I made up my
mind when we got married that my wife would never have to go out

to work and that we would give our children a better start in life than we had.' So for the next twenty years he was to work a sixteen-hour day, going off first on a bicycle, and then on a motor-cycle. These long hours meant two things: first, the roles of husband and wife were completely separate. Secondly, while important issues in their lives were discussed and mutual decisions made, there was not much time for general conversation. The spoken word was not much practised. And in particular they never discussed politics – nor, really, had any, though William vaguely believed he was a Liberal.

So the boy inhabited a peaceful, quiet home, enjoying longer hours alone in his mother's company than most babies do, due to his father's long hours at work, and in the serenity of a feminine aura and order. 'The mother runs the home. Teddy's mother was wonderful in the home – everything ran like clockwork,' says William. Edward's spiritual welfare was one of her prime concerns, and it was she who watched him each night as he knelt to say his prayers; afterwards his father came upstairs to give him a goodnight kiss. His father was a considerable presence on Saturday afternoons and Sundays; in his determination that his family should go short of nothing he himself made Teddy a wooden fire-engine, painted bright red and big enough to sit on, which he loved, and a little wicker armchair all to himself.

This emotional security was perhaps consciously boosted by his parents because there was no other kind. The First World War had been taking its toll for two years when Edward was born; when he was five months old, his father was sent to do war work in Vickers' aircraft factory at Croydon – close to Bexley, his own future constituency. Both at the factory, where he was making woodwork, and at home, there were things William Heath found hard to swallow.

At work it was the union that troubled him. All the men in his division belonged to it, and he joined as well – only to regret it. 'I had to join, but it was terrible,' he remembers. 'The union was all right, it was the way it was run. There was a clique of people in control, and unless you were in the clique you couldn't get anything past.'

Plainly his son was too young to remember any remarks William might have made at this time, and he was, in any case, not the sort of man to complain, or even to share his troubles with his wife in case they worried her. But the Prime Minister's basic attitude towards trade unions may have been affected by his father's difficulties. At any rate William Heath succinctly conveyed to me that he had found the situation almost intolerable.

As a proud and loving provider he was desperately worried, too, by the family's financial plight. His wages might have purchased country produce, eggs and vegetables, at home in Broadstairs, but in urban Crayford there was a dire shortage of essentials, which seems almost incredible to those who remember only the well-organized rationing of the Second World War. 'There was a terrible shortage of bread, potatoes and coal,' he said when I pressed him to know if things could really have been so bad in the winter of 1916–17. 'We had a ramshackle house in Crayford, and the wind used to whistle round it like a pack of wolves. I remember begging in the street for coal and potatoes – the coal came round on a cart, and I used to go into all the greengrocers' to try and get potatoes. It was a terrible time.'

Life went on as normal for Edward. At three, he had whooping cough – quite an event, as he was an exceptionally healthy as well as a rather too chubby child, and most of the childish ailments by-passed him. In 1920, his brother John was born: a blond baby who was to turn out the opposite of him in interests and ambitions – 'as different as chalk from cheese,' says their father.

This, if anything, must have been the event that changed Edward's early life. He was now the elder. He started to go to an infants' school in Crayford (dismissed as 'a little tin-pot school' by Will, but the best available in the circumstances) and showed immediate interest. The childish tantrums later extrapolated from family lore by Marian Evans may perhaps have been due to the arrival of the baby intruder; they disappeared with the discovery of an outside world. And, fond as his parents were, there was absolutely no over-protectiveness: rather the opposite. 'From the age of five or six we sent him off to places on his own to give him confidence,' says his father. 'When we were in Crayford we sent him down to Broadstairs on his own to stay with his grandmother – my mother – for six weeks, and another time we sent him to Southampton to a friend for three weeks. We put a ticket round his neck and another in his pocket and put him in the guard's van, with the guard.'

Edward had had his first taste of Broadstairs, and of freedom. Small wonder that this combined with his parents' longing to return to Broadstairs made him think of the fresh little resort, with its sprinkling of ready-made contacts in the form of relations, as a more immediate kind of heaven. He later said remembering when they finally returned he felt that 'life began when I got back to Broadstairs.' It was July 1923 and he was then seven years old.

3

An Unsentimental Education

Each time William Heath really pauses to consider his son, he comes to the same conclusion: 'He hasn't changed. He's always been the same. He's just got bigger.'

This is a remark that most parents could make about their adult offspring with some truth, but seldom with such obvious outward credibility as in Edward Heath's case. Phenomenal growth was to take place later in his intellectual life, and some changes in his emotional life, but the cornerstones of his character and still more of his demeanour seem to have been placed when he was very young indeed – perhaps at about the time the family returned to Broadstairs, for Jesuits have much experience behind them when they assess seven years as the age of reason, and reason has been Heath's conscious lodestar ever since.

James Bird was a young master (later to become headmaster) of St Peter's Church of England School, a free primary school to which the Heaths decided to send Teddy on their return to Broadstairs. Now, like Mr Heath, in his eighties, he is very spry and has retained his devotion to detail. He remembers the little boy quite clearly, partly he thinks because on the day of enrolment, when he was only one of many new boys, he presented himself with a paper from his previous school. It was then very unusual for incoming pupils to bring a report with them. It said that he was 'excellent in reading and number' (arithmetic), and Mr Bird noticed that he also had quite nicely formed handwriting. As the terms passed however he made an impression for another reason: he settled in, and yet remained slightly apart; noticeable, remembers the master, 'for his general cleanliness and wholesomeness and a certain aloofness – even as a small boy he was self-contained and purposeful'.

Among his contemporaries were a coastguard's son, Arthur Pay, who is now deputy harbour-master at Ramsgate and barely remembers him, and a Broadstairs taxi-driver who thinks that he was 'very clever'. But not at everything. Friday afternoons were devoted to hobbies, and on fine days the children were encouraged to make things from wood and plasticine in the playground. Mr Bird still has a vivid picture of him 'crouching there with some tools and pieces of wood, looking rather awkward'. It is a description which rapidly rings a bell of sympathy in the mind of William Heath, who says with a note of paternal protection, 'He's no good with his hands. If you watch him trying to make something you feel sorry for him.'

It was plain that he was not destined to follow his father as a craftsman: but his parents were concerned, if not specifically ambitious, for him. Before long Mr Bird had grown accustomed to interrogation from his pupil's mother. 'She was constantly stopping when we met in the street to know how her Teddy was getting on. She was a charming woman, but always looked very tired. I thought she probably over-worked. They used to take in summer visitors at home.' 'She was a very docile sort of woman,' says another regular visitor at the home; while this was true of her demeanour, it was a docility that hid many strengths. The sums paid by the visitors – usually one family at a time – who stayed with the Heaths in the summer helped considerably with their tiny budget. Wages did not increase after the First World War as they were to later after the Second, and with two children it was not easy to save. But save they must, if they were to move from the home they were sharing in Albion Road with the widow of Mrs Heath's brother to a house of their own. William Heath stuck to his decision not to let his wife go out to work – and with her sense of devotion to the home this would have been virtually inconceivable anyway – but raised no objections to her own cottage industry; and it did well enough for her to claim that she could pay the rates out of her own takings. Since he was out working such long hours himself, William probably did not fully realize how much his wife had to do in the house, with laundry and cooking for guests as well as themselves, nor exactly how constantly and carefully the wheels for their clockwork existence were oiled. None, however, could have been more appreciative of the results, though he is still not a man to like *haute cuisine*.

'We had good, wholesome cooking, and her children went out like children out of a bandbox every day. Teddy would come home after school looking exactly the same as when he went out and John – well, John came home looking exactly like all boys do. The boys were their mother's life – she lived for the family.'

In fact they both did, and in this were typical of a section of society with strong, proud attitudes that has largely disappeared with today's greater affluence and ease. They were working class, true, but they were determined to be at the top of that class, and had the best of qualities to enable them to do that – loyalty, tenacity, industry, and deliberate pride in themselves. Appearances were considered extremely important: shoes always gleamed, and special house shoes were worn indoors; visits from the dressmaker reconciled quality with low cost. They had an almost tribal togetherness, and held themselves slightly apart from those among their acquaintances and even their relations who did not perhaps hold quite the same hopes and standards. So though he was the first Conservative Prime Minister born to working-class parents young Edward Heath never experienced, nor even saw, the slum life of the poorest and least privileged; nor has he known the despair of squalid living conditions compounded by exhausted inability to cope, apathy or ignorance; nor the disasters multiplied by gaps or lapses in character.

Richness of character, a few tenets and more common sense, good health and good management lifted the family into a self-contained milieu where they were safe from the fears of those a few steps behind in solidity or self-control, and gave them a start where they could prepare for greater efforts in this rather snobbish and hierarchial small town.

Broadstairs of course was a good background for this phase of family development, since it was far from the distractions of gayer resorts and the capital. Few flappers found it enticing. There was less of the Charleston than military music played by the brass bands along the front. There were no colossal amusement emporiums, just one small arcade and a popular minstrel show where 'Uncle Mack' played to visitors and residents alike.

Most residents, including the Heaths, had their allotted space on the beach where they could pitch a tent – a facility which was used a fair amount, since this was before summer holidays away from home became a possibility for many. Mr Heath's own measure of the difference between pre-war and post-war Broadstairs and today is calculated on the inches of leg shown on the beach! 'Before the First World War you wouldn't see an ankle . . .'

Even if more worldly pleasures had been available, the Heaths would have been unlikely to indulge themselves. 'We kept mainly to ourselves,' remembers John Heath. It was on Friday that William had his night out, playing snooker. It was nothing less than an event. With his personality one would expect him to be a tremendously popular man, yet he says, 'I've never had a lot of friends, I've been a loner all the time. I don't know why.'

The explanation may be three-fold: apart from a genuinely independent character, there was the slight sense of apartness deliberately fostered in the competitive family, and there was little time.

Occasionally the family together visited friends or relations. The boys' grandmother was still alive, although her husband (unlucky at work and a staunch Tory, strongly for the Empire) had died when Edward was a toddler. There were various other Heaths and Pantonys, mostly engaged in trades or crafts, and one uncle who was an accountant.

But for the most part in the early years it was a routine for all of them of work, eat, play cards or listen to the radio, and go to bed. 'It wasn't easy but I'd do it again,' says William; and then, after a pause, claims something that in the 1970s is so astonishing as to cause momentary disbelief: but it is plainly absolutely true. 'From the time we were married we never went out to a show or a cinema for twelve years. And then we went to the cinema . . . I remember that evening!'

A smile of pleasure brushes across his face as he thinks of it. The evening he remembers must have been when Edward was nine and John five. William had saved enough money to pay a deposit on their own house at last, and for the first time they could allow themselves the slightest financial relaxation. He also remembers the evening vividly because it was the occasion of an incident that demonstrates very clearly the working of his elder son's mind, and suggests a good deal about his fundamental attitudes.

The seats in the cinema were bookable. William made his reservations, gave Edward the seat numbers, and told him that if he wanted anything he was to telephone him at the cinema. He took the precaution of explaining this to the cinema manager before they took their seats. During the interval the manager called Mr and Mrs Heath to the phone: it was Edward, who just wanted to tell them that he and John were absolutely all right.

A sense of responsibility and maturity, an ability to cope with the technicalities of life – telephones and strangers – that some children would have found difficult or embarrassing, these were all there, together with a certain self-importance. Protectiveness is a rather elderly quality in a child, and more often found where there has been hardship. It is easy to speculate too that for two or three years with his father away at work for so much of the day, and his mother coping with her younger child, Edward may have felt increasingly like the man of the house and decided that he should be a tower of strength to his mother. This was perhaps his first opportunity to do something positive about it, although for a long time he had been adhering to her standards at home and making as little extra work for her as possible, keeping his clothes spotless, with spills the exception rather than the rule.

For a watchful child with a highly developed sense of responsibility the experience of daily life must have had a deeply formative effect. Almost any child would feel concerned at seeing both or one of his parents struggle against adversity, even of a mild kind such as keeping to a very strict budget, having no help at all with the extra work for paying guests, and visibly tiring. A child with a more introverted nature, secretly passionate and idealistic, could suffer considerably on behalf of such a parent. It is also the nature of childhood to supply the remedy, in daydreams: perhaps of supplying the money to solve all problems. Another response, which might have worse consequences, could be a decision to be tough; having seen his mother leave herself open to extra difficulty and worry on behalf of others, he might almost instinctively decide that he would shape his own emotional nature differently. Therefore he might allow himself to feel such concern again for very few people indeed. It is impossible to know for certain whether the very young Edward Heath responded in this way, but one would judge from the mature man that he is certainly no masochist, and that therefore such a pattern of response was at least theoretically possible. From this would spring not only intense ambition, to provide both financially and in career terms the fulfilment his parents lacked, but also great wariness of emotional involvement. A determination could also follow to achieve proportionately more than his father in material terms before contemplating matrimony. At the age of nine, of course, these would probably not all be conscious thoughts, particularly the last: but it is after all before puberty and consequent immersion in themselves that some children tend to worry and plan most about their mother and father.

Their new house, Helmdon, in King Edward Avenue, the first house of their own, was to be the family home for nearly forty years. It was semi-detached and three-bedroomed. Occasionally when they had their summer visitors the boys would share a room, but the age difference and, still more, the difference in tastes meant that in spite of their mutual loyalty, they were never the closest of brothers. John Heath now works for Harrow Corporation as a building surveyor.

John remembers the new house, it was exceptionally well-equipped for the time and their income: 'We had a three-piece suite, a sideboard, and a piano. I can't remember that house without a piano. We always had a wireless – ever since I was seven or eight. With the earliest set we had four pairs of earphones, and all sat round listening. Ever since they came out we've always had a radiogram.'

The piano was an expensive investment, bought for Teddy who had started taking music lessons when he was eight; an added burden before they moved to the new house but another indication of the parents' eagerness to give their children all the advantages they could. Edward was to benefit financially and spiritually from this. Musically he quickly showed aptitude and pleased his teacher, a Miss Locke. While he practised his mother would sit with him and knit, and his father made him a music-stool which still stands today in his bedroom in the new 'Helmdon', which took its name from the old.

The Heaths were scrupulously fair parents, and arranged for John to take music lessons too. There was a thought that if he could play the violin, the boys could perform together. They soon realized their mistake – 'to one it was a joy to practise, to the other it was an agony' – and John gladly gave up.

He was immensely proud of his elder brother, and always rushed home to be the first to tell his mother of any success Teddy had had, but had no desire to compete with him. His pleasures were dashing down to the beach tent – which he could make in three minutes flat, downhill all the way – and going out to the farm owned by the couple with whom Mr and Mrs Heath were by now going to the cinema every Saturday. 'They had a son and daughter about my age. I used to spend quite a lot of time out there, and I learned to milk cows and so on. Teddy went out there too, but not so much.'

The boys were very different. John was extremely accident prone: 'Every summer I had an accident, invariably; I was usually laid up for a month or two with scarlet fever, or stung by a jellyfish, or got pneumonia after playing hockey in wet clothes – you should never play hockey twice in one day in wet clothes.

'One day I was playing cricket at school and got a ball between the eyes. I was taken home in a taxi with a bloody nose, and I was wearing a white shirt, so you can imagine . . . Teddy opened the door. Mother was in the garden. She never saw me. I was laid out flat and the doctor called for before she was told I was home.'

Sometimes her elder son's conscientiousness worried Mrs Heath a little. Friends remember that years later, in Bexley, she told the story of going up to his room one day when he was, as usual, studying hard, and asking him whether he wasn't working too hard. He looked up at her and replied distinctly (according to her recollection), 'Mother, sometimes I don't think you *want* me to get on.'

Often keeping him company while he worked, or went out for walks, was a very close companion – a dog called Erg, after his own initials, which he had been given when he was ten. Erg consumed a fair amount of attention and affection. Teddy had some friends among his peers too, but he never, as most small boys do, indulged in a heart-to-heart sworn friendship with a bosom pal. As this was rather like his parents themselves, it did not particularly worry them. 'The boys are naturally reserved, and we brought them up to be independent,' says William Heath, proudly. His elder son has always stressed that their mother too, gave them autonomy: 'She left us boys free to go ones own way.' Consequently, he says, he felt no sense of rebellion against his parents. In line with William's theory of independence they were not encouraged to do anything like join the

Boy Scouts – 'I don't believe in it. You should make up your own mind what to do' – a somewhat mixed argument, but one that held good at the time.

John remembers how their independence was fostered. 'If you had a problem, Dad's attitude was – try and sort it out for yourself first, not to rely on him to sort it out for you. The idea was to stand on your own feet as far as possible. Of course they were always there, but there was no group analysis at home.'

Talking in fact was not particularly encouraged at all – it was regarded as a somewhat dangerous pastime. The two main tenets impressed on the boys were: (1) Never to tell lies, (2) Never to speak outside the home what they heard in it.

Anyone today who has seen Edward Heath's contempt for deliberate deceit and, still more, who has realized just how closely he guards the recesses of his emotions and personality, will recognize how well the first lesson was learned and to what lengths the second has been taken. It would be hard to find anyone who has learned to keep his own counsel so completely. It is this that has made him unattractive to men he has had to deal with, sometimes to his own colleagues and more often to those on the trade-union side; he is unfathomable to many of his own closest friends, and – because he is so self-contained – occasionally hurtful even to his family.

William Heath knows that his son's silences and self-containment spring from the best of intentions. 'He always wanted to avoid worrying his mother. If he had an exam he wouldn't tell her anything about it until afterwards.' This was matched by equal sacrifices from his mother; though she worried terribly about his first trip abroad with a school party, she said nothing in case it spoilt his holiday. As for his father, silence was in his case partly natural, partly the result of tiredness – 'There wasn't much time to talk after sixteen hours at work. We asked them about school, that sort of thing.'

Thus while it is true that, as the Prime Minister says today, 'We were a very closely-knit family', there was a curious tendency to isolation even within the safety of their own four walls. Even so, communication, if it did not take place verbally, took place by look and instinct and often still does.

Instinct may reveal but it does not fully explain. One sees the Heath home as a haven of strength and affection, where nevertheless four individuals were deliberately cutting themselves off not only from the outside world but even from part of the mutual help and support they could have given each other. The image of them listening to the wireless through four sets of earphones symbolizes, in a sense, their whole attitude to verbal communication. The result in Edward Heath's case was certainly to exaggerate an inherited tendency towards brevity of speech, and to render him inhibited and even inarticulate when it came to discussing, or even expressing, deep *personal* feelings and problems. Since he was to grow into a man of forceful, if seemingly somewhat cold passions overlying a basic sensitivity, and underlying great self-control, the habit of not talking things over at home was to lead to great tension in his character and his relationships in later years.

Meanwhile it had other, more immediate effects. It encouraged some aspects of the boy's personality to go underground and to grow in isolation. It also encouraged him to externalize his interests at an early, even precociously early, age, to turn outside the family for discussion and stimulus on subjects that interested him, and where there were no emotional undercurrents. 'As a little kid he could talk with anyone and hold his own,' says his father. 'He always chose people who were older than himself.'

Religion was one of his private explorations, music another. The boys were never forced to go to church or Sunday School, but had been encouraged to attend by their mother, who was herself a regular worshipper. At the Norman Church of St Peter's-in-Thanet, Edward combined the two interests, singing in the choir, and later, after his voice had broken, learning to play the organ. A friend, Ronald Whittell, attended confirmation classes with him and told George Hutchinson he thought that 'the vicar was the first man to have a very considerable influence on Heath'.[1]

Apart from the enormous influence already exerted by his father, which at this age he probably did not recognize – and indeed may not yet – this was probably true. It was not just the man: it was what he revealed. Religion was one of the outlets through which his reactions to the world, his beliefs and bewilderments, would surge as they were turned back by the dams of control, and inhibition, from more mundane expression. Gradually they would swell to form a reservoir

[1] *Edward Heath*, by George Hutchinson, Longmans, 1970.

of uncommon, if largely unchannelled, strength. And music was increasingly to become his emotional vocabulary when expression was needed: it could convey every mood without words, and it was unlikely to betray.

But it helped to lead him into a friendship which was to have a considerable effect, perhaps greater than is yet realized, on his mature life. Riding his bicycle – a proud new acquisition – through the narrow streets of Broadstairs one day, he collided with a car and was knocked into the road. 'The car was driven by my husband's partner,' says Mrs Jean Raven, who was married to a general practitioner, Dr Hugh Raven. They had a family of six – five girls and one son – all of whom were musical. Teddy's first glimpse of them was when he was taken back to the doctor's surgery after his accident. Gradually the Ravens got to know him better through his singing in the choir and his work for the local carol service, in which they were also interested. He became friendly with the children, and particularly with one of the daughters, Kay. In the drawing-room and old nursery in the Ravens' fine house, he breathed a new ether.

His parents were told nothing of the accident – the first his father heard of it was from me; but they were happy that he was invited sometimes to the Ravens' house.

These different surroundings and society stimulated the adolescent boy and nurtured his sense that there were unknown worlds to explore. But he was not the type to lose himself in fantasies; his mother, he says with an emphasis that shows his approval, 'kept our feet on the ground': sensitive she might be, silly she certainly was not. And many of his father's traits, for all the difference between their approaches to the world, were coming out in him. Even as a boy he was strong-willed enough to be called obstinate. 'He takes after me, that's all there is to it,' declares his father on this point, with some satisfaction. And both boys learned from their father a little trick that coincidentally has been shared by a fair number of outstanding men, including Churchill: William Heath whenever possible took forty winks after lunch. Edward and John found that they too could cat-nap at will.

The home influence remained paramount, although now it was leavened by outside influences. Apart from the Raven household, the most significant of these was school.

4

Scholarships and Depressions

The happy but humdrum routine of everyday life was broken, when Edward was ten, by the chance of sitting for a scholarship to Chatham House Grammar School in Ramsgate, which was the largest public secondary school in Kent. He was tremendously keen to sit for the exam, but uncharacteristically fell ill a few days before it was due to take place – surprisingly, because he was an extremely healthy, almost hardy, little boy. Two years earlier, on 13 October 1924, a medical examiner at St Peter's School had noted these features:

Height:	four feet, four and a half inches.
Weight:	four stone, nine and a half pounds.
Condition:	5
Cleanliness:	1
Tonsils and adenoids:	marked
Eyes: R	6/9
L	6/9
Deafness: R	W/6
L	W/6
Measles:	1923
Whooping cough:	1919
Mental state of child:	Good.

It was a comparatively clean bill of health, and the low mark for condition probably reflected his somewhat chubby build which, as he did not care for games, was not all represented by muscle.

Of course, small boys are susceptible to germs, but his father
explains the pre-scholarship illness in a surprisingly modern way: he
thinks it was exam fever. There was not really much need for anxiety.
On 17 April George Taylor, his headmaster at St Peter's, had written
to Dr H. C. Norman, the headmaster of Chatham House, describing
him as: 'In advance of his age. Is easily ahead of any other in his
group.' In a space left for any marked ability, he had written
'mathematics'.

Even so it seems that his father's theory was correct, and that
Teddy already had enough of a burning desire to get on to send his
temperature up – the corollary of ambition being of course fear of
failure and of disappointing his parents. When the day came he was
well enough to sit, and he did well, backed up by another testimonial
from Mr Taylor giving assurances that he was 'a good boy . . .
earnest, painstaking and thoroughly well-behaved'. He had to
undergo the ordeal of an oral as well as written examination, and
when he returned to St Peter's, Mr Bird asked him what had taken
place. He had been asked what career he would eventually like to
pursue, and had said he would like to be an architect. This comes as
a surprise to Mr Heath, who thought his son had vague ideas of
becoming an accountant, like one of his uncles.

Scholarships were awarded to about a quarter of the boys at
Chatham House School where the fees were £12 a year, and Edward
Heath was one of the lucky ones. He was given a free place. On
23 September 1926 it was recorded on a school form that his father's
total income from all sources (after deductions) was £120 a year.
This was not as appallingly low as it sounds, since some three-
quarters of the population lived below an income of £200 a year;
many had sunk far below this during the General Strike in the
spring, which had been protracted in the mining areas by the
employers' lock-out till the autumn when the miners finally capitula-
ted, with half a year's wages lost. However £120 was low enough to
make Teddy eligible for a travelling allowance of 18s. 9d. (94p) a
term. This, it was sternly decreed by the local authorities, was not to
be spent on the railway: schoolboys were unpopular with many train
travellers. So each morning he rattled his way to Ramsgate in one
of the trams that ran along the front, past its brighter amusements
and more elegant architecture ('salubrious', the town had been

described in 1890, and on the whole it still was); and each evening he rattled back again to quiet Broadstairs.

He spent nine years there. The grammar school was founded in 1909, under the name of the Ramsgate County School for Boys, and had changed its name to Chatham House (Grammar) School in 1923 when it acquired the premises (built in 1879) of a former independent school of this name. Its headmaster from the time of the school's foundation and throughout young Heath's years at the school, was Dr H. C. Norman, who was also Director of Further Education in the Isle of Thanet.

Dr Norman was forty-one when Edward entered the school and later was to become his pupil's staunch ally. He himself had been an exemplary boy at Rugby, outstanding academically, head of the school, and captain of games. He had obtained an exhibition to Oriel College, Oxford, to read history, and after a period of teaching undertook a further period of study at the Sorbonne. He then taught French at the Liverpool Institute where his methods were so much talked about that he was asked to give demonstrations of the 'direct method' of teaching French, and also became Captain of the Institute Cadet Corps. So he was both a disciplinarian and a progressive. In 1922 he wrote, 'The world since the War has itself entered upon a new phase . . .', but evidently he intended to maintain the aim of the school – 'all our efforts have been to teach the individual to subordinate himself and his own interests to that of the community. This is the very essence of our House system.'[1]

The first two lines of the school song were redolent of the Anglo-Saxon history of Kent:

> Here, where the feet of Englishmen first trod the English soil
> And marched in strong battalions on the foe . . .

And in the House system, the fagging and occasional corporal punishment the school was attempting to be as traditional as a public school; but far from being a pale imitation it had tremendous energy and pride of its own.

In 1926 it had a philatelic society, photography society, chess club, cycling, literary and debating society, wireless society, musical

---

[1] Headmaster's foreword, *Records of Chatham House School*, 1923.

society and dramatic club. These were all evidence of strong interests from a fair number of boys, and other clubs which came and went with pupils included the natural history, the astronomical, the rambling, and even the microscopal. Among the sports enjoyed (though not, on the whole, by Heath) were cricket, football, shooting, boxing, cross-country walking and swimming – the last of which he did, and still does, like. But what was really astonishing was the curriculum. Economics was taught regularly to certain boys who had passed the London matriculation, and the Sixth Form curriculum included a one-year course in logic and psychology: this was forward-looking indeed.

Heath's school career is remembered in some detail by one of the senior masters, Cecil Curzon, who got to know him well as he progressed through the school. 'He was never exceptionally brilliant, but I still maintain he *could* have got a First at Oxford. His academic career really fell into two parts – up to the end of the fourth form he was in the junior school, and during the first four years of his career the head was keen on the "marks system", during which marks for various subjects were totted up by the form master at the end of the week, and graded: 80 per cent was honours, 70 per cent first class, 60 per cent second, 50 per cent third, and 40 was fourth class . . . Teddy was never higher than second class – very average. But some of the boys were mark-grabbers.

'And of course Teddy was two years below the average age of the form. He seemed satisfied with marking time, and average marks.'

It must in fact have seemed to him that he was far from marking time. He was only ten years and eight months when the average age of the form was thirteen – yet he came twelfth out of thirty-one boys: he was, without excelling in any one subject, doing more than hold his own. It also seems, perhaps as the result of being the youngest in the form, that he became more obviously boyish at this time. On 9 December 1929 the headmaster had to send a report to the Director of Education about him: 'running along a passage – in which running is forbidden – he hit his head against a pipe and cut it so badly that I had to send him to a doctor who put a stitch or two in it. The passage was well lighted and I cannot discover that anyone was to blame but the boy himself.'

Earlier the same year he had rebelled against school meals, and his father had sent a letter to the school asking for permission for him to go to Carr's café 'for his dinner, as we find the school dinners do not agree with him'. This received a rather tart reply saying that such a request should be substantiated by a medical certificate, as 'there is nothing in the school dinner which should be unsuitable for a boy in ordinary health'. It seems that Mr Heath and a doctor won the day, since he succeeded in going outside for his meals.

Another letter typed to Mr Heath by the headmaster's secretary on 8 December 1930, reads with extremely individual punctuation:

8 December 1930

Dear Sir,

At the recent Medical Examination the doctor was sorry to find that you had not yet had any treatment given to your son for a Deformed Chest, and that his teeth were still in need of attention, he hopes that you will be able to have him attended to in the near future.

Yours sincerely

Headmaster's Secretary

William Heath has no recollection of receiving this or any similar communication – 'I don't remember it,' he says. But he is emphatic that the contents, in any case, were untrue. 'He never had a deformed chest or bad teeth.'

There was no doubt that he was an extremely healthy little boy, who had only forty-three *half*-days absence from school in all the nine years – an average of roughly two and a half days a year. But he has always walked with his arms held somewhat stiffly by his sides, and when he throws an object does so with a lack of aim that suggests a mild muscular lack of co-ordination (although his skill as a helmsman shows that some of his movements are precisely controlled). Perhaps this was what made him so hopeless at games, a deficiency which affected his status in a school where athletic prowess was so prestigious.

One of the almost inevitable consequences in a school that modelled itself along public-school lines was the hero-worship of sportsmen. 'Boys who weren't good at games were considered outside the ring – if you were to be on tremendously good terms with the other boys you had to be a games player. They were the heroes,' says one observer, adding, 'Yet I wouldn't say he was lonely.' His brother John, who entered Chatham House in 1931, remembers, 'He had a lot of friends, but no particularly close friends.'

The remark that he did not seem to be lonely shows that he was already, in his teens, remarkably self-sufficient and self-insulating. Whatever slight, or great, pain he may have felt he kept to himself. There was the love and encouragement at home to return to, and not too many questions there that would uncover the fields where he was not paramount. So, while missing out on schoolboy adulation may have increased his introversion, it led to no instability; on the contrary, it probably reinforced all his father's dicta about standing on your own feet, having self-respect, and going it alone.

Concomitant to this was a drive to work harder – both to use the energy that others were burning up on the pitch, and, half-consciously perhaps, to excel on his own ground. The headmaster's report in the spring term of 1930, when Teddy was nearly fourteen, certainly provided a trauma. The other boys in his form still mostly two years older were all preparing to take their General Schools Certificate. However Dr Norman wrote on Teddy's report: 'most promising, but I think it is tempting Providence to let him sit this term, he is too immature for an examination of this standard.'

For once the anguish was severe enough for him to complain. One can imagine the council that was held in the Heath home when he did so. His father's subsequent letter to the headmaster, dated 28 March 1930, and written, as usual, in his very graceful hand (quite remarkable for someone who had himself left school at the age of twelve) showed both soundness and shrewdness – unfaltering support for his son, together with a deft undercutting of opposition. William Heath said his son was 'very depressed' by the headmaster's decision, and continued, 'I think it would be advisable to let him carry on. He is young I agree, but even the young sometimes exceed our expectations. Your advice I believe was on account of his weakness in French in part, and Latin. I have already talked the matter over with him and made arrangements for him to study French during the whole period of his Easter holidays . . .' He concluded by offering to come and discuss the matter further with Dr Norman should he still be in doubt.

Edward took the exam, and passed, but his autumn report said,

'I do not think he has kept up to his previous high standard.' He was not very good at chemistry, where his work was labelled somewhat 'crude', and a surprising blind spot in view of his later development was geography, where until he was sixteen 'R.W.' wrote such criticisms as 'I am not satisfied with his work or results.' More predictable were his English master's comments, to the effect that he read what he was told to carefully enough, but did not bother to explore – another sign of his weakness where words were concerned, probably reinforced by now by the suspicion that reading was a waste of time unless it were directed to a specific, useful end. But with the Schools Certificate out of the way when he was fourteen, and Matriculation passed the next year, he was freer to follow his own interests. And in these he made great strides.

He did not have the same utilitarian attitude towards music, for which his hunger was developing. As well as singing in St Peter's Church choir and making good progress on the organ, he was taking a lead in musical affairs at school. By the time he was fifteen he was conducting the school orchestra, and was seriously considering music as a career. This idea was scotched, and history probably changed, at the end of March 1926 when the school wrote to his father explaining that there was a one-guinea charge for taking music as an additional subject in examinations, and asking him to send this amount – 'if you approve of his entry'.

This request seems to have caused some consternation in the Heath household. Mrs Heath was at this time acting more or less as a go-between, soothing the different ideas and objectives of father and son. 'I told his mother that I wouldn't pay for the exam unless he would promise her not to make music a career,' says William today, plainly feeling his judgment has had world-wide vindication. The promise was given, the exam of course passed. Still greater glory was to come in 1934, when Edward was just eighteen and won a prize in an inter-house piano competition at school. The judge, who was Director of Music at St Lawrence College, Ramsgate, was most impressed by his rendering of a Bach fugue – 'accurate and clear' – and of selections (whose details were unrecorded) from Chopin – 'an excellent sense of *tempo rubato*' – and Mozart, where one piece was judged 'very good technically and interpretation most musicianly', and another simply 'brilliant'. The judge, Mr P. B. Tomblings, summed up: 'A very excellent all-round performance. His playing shows sound musicianship and he is well equipped with technique.'

His success in this examination had more than superficial importance. It gave a tremendous boost to the end of term morale of his house, Colemans, of which he had been made captain in 1933 after a few months as a prefect; and his musical expertise improved his position in the critical eyes of the younger boys, and especially with his peers. This was evidenced by his winning, jointly with J. E. Hobbs, the Leslie and Douglas Prize awarded annually by the school for 'character' – according to the judgment of the Fifth and Sixth Forms.

Cecil Curzon remembers: 'In the junior school he had been a nonentity, but in the Sixth Form the attitude of the boys changed towards him. We had a custom whereby a boy from the senior school who was distinguished, but not a games player, was asked to be the scorer of the First Eleven in cricket – and he became the scorer.'

It was like a fabled account of what was to come in later life. He was still not a favourite, but he was taken very seriously indeed. The honour was in fact hard-won – he had been tremendously active over a very wide range of fields in his last three years or so at the school. Probably the least appreciated of his zealous drives was that as prefect. 'He was a bit of a stickler,' says the master. 'He was very down on kids who had their hands in their trouser pockets, or weren't behaving well in the street in their school cap and blazer. He thought that breaking a school rule amounted to disloyalty to the school.' This is borne out by Peter Veale, who said, 'Smaller boys – I was one of them – sometimes regarded him as fussy and officious. He would jump on any boy who did not wear the school uniform.'[1]

He had also won acclaim, if not popularity – whose golden aura was gained by intangible assets, according to the subtle, unfair and very worldly attitude of schoolboys – for his memorable performances at the school debating society. On domestic issues he tended to the negative, puritanical side of debate. In the autumn of 1932, when he was sixteen, he proposed that 'Sweepstakes should be abolished', but was defeated; the next year he carried the motion 'That Sunday cinemas should be abolished'. Three years later he seems to have had a great hit when experimenting in an altogether lighter vein together

[1] *The Sun*, 28 July 1965.

with eleven other speakers on the subject of 'What I hate', during an evening described enthusiastically by the school magazine as easily the most successful and entertaining the society had ever had. In the same year, 1935, he reacted strongly against the proposition that schools should be co-educational, which he called 'misguided'; this debate commanded a large audience of seventy-five boys, but forty-eight voted with Heath, so it seems that the courage of the majority was below the level of their curiosity. Women under thirty, after all, had only got the vote seven years before, and the idea was more widespread among schoolboys than it is today that females especially young ones should be accepted on sufferance only.

On international affairs Edward Heath at eighteen showed no lack of imagination about the dangers of dictatorship; and here his temperamental scorn of drifters showed up in a positive context. Whether by luck or judgment he moved, on 23 March 1934, on a visit to the Isle of Thanet Debating Society, 'That This House Deplores the Whitherance of Europe.' This was a month after the burning of the Reichstag, merely two months after Hitler had been appointed Chancellor and five months before he actually became Dictator of all Germany.

What effect did all this activity have on his work? At one stage the headmaster wrote that he should not allow himself too many distractions, in or out of school, but on the whole his interests gained him a reputation for increasing maturity. In many respects, those that could be judged immediately by outward performance, this was deserved. 'In the second part of his school career, the senior school, he was brilliant,' says Cecil Curzon. 'Not a genius, but brilliant.' This is something of an overstatement, to judge from later academic achievements, but it shows that he had won the support of his teachers, which he badly needed. As Curzon continues, 'Teddy had set his mind on going to Oxford. This was a problem, because his parents had no money and the school had no endowment fund. So he was aiming at an open scholarship in P.P.E. and came to me to prepare his Economic History and Political Science. I had a small class, just half a dozen boys, and those who did come were keen. I gave Teddy fifteen lessons a week – which was half my time – so I got to know him very well. He impressed me enormously, although he hadn't done very much history . . .'

Curzon himself had been taught by Maynard Keynes at Cambridge: a doubtful advantage, it seems, as Keynes's brilliance did not extend to his teaching and Curzon had to seek extra-mural tutorials for down-to-earth explanations. His own methods were very direct, his reasoning crystal clear, but he in turn was to have trouble of a different kind with his pupil. 'We were working on Marshall's principles of economics, and when we came to his theory of monopolies, Teddy wouldn't accept it. He was never rude – he still gives me the same respect today although he's a Prime Minister – but he wouldn't accept what I said. I had the most interesting discussions with him. Marshall's theory was that monopolies must lead to competition: as soon as one builds up a monopoly one is bound to get another large industrial unity being built up, with the result that the monopolists would have to ask for a price for their commodity which was below what could be offered by the smaller industrial unit. He didn't agree. His argument was that it fostered high prices. I had graph after graph prepared, but it was no good. He wouldn't accept it.'

It is a fascinating account, presaging his demolition thirty years later of Resale Price Maintenance; it shows, too, his independence of mind, stubbornness of will, and the fact that he was now positively enjoying the stimulus of argument.

After two years in the Sixth Form, he sat for the open scholarship examination to Oxford and Cambridge and failed. He would have been accepted as a Commoner, but there was no question of him getting an award. To understand what a high order of disaster this was, as both Dr Norman and Mr Curzon instantly recognized, it is necessary to trace what had been happening in the Heath household and the outside world during the past few years.

In 1929 Ramsay MacDonald had been elected Prime Minister of the country's second Labour Government; but like the first, six years previously, this government was in a minority in the House. Unable to assert its own policies and to introduce radical legislation, it generated insufficient confidence at home and abroad, and in a climate of increasing uncertainty unemployment climbed from just over a million in 1929 to two and a half million by the end of 1930. It was during this period that William Heath's employer died. All but one of his workshops were at once sold to a Margate firm called

Jones. As a first-class worker, Heath might have found new employment fairly quickly despite the prevailing economic tide, but even in industry jobs were not pensionable, so, with little to confirm his decision in terms of job security, he determined to set up on his own. He managed to rent the remaining workshop, which was over a garage and extremely inconvenient for his purpose because it was difficult to get the materials up and finished work down – which was probably why Jones had not wanted it. He put in his own equipment, and even made an offer for the premises, but this was refused. As he would not stoop to borrowing, nothing could be done about that.

He started off with one man to help him – at about the time Teddy was sitting for his General Schools Certificate – and recalls, 'This was a depressed area. You had to go and search for what work you got. There was just enough to keep us going.' In 1931 the country's financial crisis led to the formation of a National Government, intended at first to be temporary but given a renewed lease of life when the Labour Party expelled Ramsay MacDonald and other members associated with the coalition, so that the Prime Minister stood for re-election and stayed at the head of a similar team, seconded by Baldwin, for a further four years. The gradual easing of the national situation was reflected locally, and William Heath began to expand, in time taking on six regular staff plus some casual labour and acquiring the lease of the rest of his late employer's premises when Jones in turn closed down. Even so, money remained tight. 'Every summer was slack, and we had six weeks without anything one year – that was the worst time – but we always kept the six on. After their wages were paid there wasn't much to live on.'

Expenses were rising in the home as well. It had been decided that as usual John must have the same chance as Edward, so he went to Chatham House too – but without a scholarship. He remembers that at about this time he asked his father for a bicycle. 'My father said, "You can have one when you can pay for it," and I produced my savings certificates – he'd forgotten I had them.' William himself was still driving to work on a motor-cycle, on which he had had about nine accidents, when a friend (the head salesman of a car firm) suggested he needed a second-hand Hillman Minx, drove him to work in it for two days, and at the weekend took the whole family out in it, before the days of driving tests. 'On Sunday Teddy drove it home from Herne Bay.' Suddenly they had acquired a car and two drivers.

With all these events, and in the context of national uncertainty, it is natural that William's first thought when he heard that his son wanted to go to Oxford was; 'Who's going to pay for it?' By eighteen he himself had spent a third of his life working, and was well on the way to setting up his own home. No doubt he had hoped that Teddy's brains would be turned to good use after he had promised to leave aside a musical career; he was old enough and clever enough to be bringing good money into the home. Some relations, who seemed to find Edward a bit stand-offish anyway, regarded university as a waste of time and money. If he had won the open scholarship, the problem would have solved itself – for just as William Heath let John have his bicycle when he showed he could pay for it, the same principle would have operated over the much greater project of Teddy's future. But, as he did not, and the family budget was stretched to the limit by the recent business expansions, Dr Norman had to write to the admissions tutor at Balliol College on 8 June 1934: 'I saw his people yesterday and discovered that it is quite impossible for him to enter as a Commoner.' However, by dint of argument (Cecil Curzon says that the headmaster told Mr Heath, 'You know, Teddy is going to be Prime Minister one day') he succeeded in getting his pupil a year's grace. He could stay on at school and sit for the scholarship again.

He knew where his weaknesses lay. In reply to a request from Edward's headmaster, Charles Morris, the Balliol admissions tutor (now Lord Morris of Grasmere) had written: 'Heath's work in Economics was on the border line of being Exhibition standard, his general work was not quite so good, and his French seems to have been really rather weak.' Even this analysis did not help him, as became plain when he sat for the same examination in the summer of 1935, and the new admissions tutor, M. R. R. Ridley wrote: 'He made quite a good showing in the Modern Subjects Scholarship in Economics with an $\alpha=$ and a $\beta+?+$. This was of course his strong subject last year, though in neither year was it by itself up to scholarship standard. But whereas last year in his Essay and general paper he got a β and $\beta+?+$ this year he got the same mark on his general paper but only a $\gamma+$ on his Essay. His (French) prose and unseen were a trifle better than last year, and his Literature paper definitely worse . . . on balance he does not appear to have made any marked advance.'

It seemed that he had reached his ceiling, and perhaps the falling-off in his Essay and French Literature papers was only stronger evidence of his apparent lack of interest, except in their functional aspect, in words. But he has always tended to clipped phrasing when tense or anxious, and this may have been another reason for the results. Even so he had done well enough to be offered a Common Entrance. Kent Education authorities were willing to make him a loan which he would have to repay when he came down. Could the rest be found?

The Kent loan amounted to £90 a year, and as the lowest calculation of his expenses for a year at Balliol amounted to £220 his parents would have to supply £130 a year – more than his father's entire annual income had been when he entered Chatham House nine years before. It must have been a very tight squeeze indeed, and from one or two remarks Edward made at Oxford and afterwards it seems likely that it was his mother who was his champion in this desperate hour. Her moral strength combined with her passionate devotion to her son must have been an exceedingly strong force, and when added to Dr Norman's arguments, and Teddy's own sense of Oxford as a must, there were three determined minds made up against William's which still was not absolutely sure. But the sense of family unity and the habit of talking things over, however briefly, triumphed, and after another conference between Dr Norman and Mr Heath, it was settled – he was to go up to Balliol as a Commoner.

The triumph brought with it worry and, through responsibility, a still more intense sense of ambition.

He may himself have felt it was a ruthless decision, as indeed it was; but he had always been ready to make heavy demands on both himself and those around him when he has been convinced that a greater good would result. The agony of more than a year's uncertainty had hardened his resolve, but he had much to do to prove that his own confidence, and the sacrifices he was demanding from others, could be justified.

5

Why Conservative?

Edward Heath was one of seventy or so freshmen who went up to Balliol in the Michaelmas term of 1935, and at the time there was nothing to suggest that he would one day become the third Balliol Prime Minister. He had not, like Asquith, won a Classical Scholarship; nor even, like Macmillan, an Exhibition. He had not Asquith's gift for 'resonant, elaborately constructed, yet beautifully balanced and lucid English diction',[1] nor would he ever become, as Macmillan had, 'one of the most polished orators in the Union – perhaps just a little too polished'.[2] His attitudes were less radical than either of theirs had been at the same age. But if he had not the brilliance, the grace in speaking, the stylish manner, the physical magnetism, the intellectual curiosity that would have once made their mark on Oxford society, if it was easy to overlook him, as in fact most people did, he had hidden assets. Within the pleasant-looking boy of nineteen, as only a handful of people knew, was an avid ambition, a hunger for success, far greater than the average young man's desire to do well in the world; and it was directed along far narrower and more meticulous lines. This drive was already more than half directed towards politics. He had proved to his own satisfaction that ambition and persistent work towards a goal, combined with some degree of talent, go at least as far as a greater talent with more superficial flair, but unsupported by desire and discipline. Edward Heath

[1] *Asquith*, by Roy Jenkins, Collins, 1964.
[2] *Isis* report quoted in *Macmillan, A Study in Ambiguity*, by Anthony Sampson, A. Lane, 1967.

had the first, industrious combination. He also had a deep and as yet unrevealed potential for positive leadership on major issues. On many less important issues he could be unilluminating and rather retrogressive. Yet when he focused his attention on a great crisis or design, he seemed instinctively, without the subtle doubts and self-doubts of the more intellectual man, to understand the basic moral potential of the issue, and could spell out what he saw in tones of unmistakably clear, if not visionary, promise or threat.

During his first two years at Balliol nothing happened to evoke the performance of which he was capable; but, though embryonic, his future political self was already formed, the features there in miniature.

William Heath is fairly certain that his son made up his mind to go into politics when he was about sixteen – a few months after he had promised his mother that he would not make music a career. Perhaps this undertaking could have been regarded as a promise made under duress, and maybe he kept the possibility of a musical career at the back of his mind. But in the forefront, quite distinctly, was the idea of becoming a politician. Lord Morris remembers interviewing him during the summer before he came up, in 1935, and felt genuine astonishment when, in answer to a question about what life he hoped to pursue after coming down from Oxford, the schoolboy coolly answered that he wanted to be a 'professional politician'.

The answer was the more surprising as the boy struck him chiefly as being extremely modest – 'modest and careful', as he puts it. He said later, 'I do not think I ever heard any other schoolboy answer a similar question in these terms'.[1] It was not so much the ambition as the directness, the lack of camouflage that was unusual. The pre-war flavour of Balliol that was so well described by Aldous Huxley still persisted: 'There are Union orators of every shade and opinion and young men so languidly well bred as to take no interest in politics of any kind; there are drinkers of cocoa and drinkers of champagne. [Balliol] is a microcosm, a whole world in miniature; and whatever your temperament or habits may be . . . will provide you with congenial companions and a spiritual home.'[2]

[1] *Edward Heath*, by George Hutchinson, Longmans, 1970.
[2] *Limbo*, by Aldous Huxley, Chatto and Windus, 1920.

Edward's statement at once marked him out from the 'young men so languidly well bred as to take no interest in politics of any kind', and even from those who so wished to be thought well bred that they allowed no glimmer of serious personal ambition to pass their lips. He was direct, impatient of devious niceties, and perhaps also lacked some sensitivity as to the response his words might provoke. In any case, even if he was aware of a certain brashness in his approach, he probably calculated (and if so was almost certainly right at this stage of his career, though he could have curtailed the characteristic later) that for someone with his personality and from his background self-effacement simply would not pay. A golden boy could have waited to be called. Edward Heath was convinced of his own worth, but he was realistically aware that he had no superficial advantages; not even an aura. It was up to him to declare himself, and push. He had nothing to lose. An excess of modesty, other than in manner, would have already lost him any chance of going up to Oxford at all.

His ambition may have been inherited from both sides of the family with their inclination to self-improvement, and was doubtless nurtured strongly by his mother. Some idea of the strength of his father's ambition is given by the fact that although by most reasonable standards he had achieved a great deal – leaving school at twelve to become a master-carpenter employing a sizeable staff is not insignificant progress – he never regarded himself as successful. Perhaps a tendency to self-deprecation in purely career terms has been accentuated in recent years by his son's achievement; but when he said slowly, 'I could never have borrowed . . . that's been my downfall,' he said it with a Shakespearian finality that momentarily convinced me until I considered – *What* downfall? It was not said in the tone of one recently convinced of his failure, but rather of a man who, whatever his own achievement, had never been accorded the acclaim of his society – the world of Broadstairs.

This goes far to explain his son's determination to wrest respect from his contemporaries. But if the drive itself was a natural inheritance, the direction given to the drive was his own. Politics seems a surprising choice for a boy of his tastes and background. But, on closer inspection a variety of reasons became apparent that must have added up to a rationale. Since he was nine it had been obvious that he liked responsibility and command. Always serious-

1. Heath (extreme right, front row) in the army.

2. In Danzig in 1939.

3. With a Polish couple in 1939, who had given Heath and Seligman a lift from Lodz to the frontier.

4. Sitting on the lorry that gave them a lift from Warsaw to Lodz.

5. Edward Heath as the godfather of the Seligman's son at his christening in 1950.

6. 7 January 1958. Cabinet members seeing Mr Macmillan off on his Commonwealth tour. *Left to right:* Lord Home (Commonwealth Relations), Heath (Chief Whip), Lord Kilmuir, Lennox-Boyd, R. A. Butler and Lord Hailsham.

7. 3 November 1960. Iain Macleod, Colonial Secretary, with Heath, then Lord Privy Seal, chatting at Lancaster House prior to the opening session of the West Indies Bases conference.

8. 23 September 1961. As Lord Privy Seal, addressing a meeting of the United Kingdom Council of the European Movement at Church House in London.

9. 18 September 1962. Heath meets Erhard, Schröder and Schwarz in Bonn, to discuss the accession of Great Britain to the E.E.C.

10. 29 March 1962. Heath, in his capacity as Lord Privy Seal, signing the European Satellite convention, watched by Peter Thorneycroft, Minister of Aviation.

11. 19 March 1964. As President of the Board of Trade, chairing a meeting of the Commonwealth Economic Consultative Council at Marlborough House.

2. May 1964. Playing the organ at Durham.

13. August 1965. With Madron Seligman and his son during a holiday taken at Cap Nice on the French Riviera.

14. Fishing at Cap Nice.

minded (even when he was venting a sharp wit), he belonged to that type that likes to convince others of the rightness of their views. Many people find it almost too easy to do this, through the force of their personality, the brilliance and attractiveness of their ideas – especially when they are young and their contemporaries are most malleable. He did not have such magnetism, and to assert his views he needed power; he had been given a taste of this in the strenuous arguments when he was at Chatham House, particularly in his excellently filled role as secretary of the school debating society. Politics, of course, were not discussed in his home, and this too may have acted as a stimulus. He and his father, so similar in character, were yet so different in tastes and talent that as a young man he may have felt more than the usual reaction against the paternal pattern; if so, a sphere right outside the familiar world would seem both better and almost easier to aim for than just a better job of a known variety: easier to set his sights on the Cabinet, almost, than to work to become a better accountant than his uncle. A political career would also be more impressive to Broadstairs: he had for a long time cherished personal dreams concerning this, and also, realizing that he was socially mobile, needed a sphere that would allow him sufficient movement.

So he chose politics – but why on the Conservative side? This was hardly a choice, more a matter of temperament and of his own particular experiences in the light of that temperament. The prevailing winds in Kent were forcefully Conservative. Thanet itself has returned a Conservative (or in the case of Esmond Harmsworth, now Lord Rothermere, a Unionist) member in 1918, 1922, 1923, 1924, 1929, 1931 and 1935. (It would later continue in its loyalty even against the Labour landslide in 1945.) A comparison of returns in the eleven Kent constituencies throughout the seven elections from 1918 to 1935 shows that seventy Conservatives were returned to the seventy-seven seats.

Chatham House School had reflected the enfranchised opinion in most of its attitudes, and a mock election in 1929 produced the results:

Conservative	215
Liberal	118
Labour	38

KENT	1918	1922	1923	1924	1929	1931	1935
Ashford	C	C	C	C	L	C	C
Canterbury	C	C	C	C	C	C	C
Chislehurst	C	C	C	C	C	C	C
Dartford	L (Lab)	Const	Lab	C	Lab	C	C (Lab)
Dover	C (Ind)	C	C	C	C	C	C
Faversham	C	C	C	C	C	C	C
Gravesend	C	C	Lab	C	C	C	C
Isle of Thanet	C	C	C	C	C	C	C
Maidstone	C	C	C	C	C	C	C
Orpington	—	—	—	—	—	—	—
Sevenoaks	C	C	L	C	C	C	C
Tonbridge	C	C	C	C	C	C	C

And this at the time of a Labour victory in the country, albeit a lukewarm one.

Edward Heath had a sufficiently independent brain and will to have chosen a different course if this had seemed to him right. That it did not is probably doubly due to his father: it was a matter of inherited and encouraged character traits and also of example – *self*-help.

Harold Wilson, four months older, was already up at Oxford when his unknown rival came up. He too was a grammar-school boy, he too had a firm religious background, he too was reading P.P.E. Here the resemblance, for the moment, ended. Wilson was academically advanced and acquisitive for more knowledge; he collected the Gladstone Memorial Prize, the Web Medley Economics Scholarship and finally, two years ahead of Heath, a First-Class degree. He did not use the Union to launch himself. Wilson was later to admit, 'I think I was born with politics in me,' and his Nonconformist family predisposed him towards the Left; but his natural inclination towards the Labour Party was probably clinched – at least in rational retrospect – by the vivid impression made on him at the age of fourteen – in 1930 – by seeing a weaver friend out of work[1] and realizing that there was no hope for him. At precisely the same age and, presumably, roughly the same stage of emotional vulnerability and empathy, Edward Heath had seen his father (thrown out of work by his employer's death) set up his own workshop and start up as the Boss with a single employee.

[1] Interview with Brian Blake of the B.B.C., February 1964.

Their experiences typified the difference between the depressed areas in the South and North, where in some towns employment was a luxury enjoyed by well under half the population: in Jarrow unemployment reached 67 per cent in the winter of 1932-3, in Merthyr Tydfil nearly 62 per cent, and many towns in Cheshire, where Wilson spent part of his boyhood, had rates approaching 50 per cent. It was the difference between short rations and hunger, between difficulty and despair.

Heath himself later discounted the possibility that living in the other environment would have changed his political formation: 'My part of the country wasn't as bad as the North, but nevertheless one realized this, and I don't think that the answer to it was to take everything into the hands of the State, which is what the Socialists were saying, and so this is one of the reasons why I was a Conservative . . .'[1]

Almost certainly he read his own character aright, but exposure to the dreadful conditions in the North might have triggered off an unexpected type of emotional energy in him such as he may have only experienced otherwise in relation to his mother. Even so, this would probably have been less intense than that which fuelled Harold Macmillan, who wrote: 'I shall never forget those despairing faces as the men tramped up and down the High Street in Stockton or gathered round the Five Lamps in Thornaby',[2] and who, partly because of those faces, was for long a rebel within the Conservative Party. For Macmillan, this terrible vision of a life he had never had to endure himself was profound, even in his late thirties, and vibrated through him to the foundations of his beliefs. Edward Heath came from a stratum much closer to hardship, where nevertheless good management as well as some luck managed to fend off disaster. He was therefore less sympathetic to its victims. If Edward Heath as an adolescent had seen those who, in spite of possessing strong characters, had still gone under, he might have felt a similar compassion for the despair of his countrymen. Instead, his later concern for them developed along more combative and demanding, less paternalistic lines. Later he believed he had joined the Conservatives 'because

---

[1] The Prime Minister interviewed by Herr von Troschke, on German television, March 1971.
[2] *Winds of Change*, Macmillan, 1966.

they're the party that get things done'. A less practical young man might have been converted to radical solutions nevertheless, but one of his former tutors says, 'I don't think he ever tumbled over the other side of the line – his temperament and background, I think, were both pretty tough pulling to that side: conditioning him.'

Almost exactly one year after he came to power the Prime Minister himself told me flatly, if hardly surprisingly, that he did not think there had ever been any chance of him becoming anything other than a Conservative.

In this apparent intransigence he was very different from the average undergraduate, who took his politics a little more flexibly. He was also different from the obviously outstanding undergraduate, for instance, with his powerful curiosity, Denis Healey, who came up a year after Heath and was, for most of his undergraduate life, a Communist. A former member of the college remembers, 'Healey was a very interesting case – a member of the Party, but he was on an intellectual Odyssey, seeking an intellectual answer to the problems that that generation were undergoing. He explored streams of intellectual inheritance outside his formal work. We all felt sympathy for the plight of that generation. Nothing much could happen in the political life of the country. But it was not as bad for Ted as the Healeys – he didn't feel, I've got to find an alternative; the party he was going to join was in office.' Denis Healey shared Heath's dislike of sport and love of music. He also loved to argue, but failed, it seems, to find a furious opponent in him. 'He wasn't very didactic or dogmatic,' he remembers, with a note of disappointment over battles unfought.

His tutors noticed something of the same thing: he was most eager to listen and to learn, but, according to one, 'he wasn't very argumentative', according to another, 'he probably had a very great respect for the tutors – even Etonians think the tutors are immensely clever'. It was rather as if he was taking a deep breath which was not to be exhaled for many years.

In 1935, four years after the Tory landslide and his exile from the Labour Party, MacDonald gave way as head of the National Government to his Conservative second, Baldwin, who had been officially Lord President of the Council. The two had worked well together,

fusing their abilities and abandoning their differences to surmount
the crisis, but to Harold Macmillan, MacDonald's speeches now
seemed so 'tortuous and so mystifying as to have no meaning . . .
always high-minded, he became woolly-minded'.[1] Another Conservative considered simply that, 'MacDonald had a well-stocked
mind, but he had a very weak character'.[2] This was hardly a combination to appeal to the young Heath, who was already inclined to
suffer weakness still less gladly than foolishness, and must have
found the wasted ability most exasperating as an example of leadership. Baldwin was often slow to make decisions, but made them with
moral certainty and held to them trenchantly – setting another seal
on Heath's view of Conservative power. Heath made a moving
speech about Baldwin, showing the depths of his admiration, at a
centenary dinner for him in 1967. When Baldwin went to the country
later in 1935 his position was confirmed: the Conservatives and their
Liberal-National and National Labour allies had a majority of 249
over the remnants of the torn and tattered Labour Party. So yet
again the National Government was reinstated, with its first Conservative Prime Minister.

Events were moving towards a climax which was to reveal the man
within the undergraduate. The Government had been returned with
a mandate for rearmament, but the Conservative Party was divided
and uncertain in its views on defence; *The Economist* dubbed the
1935 White Paper on Defence the 'Black Paper'. The long-expected
attack by Italy on Abyssinia began on 3 October 1935. The next
month the League of Nations tried to introduce economic sanctions
against Italy in protest; they were to prove ineffectual, and were
scorned as 'the height of midsummer madness' by Neville Chamberlain, but the debate on the fate of Abyssinia aroused stronger feelings
and arguments than had recently been shown in Parliament. When
the sanctions were finally abandoned, Macmillan and a fellow
Conservative resigned the Whip. Baldwin's concentration was not
helped by the abdication crisis at home, when a different attitude
from Edward VIII could have weakened the Government. Baldwin
resigned in May 1937. With the accession of Chamberlain the slide

[1] *Winds of Change*, Macmillan, 1966.
[2] *Memoirs of a Conservative, J. C. C. Davidson's Memoirs & Papers 1910–1937*, by
Robert Rhodes James, Weidenfeld and Nicholson, 1969.

towards appeasement accelerated; before long the full clamour of combative patriotism was to be provoked in Heath, and both his brand of Conservatism and his character put to the test.

The revelation of his true passions, when it came, must have seemed as startling as his political ambitions had seemed to Lord Morris. When he went up to Balliol he was, according to one contemporary, 'very intense, very middle class, rather grey'. He was not a great disputant, nor a great chatter – several people noticed that though he spoke of his parents with pride he never actually described his home or his home life. He struck his tutors as solid rather than brilliant. Yet within two years or so he had become, as Julian Amery remembers, 'clearly somebody one noticed. One found him in all kinds of groups and parties, but he was in a way rather detached from any of them – I'm using "party" not in the sense of cocktail party but of a group of six or seven talking late at night.'

From the first, he had not attempted to explore Oxford in either the headlong or the rather haphazard way of most undergraduates. Instead, he plodded through his early career there with his usual deliberation, and applied himself to the problem of establishing himself with what may at the time have been the defensive reaction of an anxious freshman, but was nevertheless as effective as a campaign of mathematical precision. He was fully prepared to watch and learn from others until his time was ripe; meanwhile he broadened his activities as he had done at school until eventually a variety of functions grew out of his particular interests.

There were indications of this approach in his first term. On 28 November 1935 he went to a concert to hear Beethoven's Ninth Symphony conducted by Sir Malcolm Sargent. When he got back to his rooms in Balliol late that night he sat down and wrote to his old school sponsor:

Dear Headmaster,
    I wondered at first should I put 'Dear Sir', but this seemed very much as though I were asking you to sign another form of some sort. Dear Mr Norman sounded very strange to my ears and 'My dear Headmaster' is how I imagine the Governors address you. So, Sir, I think I had better stick to my compromise.
    . . . settling down and work . . . have left no time for doing great

things, and I am now very sceptical of biographies in which it is related how great men 'hit' Oxford in their first week.

The college is delightful. Of course, not an architectural wonder, but it has its own, to me, very pleasing atmosphere. The dons are very nice, as nice as the helpful letters they used to write. Here too everybody mixes very well, unfortunately not always the case.

I have joined the Union where I have spent the term sitting at the feet of the great men of the day, so that next term perhaps I may speak the better. The Bach choir gives me an opportunity to sing – it is great fun, and I've also joined the musical society . . .

My tutor advised me to have a shot at the organ scholarship here. I feel you may think it strange that I, already up here, should compete for an award which would allow someone else to come up, but I feel from the financial point of view that I must.

After a few more phrases about his shortcomings in letterwriting, etc. he signed himself, very formally, E. R. G. Heath.

It is a revealing letter – particularly for someone so guarded against displaying introspection and so loath to commit himself on paper. His new scepticism about how 'great men "hit" Oxford in their first week' might be a hint that he expected in time to be among them. He had not lost any time in ascertaining that his path was to be through the Oxford Union; but, with that characteristic watchfulness and patience, he would wait until he was prepared for the despatch box.

Socially sensitive, though too sensible and believing too much in his conception of his moral worth to harbour any feelings of real inferiority outside the social sphere, he searched long for the correct mode of address to Mr Norman. He dreaded the thought of making a blunder through ignorance. But the remark about mixing well – 'unfortunately not always the case' – shows that he was evidently less aware of snobbish attitudes at Oxford than at Broadstairs. There were more of his own kind here, and different strata mingled intellectually even if afterwards they went to different parties. He is not explicit about the experiences that produced this reflection: maybe it was his somewhat isolated career at school or, more probably, the social snobbery of Broadstairs towards the sons of craftsmen and trades-men. But this rather dignified comment is the only complaint so far on record about the loneliness he had felt before Oxford.

It says much for Balliol. Its modern outlook, ahead of the general pattern of colleges in so many ways both socially and practically, had been developed by the Master, A. D. Lindsay, himself a remarkable man, on lines laid down by the far-seeing Benjamin Jowett, Master from 1870–93; he had insisted that the college existed primarily for the sake of the undergraduates, not for research, and should educate men of affairs, not only academics. When Lindsay took office he said he had been brought up in this faith, and hoped the college would never abandon it. Under him its scope increased. There was still a large entry each year from Eton. But also, in the words of a contemporary, Lindsay 'thought the more diversified Balliol was, the better, that the entry of a black man and a bus driver from Bristol as an adult scholar were moves towards an ideal society. Balliol was pioneering, whereas Trinity thought it had fallen from grace if it took in a Ted Heath or a black man or someone who didn't come from one of the more refined public schools.'

In fact J. E. Hobbs, who had been Captain of Chatham House during Teddy's last term, had got a science scholarship to Trinity, but although the two might go to the same concert and were not unfriendly, they went separate ways. This was partly a matter of individual personalities; but there was a genuine friendly feud between the neighbouring colleges, and one tired entry in the Balliol J.C.R. suggestions book (in which undergraduates could proclaim their desires or criticisms of society) read:

Sir:
   May I call the attention of certain gentry to the practice of yelling 'Bloody Trinity' across the quads.
   May I respectfully suggest that they
      (a) sing in tune (if possible)
      (b) cease at a reasonable hour, say 1 a.m.

But the answer came that the practice was 'tradition'.

It was a different world from Broadstairs, and 'inevitably it was part of the education of the Balliol undergraduates who came up from below, socially speaking, to bring himself to take on the ways and manners, and the values, of the sons of the governing classes. At the same time the latter were considerably affected by the able young men who came up from less privileged schools and homes, partly because of their sheer ability and partly because of the individual determination and character without which they would never have arrived at the college.'[1]

These ways and manners might, in their more subtle and sophisticated forms, elude him for some time yet; some he would never care to adopt, although he was always polite to his elders. As for the values of the sons of the governing classes, some of these he already had – not only his apparently instinctive identification with the Conservative Party, which was to become more important as his Oxford career progressed, but also the expansion of his enjoyment of what he today calls The Good Life. There were many types of good life to pursue at Oxford. Racing, or beagling, or going to parties that glittered socially but not intellectually, were emphatically not for him; they would have seemed little removed from yelling 'Bloody Trinity' across the quad late at night. In any case he was not the type to attract invitations from those outside his own social sphere. One man remembers, 'You certainly wouldn't have expected to meet him at a party with Hugh Fraser or Philip Toynbee.' In the first two years at Balliol his enjoyment consisted largely of music, which now became a means as well as an end. At the end of his first term as he mentioned in his letter to Dr Norman he sat for the organ scholarship on the suggestion of his tutor, and won it. It was worth one hundred pounds a year, and a corresponding weight was removed both from his parents' expenses and his own worries. Since the organ scholarship was valid for three years, and would run from the beginning of the next Michaelmas term, it also gave him the opportunity of spending four years at Oxford instead of the three years normally needed to read P.P.E. The night that he got the good news he telephoned at once to Broadstairs – typically, he had not told them about the exam beforehand. His father remembers him saying, 'We are celebrating with a cup of tea in my rooms.' He was not yet one of the drinkers of champagne, although his vision of the good life would later expand to include this among his delights.

For the time being it was enough that he could buy things of his own, particularly books. One of the people who had found him lacking in literary knowledge when he first went up wondered, 'Where are the books in Broadstairs?' and it was a well-founded query. He had often asked for, and been given, books as Christmas

[1] *A History of Balliol,* by H. W. C. Davis, Blackwell, 1963.

and birthday presents, but these were not the final embellishments
to a sound family library; he was not so fortunate as another budding
politician who had just gone down from Oxford, Barbara Castle.
In later years she proudly called herself working class, but her father,
an inspector of taxes and self-taught scholar, translated Lorca and
Greek plays into English at home in a study literally lined with books.
Edward Heath was closer in possessions, but not aspirations, to
Chaucer's scholar, who had at his bed's head

> Twenty books clad in blak or reed
> Of Aristotle and his philosophie.

Now he set about adding to his nucleus with whole sets of volumes on
philosophy and economics, usually buying the good cheap editions
(before the days of widespread paperbacks), but still not venturing
very much into the spheres of imaginative writing. But, as he passed
from nineteen to twenty, he himself felt that the transformation in
his life was beginning: 'Never until my second year at Oxford did I
buy a record . . . I never bought a book of my own until I was at
Oxford . . . I like to have things of my own, pictures of my own, even
if they are poor pictures.'[1,2] It is not really surprising that he regarded
money very highly indeed, and looking back to that time and gradual
materialization of his hopes said later, 'Without some prosperity you
can't have a full life – travelling, theatre, books – books of your own
and not borrowed from the library.'

He had an account now with Lloyds Bank but he was not (he
told friends who asked why he did not smoke) going to waste his
mother's money. Unlike the 'clerke of Oxenford', who eschewed
owning a fiddle, he had his piano sent up to his rooms – an extremely
unusual thing for an undergraduate to do – which were now, according to the traditional abode of the organ scholar, no. 1 on staircase 1.
He had to be in chapel in his lay scholar's gown in time to start the
daily service at five past eight each morning – an early start for him
at any age, but unprejudiced by late nights.

It was the end of his first year, on 16 June 1936 that he made his

---

[1] Interview with Terry Coleman from the *Guardian*, 9 June 1970.
[2] At Chequers in May 1972 he told me that he had bought books before going up
to Oxford, but not records.

voice heard for the first time in college affairs. On being elected secretary of the Balliol College Musical Society, he immediately proposed that a choir should be formed, consisting of Balliol men, as far as was possible, for the tenors and basses, and of women students of the university for the sopranos and altos. The following term he suggested that this choir should take part in the society's one thousandth concert. Since the society had a deficit of £11, the minutes record that a serious discussion then took place on the fees to be paid to the artists, 'the secretary [Heath] pointing out that he thought the society could save a considerable amount by direct contact with the artists'. More hints of his future fight against Resale Price Maintenance.

At this time the concerts were open to any male members of the university, but female undergraduates were classed with 'the town', and only admitted on the production of tickets obtained from and signed by members of Balliol College personally known to them. One member of the society asked whether this was really necessary (women were gaining ground in the university, and two years before, in spite of protests voiced in the Oxford Magazine, had been admitted to dinner in the Union). It was left to 'the secretary to ascertain whether many women students of the university would take advantage of alteration in the society's policy'. Most uncharacteristically for someone so thorough, when the group next met in his own rooms on 5 March 1937, Heath made absolutely no mention (according to the minutes) of any findings he had made on the question entrusted to his researches, and women members of the university could not gain entrance to the concerts simply by wearing a gown until ten months after Heath had resigned as secretary. It was shown, however, that the deficit had been converted into a credit of £12.

Heath was chosen to conduct the one thousandth concert on 28 November 1937, and his parents drove up from Broadstairs to don evening dress and see him. The evening was a great success.

It was about this time, in his third year, that he began to be taken a great deal more seriously by his contemporaries. He had made a number of friends, but still not very close friends – although having survived his teens without a bosom pal, he was not likely to miss this at Oxford. At the end of his second year he gave the impression of being rather smug, and the J.C.R. suggestions book carried the entry, dated 15.6.36,

Overheard on Staircase X
Mr E. R. G. Heath:
'I'm cultured.'

A joke, perhaps; but, if so, one only too easily capable of mis-interpretation.

In his third year he was acquiring a wider general circle of friends, and even overcame his general weakness at games so far as to fling himself whole-heartedly into playing table tennis, which, according to *Isis*, 'he plays with the more wizardry as he appears to hold the racket as if it were a soup-spoon'.[1] He even took the trouble to wear a 'specially constructed glove' for the purpose. During the summer of 1938 he directed the music for the O.U.D.S. (Oxford University Dramatic Society) production of *The Taming of the Shrew*, and com-posed the choric odes for the Balliol Players' production of the *Acharnians* of Aristophanes. One of the players was Madron Seligman, a good-looking middle-class undergraduate who had come up in 1937, two years after Heath. He was, Lord Morris remembers, 'very very good company'; he liked skiing and was later picked for an Olympic team. It seemed to one person who remembers them that the two had superficially very little in common – an impression not minimized by their different years – yet they became friends, and very good friends, remaining so today some thirty-five years later. Today Seligman is an industrialist, managing director of his family engineering firm which won the Queen's Award for Export in 1966. Perhaps it was the first time that young Heath had met someone who appealed to him sufficiently in outlook, temperament, and tastes – they played duets on the piano and looked at paintings together – who also had the confidence and charm to break through his own reserves and prove that some people outside the family could be trusted too. Seligman had a certain glamour, but more important were the qualities he has retained – an evident straightforward niceness, combined with an objectivity that, if no match for Heath's caustic eye, at least showed a refreshing freedom from impractical aspirations. 'We shared P.P.E. tutors and he sponsored my Union

[1] *Isis*, 25 January 1939.

career,' he remembers today. 'Uncle Bertie, my favourite uncle, took us both to dinner at the Royal Thames Yacht Club – and I think that meant quite a lot to him then.'

Such an outing was indeed quite an event for him at this stage, although within the university he commanded increasing respect. Wherever he was, the influence of his home crept through in his standards and his ways. One friend noted, 'If we were going swimming he wouldn't strip off in front of me – but he wouldn't obviously *not*, either. He's fairly "pi" – I think that may be his mother's influence. She was very pure.'

He did not appear to be very much at ease with the women undergraduates, sharing the general tendency of the young men of the time, other than those from sophisticated circles, to hold them in rather low, if nervous, esteem. 'He's always been rather tight with women,' comments an acquaintance of very different demeanour. 'Some people think it might be a reaction against his father.' (It is true that his father's naturally flirtatious manner still earns him a degree of envy from octogenarian contemporaries.) Some of his friends cannot remember seeing him with a girl. Madron clearly remembers going up to London with him and two girls to hear the Ninth Symphony; they stopped at Henley to picnic on the way. The very clarity of the recollections suggests that this was something of an event. His friendship with Kay in Broadstairs continued (and of course the vacations, most of which he spent at home, lasted for about half the year). When he was told about the love lives of other young men, he was shocked if they indulged in fornication – both his religious and his home upbringing had left him in no doubt that this was wrong. But it was quite impossible to go through four years at Oxford leading a sheltered life, untouched by the exploits, the fears and desires, the arguments and sometimes the inanities of his contemporaries. This was particularly true of his last year, when he was voted President of the Junior Common Room. Though this was considered a dull job in some colleges, it evidently carried a certain cachet at Balliol: Denis Healey and Roy Jenkins succeeded him.

The very fact that Balliol did consist of such an individualist and mixed group of young men made this office fairly taxing. 'They were an awkward lot of cusses to deal with,' a Fellow remembers. One of Heath's duties was to deal with the questions and comments in the J.C.R. suggestions book. The text of this unusual volume included practical worries about whether porridge and cereal should be served every morning, and whether people preferred poached or fried eggs. All these were examined most seriously by Teddy Heath, who wrote lengthy replies about the costing of the various items that would have shamed the average housewife today.

Personal problems were also aired. The normal anxieties of their age were increased by the gulf between their life in Oxford and the world outside. A young Ann Todd appearing at the Playhouse was 'breathtakingly fresh', Charles Laughton was being shown at the Scala in *The Private Lives of Henry VIII*, and the Oxford Magazine carried such pastoral advertisements as: 'Cottage on Cotswolds, suitable for Scholar. Six small rooms; beautifully quiet and secluded; all services. Rent £36' (per year, of course). The setting for this was a nation still suffering from unemployment, from guilt over the First War, fear of the military.

Some of the writings in the J.C.R. suggestions book might have been written by undergraduates at any time; others reflect their particularly savage predicament. 'Overheard' comments were extremely popular:

> 'I'm very tired tonight; I've been up all the afternoon.'
> 'I'm sort of reacting from my Liberalism you know – my *pure* Liberalism that is.'
> 'The worst of the word fornicate is that it will only fit in to trochaic verse.'
> 'A damned good thing, I'm all for these bloody unemployed joining the recruits.'
> 'If only you could get these bloody unemployed fit you'd have half the battle won.'
> 'I like my sex straight from the shoulder' was followed by the comment 'Deformed, by God!'

There were some cruder sexual remarks, a few of which drew written comments from other readers and must have been blatantly educational to a fair proportion of the undergraduates, judging by the tone of fretting frustration in which they were often written.

Teddy could even be a little risqué himself in the Union, where people were also beginning to take notice of him. *Isis*, reporting a speech in which he deplored the decline of frivolity, said, 'reasons of space (and in one instance decorum) forbid repetition of the string of jokes and stories of which it was composed'.[1]

In general he favoured less levity, and the Left-of-centre Conservative would have found little to praise in, say, his solidly traditional views on education. He strongly supported the elitist system, an attitude that foreshadowed his support of the grammar schools in the comprehensive battle more than thirty years later. In March 1936 on a motion that 'The present system of education is unsuited to a democratic state', he pointed out that 'equality of education meant equality of wealth, and equality of wealth meant Communism'.[2] Therefore he voted against it. Nearly a year later he opposed a motion 'That the public school would be an anomaly in a civilized society'[3] – the very theme that Harold Macmillan had considered in the Union precisely twenty-four years before. But he, perhaps *de rigueur* as an old Etonian, had taken another point of view altogether, arguing 'that a public-school education did not produce active citizens'.[4] However much the two felt trapped by their own educational backgrounds into defending the opposite, they both did so with a spirit that went beyond the formal: it is an interesting clue to an essential difference – Macmillan's tendency to the left of his party, Heath's to the right – between them, although very soon their paths were to converge.

Soon new allegiances were to be formed, old ones broken, in British political life. At first young Heath had been more aware of himself than simply concerned with the issues. On 7 November 1936 he had written again to his old headmaster, in tones much easier and more confident than the year before:

Dear Dr Norman,

To my great joy I was given a paper speech ten days ago moving 'that this house would not approve the return to Germany of her former colonies', which we carried by a large majority . . . Fortunately the speech went down very well indeed and I think it will lead to an official nomination for the Library Committee.

[1] *Isis*, 25 May 1938.   [2] Ibid., 11 March 1936.
[3] Ibid., 24 January 1937.
[4] *Macmillan: A Study in Ambiguity*, by Anthony Sampson.

This time he signed himself simply 'Teddy Heath'.

Anti-German feeling was mounting in the Union, as in the country, but in a somewhat nervous and irresolute way. In the words of another speaker 'unpleasant facts must be faced. Germany is now so strong that she must be appeased as we could not stand up to her in case of war.'[1]

Heath's own speech, which neatly refuted every possible point Germany could put forward for the return of her colonies, showed that he already had strong feelings about that country; but he wanted to see Germany for himself. So in the autumn of 1937 he arranged an exchange visit with a German boy (who was later to be killed in the war) and after spending some time with him and his family, he travelled on alone. For a time he stayed with a retired teacher, Dr Winckler, and his wife, whom he has since described as 'a German Liberal of the old school and he hated the Nazis and everything they were doing.'[2] The old couple suggested that he should go to Nuremberg and see for himself what was going on. He spent three days at the rally, and says, 'This was when I realized what they were really like.'[3] With an emphasis very understandable in the context of his liking for reason and emotional control he also says, 'I can still recall that rally, every moment of it. What struck me was the hysteria of the whole thing.'[4]

The realization confirmed his convictions as a Conservative, vehemently opposed to the Labour Party's pacifism. But he was also increasingly finding fault with sections of his own party, and particularly its leadership. It was an unforgettable lesson in political judgment. 'I could foresee that the war was coming and I was bound to be in it, and this, I think, influenced the whole of my attitude towards foreign affairs.'[5] He told me, 'It was very clear to me what the doctors meant.'[6]

His acute sense of danger lent an equivalent power to his speeches. His first notable victory – and a Conservative win was a rarity at this time – came in the autumn of 1937 when he demanded of Dr

---

[1] *Isis*, 4 November 1936.   [2] *Edward Heath*, by George Hutchinson.
[3] Ibid.
[4] Interview with Herr von Troschke on German television, March 1971.
[5] *Illustrated London News*, 7 August 1965.
[6] Interview with the author, June 1971.

Hugh Dalton, heavyweight opponent indeed for any undergraduate speaker, 'With regard to foreign policy, what would the Socialists do now? Let them tell us, and be appallingly frank about it.'

Anthony Eden resigned in February 1938 in almost silent protest against Chamberlain's policies. One of the few undergraduates to have a radio set in his rooms was Philip Kaiser, an American Rhodes scholar, and a group of expectant Balliol men gathered with him that night to hear Eden's decision. Phil Kaiser later became Minister at the American Embassy, and was already, in his early twenties, both politically curious and an interested spectator of his fellow humans. He says now, 'I never remember Ted talking about anything but politics.' However, on the night of the resignation, 20 February, his behaviour was characteristically enigmatic – 'He made no comment, just looked very serious, thanked me, and left.'

Edward Heath's vituperative comments came a little later. First, in the spring, as secretary of the Union, he led the attack on the policy which had brought about Eden's decision, in a speech which earned him somewhat surprised regard as a rebel to contend with in the Conservative ranks. In the autumn he returned to the despatch box to make two withering speeches that left no doubt about his position. *Isis*, falling back in some amazement, reported on the motion disapproving the policy of peace without honour, that, 'As a Conservative, Mr Heath must have astonished some of his confrères by his bitter attack'.[1]

He had spent part of the summer vacation of 1938 in Spain, as one of a four-man student delegation which visited the region still held by the old Government but now under siege from Franco. He and his three companions were lucky: their hotel in Barcelona was bombed, and people who had taken shelter in the basement were killed, but with a boyish desire to see it all they had stayed upstairs and were unhurt. Streams of young men had gone out from England and other countries to fight in the Civil War; some who stayed at home tried to help by contributing to appeals, in Oxford and elsewhere, for clothing and blankets. It was Heath's first experience of war, and while he was not stirred by any quixotic desire to stay on and fight, he was certainly far from unmoved by the realization of what war meant in personal terms. On his return to Broadstairs he

[1] *Isis*, 19 October 1938.

wrote an account in the local newspaper of what he had seen that was both graphic and unusually, openly sentimental. Perhaps a helpful sub-editor had changed a phrase or two, but the small-town boy is very plain in his description of the Spanish families: 'They are calm but on their faces is a look of anguish as they hear the bombs drop and know that nearby men, women and children are lying dead. And who can tell when their turn will come? In the day-time, shopping, or suddenly at night in their beds? Who can tell?'[1]

He was also impressed by the shortage of food, by the Spanish Opera Company which gave performances four times a week, and scathing about the French players whose 'first performance was interrupted by an air raid and the company hastily returned home'.[2]

It seems that, as with his visit to Germany, the sight of Spain had sharpened his sympathy and his tongue in regard to the oppressed and their dictators: an important point since it suggests that he had sufficient imagination and judgment to reach the outline of his decisions in the abstract, on the basis of reason alone, but that only personal experience could unlock the reservoir of his feelings to add the force of emotion to the weight of his arguments.

Briefly, he seemed carried away. In November he declared that the Government was 'nothing more or less than an organized hypocrisy, composed of Conservatives with nothing to conserve and Liberals with a hatred of Liberty'.[3] In a witty admonition to Chamberlain, which gained a cartoon in the week's *Isis*, he parodied, 'If at first you don't concede, fly, fly, fly again.'[4] The division in the country was reflected in the Union, where the motion of no confidence in the National Government as at present constructed was carried by a relatively narrow margin: 203 votes to 163.

It happened that Heath was also writing the reports of the Union proceedings in *Cherwell* at this time, and he took good (if somewhat unfair) advantage of his position there to back up his arguments and reclaim his own integrity with a deftness and wit that appeared briefly and as suddenly disappeared again from his public style. Describing himself as 'the ex-librarian from Balliol', he said he was 'opposed by the Librarian, Mr J. R. Kerruish (Magdalen), who began by quoting from the collected works and speeches of the ex-

[1] *Thanet Advertiser*, 19 August 1938.   [2] Ibid.
[3] *Isis*, 23 November 1938.   [4] Ibid.

Librarian to show how he had at one time held different views from those he had just put forward. This he did with great effect – but the ex-Librarian still agrees with the quotations when read in their original context!'[1]

It had taken a major, perilous and international issue to rouse Heath to the height of his argument. His remarks had been gaining a momentum since his disapproval of the return to Germany of her colonies two years previously. He had established his position in the Union sufficiently to win the coveted Presidency in Hilary 1939. This remarkable achievement was underlined by an apologetically give-away remark in the *Isis* Idol profile of him – 'his election to the Presidency . . . was due not to his politics but to his ability and character'. But, if he had reached the acme of the undergraduate politician, what had he done to his prospects as a serious contender on the Conservative side?

When he came up he had been regarded with faintly sceptical eyes as worthy, yes, but not a front-runner. One man had envisaged him as, at best, a future Minister of Works. Ian Harvey had foreseen that he would probably follow in his footsteps as the President of the Oxford University Conservative Association (which indeed he had, in 1937) but had not imagined him taking the lead in any unorthodox politicking. Entirely through his own efforts he had now become, as Julian Amery remembers, 'the leading Conservative figure in the university'. As President, he restored the Union with excellent speakers and serious subjects.

Now that action followed words, it must have seemed to the more calculating of the promising politicians there, as well as to the older generation, that Heath was throwing away every chance he had of a political career when, in October 1938, he took an active part in the Oxford City by-election.

The Candidate for whom Edward Heath campaigned was a member of the Labour Party, standing this time as an Independent Progressive against a Conservative candidate. The choice becomes clearer when the figures are identified as the Master of Balliol himself, A. D. Lindsay, who was put forward by Oxford City Labour Party, while the Conservative was the pro-Munich Quintin Hogg, now Lord Hailsham.

[1] *Cherwell*, 26 November 1938.

Lindsay's remarkable personality has been well described by J. P. Corbett, a Fellow of Balliol from 1945 to 1961, who wrote that he had 'extraordinary mental zest and an equally extraordinary power to bring that zest to bear on people so as to excite them in one way or another . . . and as often to hostility as to affection . . . he just shook one up.' His lively intellect, his overriding trust in democracy and depth of feeling were all made clear to the undergraduates, including Heath, who were invited to discussions in his rooms and heard him preach – he was a fervent Christian.

His reaction to the Munich settlement was expressed in words at once poignant and strong, which conveyed the keenness of his sensibility to all the aspects and implications, moral and practical, of appeasement. Urging that rearmament be tackled as a truly national effort, he wrote, 'I deplore the irresolution and tardiness of a government which never made clear to the Germans where this country was prepared to make a stand . . . I am unable to forget the unutterable harshness of the terms imposed on Czechoslovakia . . . Be neither against Bolshevism nor against Facism but for democracy.'[1]

This was Lindsay at his most recognizable and rousing. The candidate went further than the canvasser, however. Four months previously Heath had suggested, in a Union speech, that Mr Churchill had made it perfectly clear to Berlin how Britain would stand in the event of a German invasion of Czechoslovakia. Furthermore, he had argued (in phrases strongly reminiscent of William Heath on very different subjects) that 'to have given Czechoslovakia a written guarantee of our assistance would only have made her overconfident and unwilling to solve her problems'.[2]

This was a noticeably cooler approach than Lindsay's own, but, despite their differing degrees of feelings, there was enough common ground in their reasoning for them to fight on the same side, together with Harold Macmillan, who wrote to Lindsay promising his support and asserting 'the times are too grave and the issue too vital for progressive Conservative opinion to allow itself to be influenced by party loyalties or to tolerate the present uncertainty regarding the principles governing our foreign policy.'[3] Macmillan travelled up to

[1] *Isis*, 26 October 1938.   [2] 8 June 1938.
[3] *Macmillan: A Study in Ambiguity*, by Anthony Sampson.

Oxford to speak for Lindsay, and later noted in his memoirs that Heath was 'conspicuous for skill and enthusiasm'.[1]

Strategically, the dilemma was great for both the established and the would-be politician. But for many of them the moral choice was clear. The consequences of that choice were far less clear at that time. Were they all committing political suicide? It was a remarkable choice for an undergraduate who had no outside resources, no record, no background, and no connections to sustain him if he lost everything by this decision. Julian Amery, whose father Leo was a fierce opponent of Chamberlain and Munich, fought for Lindsay beside him. To the suggestion that some courage was required, he replied, 'At that age one doesn't calculate.' For him, this was true; but Heath had already learned to consider the effects of his actions, and had not even the inherited benefits of his ally. One is therefore left with a number of possibilities: maybe he felt that war was inevitable (as he later claimed) and therefore that joining the rebels was the lesser of two dangers; maybe he felt that he was doing the right thing, regardless of consequences; or maybe he felt that his own view (and that of the leading opponents to appeasement within the Conservative Party) would prevail.

In everyday terms the first possibility would have meant that he felt his own home was threatened, and that time lost would worsen the situation; the second would have meant that his neighbour's home was threatened, and that he had a duty to protect it; the third would have meant simply that, whatever might happen, his own view and that of the leading opponents to appeasement within the Conservative Party, would prevail, because it was morally right, not just safer.

If he was wrong, of course, it was a far from safe opinion to hold.

No doubt each contributed its part to his decision, but, judging by the way he has made difficult party decisions recently, the last two reasons probably weighed more heavily than the first. He is not a man who enjoys compromise, or even who sees it as particularly useful: rather the opposite. Perhaps at the age of twenty-two, and with a young man's self-belief, he did not realize precisely the magnitude of risk involved; but, even if he had, he would probably have done exactly the same.

[1] *Winds of Change*, by Harold Macmillan.

A friend comments, 'It was astounding that Teddy was able to bring the Conservative Party into the anti-Chamberlain camp – you would have thought that coming from his modest background he would have wanted to ingratiate himself with the Establishment.'

Much of the undergraduate opinion belonged to those under twenty-one, too young to vote, and Lindsay lost. The policy of appeasement for the moment triumphed; and Heath's future looked as uncertain as Europe's. But his political character had been hardened in the fire. Ambitious as he was, the pattern was becoming plain; principle would come even before personal advancement.

Meanwhile, in social life Teddy Heath was still recognizably the boy from Broadstairs. In January 1939 he was the subject of *Isis* Idol, and the reporter wrote cosily that, 'a wide circle of friends is to be found regularly in his rooms after 10.30 p.m. indulging in unbridled orgies of tea and plumcake, but conscientiously uplifting conversation is rigorously avoided.'[1]

This was still the side of the coin most people recognized.

[1] *Isis*, 25 January 1939.

6
The Adj

When he came down from Oxford Edward Heath was just twenty-three. Photographs of him at about this time show that the corners of his rather full mouth still turned up naturally and sweetly, like his mother's; but his eyes had lost a little of their earlier dreamy look, and while they were not yet the gimlets of today they contained a more concentrated and watchful gaze. According to his ex-sister-in-law, 'His rather odd accent dates from then . . . it is a mixture of rural Kent and Wodehousean Oxford.' It is a fair description although she first met him seven years after he came down. His family did not notice any great change in him or his voice – possibly because they were looking for, and therefore finding, the familiar. But it does indeed seem that the impact of Oxford on Heath's inner life was really curiously small – perhaps because it accorded so well with the imaginary world where he had always thought he would be at home: a world where right was highly considered, where culture and hard work were not mutually exclusive, where goodness and decency were respected as much as birth, and where possessions meant more than money.

He does tend to dislike and deny suggestions that he has been greatly influenced and formed by other people – for instance he claims that Lindsay's Socialism in a way 'strengthened my own Conservatism' – although he can readily admit the effect of experience and reading. It may be a dislike of being wrongly categorized, but even an over-simple question I put to him about the importance of Locke, Pitt and Disraeli in his development (he has admired them all) evoked a cautious disclaimer before he agreed that yes, Locke's empiricism had had an impact on him.

He has certainly always had an immensely strong and instinctive inner resistance to all efforts to change him, except those initiated by himself. It seems that only a first-class argument can change his outlook or opinion. This has so far been mainly an enormous strength, since he is seldom divided against himself by seeing both sides of a question; but it has also occasionally proved a weakness since few people are capable of putting their case with maximum clarity.

Nevertheless some of the influences on him were so complete as to be entirely unseen by himself, like the air he breathed: and the chief of these was still the one he had talked about least at Oxford, his home. The continuity of this side of his life, which underlay his new activities, goes some way to explaining his increasing division into selves that were kept separate – the public, the private and the secret. These different sides of his personality had existed even at school, but they were gradually deepening, and as they did so the gap between them widened.

His public confidence had vastly increased. It had not been in the least diminished by his solid but unspectacular achievement in his final examination schools, when he was awarded a second. Academic glory in itself had never greatly interested him; the Presidency of the Union had been far more important. But just as by the despatch box he had been assured and trenchant where others were often self-conscious, so there were moments in his ordinary relationships when others were relaxed while he was reserved and even extremely shy.

There were some areas silently but unmistakeably marked 'private' which even his closest friends did not dare to explore, although they might sometimes be given a glimpse of what lay within. Perhaps he did not want to, perhaps by now he really could not – but at any rate he did not confide even in Seligman. When they had chewed over the political issues of the day, Madron sometimes liked to relax and chat about everyday events and people. He found Teddy an attentive listener, but usually completely uncommunicative himself. When Madron talked about his girlfriends, he received little reciprocal information. 'I just noticed when one wasn't around any more.' 'He was always upset when they got married.'

Little of the undergraduate crudeness seems to have rubbed off on Heath: he might use an obscenity for effect, but without relish. His mother affected his view of women: she was one of the people he most admired in the world, but apart from her and a tiny number of girls who were either genuine friends or friends of his friends, his attitude to women tended to fall into stylized categories: the respectful, the defensive, the bored and the superior. The same pattern could and still can often be traced in his relations with men he does not know well; but there is an alternative here even for those outside his circle and even his field of interest: that of the attentive listener which, with women, is usually reserved for those with whom he is on good terms professionally.

Unless he was feeling shy or ill at ease, his attitude to women had some advantages: he was, for instance, no more likely to argue with one than with a child. To older women he was often most attentive. 'He was so charming to my wife – not in the French way – that she really got to love him,' remembers Cecil Curzon. But with his contemporaries he was not always so chivalrous (there was one girlfriend who blotted her copybook irredeemably by, in the words of friends, 'getting tummy ache at the wrong moment') and some of the women he has known could be forgiven for wondering whether he regarded them as more than useful and decorative accessories.

The first exception to this was Kay Raven. Their friendship had been growing now for some eight years. She was a feminine, lively and intelligent girl, who as secretary of the Carol Society had given him a great deal of active support. With her he probably felt more at ease than with anyone outside the family – except possibly Madron.

She was a girl everyone liked. 'A pretty girl – full of beans,' remembers Mr Bird. William Heath declares, 'A nice girl. A very nice girl indeed. I liked her.' She was home from her teaching job in a boys' school for much of the time when Teddy was on vacation, and together they went on picnics, to concerts, for walks and to dances. They spent some little time in each other's company – far more than he would have spent with anyone he did not like enormously. But, according to the general custom of the times and more particularly, no doubt, their families' attitudes, they did not spend holidays abroad together as might have seemed the normal thing to do a generation later: this was still the age of safety in numbers. Her mother, a woman of rather noble features and severe manner recalls,

'He danced with all my daughters. He wasn't such a close friend.'

Nor was he probably in the searching eyes of Broadstairs such a good prospect.

So it was with Madron that he arranged to spend his summer vacations abroad in 1939. Dressed in Balliol blazer and tie, with shorts and socks both to the knee, he set out again, this time as one of the last pre-war Englishmen in Europe to see Germany and Poland.

Madron Seligman says, 'I provided the initiative and he had very good contacts' – a fair bargain since Madron's family had come from Germany and (he is half-Jewish) he spoke the language excellently; while Teddy's German was worse than his French, virtually non-existent, but his Union position gave him good introductions. 'Our real interest was political,' continues Madron.

> We used to meet all the Embassy people, and Polish politicians. In Warsaw we stayed at the Y.M.C.A. The heat was terrible, but we stuck it out – I remember lying on a bed with flies all round.
>
> I took a penny whistle with me as I thought we ought to have some music to march to, and I played 'Colonel Bogey' and Swiss skiing songs on it – it nearly drove him mad. He hardly ever reads a novel and he was the same then – his joys were music and painting. In Dresden we went to see the 'Sistine Madonna' by Raphael. It was in a separate room with red velvet chairs and settees. We sat there for two hours and thought it was the best painting in the world – and outside the world was collapsing about us.
>
> We were stuck in Leipzig on the way back. People wouldn't give us lifts because we were British – and we had a row at the station when we were trying to get tickets. He told me to get a move on, and I was trying as hard as I could to get to the booking window, and I blew up – but that was me, it was my fault . . . Sitting in the train – I think it was on 23 August 1939 – we saw the headlines in the German newspapers saying that Ribbentrop had got to Moscow . . . He showed a complete lack of fear in coming with me – I was half-Jewish but he never hesitated.

Teddy got back to England two days before war was declared, while Madron went on to stay with his family at their holiday cottage in Brittany. Heath's own war started slowly. Although as a passionate patriot he quickly volunteered, he was not likely to be called up for some months, and was therefore free to fulfil another official engagement that he had undertaken while still up at Oxford – to go on a debating tour of U.S. universities with a fellow graduate, Peter Street.

It was his first sight of the New World, and as the tour (a biennial event) lasted two months and covered twenty-six universities, he had a fair chance to observe it. They arrived in the autumn and stayed until Christmas. Afterwards he mentioned that he had been struck by the 'classlessness' of the States – another indirect admission of the different attitudes he sensed in England, although he continued to say that he had never been struck by class-consciousness in this country. Presumably pride and determination prevented him from either admitting or brooding on it. He was utterly dedicated to overcoming all opposition.

Very much on his mind while he was in America was the war in Europe. He wrote – for him – a long letter of four pages to Madron saying he wished he were back and in the thick of it. There were constant reminders of the war from questions in the universities they visited, but he was struck by the essential remoteness of his audiences from the fighting. On his return home he was invited to broadcast a talk. In this he gave a clue to much of his future Atlantic policy. Talking to me in 1972, he said, 'what that visit did was to show me what was then a very live society. New York had a champagne quality about it which was very exciting for a young man.' At the time it was evidently different.

He had been severely shaken by the mental removal that physical distance from danger or disaster produces in the average man, however well-informed. When American students asked, 'Should America enter the war on the side of the Allies?' their detachment of tone was not so much more extreme (though it hid far less basic commitment) than his own when he had suggested that to give Czechoslovakia written guarantees would inhibit her from solving her own problems. 'I sometimes felt that when he spoke of the war they thought we were speaking of their Civil War,' he said.[1]

The 1939 visit provided a lesson in perspectives. It fired his determination to fuse the resources of Europe into a single entity of energy; that could stand united under attack and need not look for

[1] B.B.C. broadcast, in *Thanet Advertiser*, 16 February 1940.

help to a transatlantic ally whose kindly but distant gaze might well be focused on problems elsewhere.

From this seed sprang the thought on European Defence which he delineated in *Old World New Horizons*, prepared as a series of lectures and delivered at Harvard in 1967.

> Europe [he said] should be left free to crown its experiment in economic and political union with a defence system if at the time that is seen to be necessary.

> At this point the labels become dangerous. If you mention a European defence system nowadays you are accused of being anti-American . . . It has been argued that Europe must provide for its own defence because the Americans cannot be trusted to risk nuclear war for the defence of Europe, or alternatively because the Americans cannot be trusted not to plunge Europe into an unnecessary war in defence of her non-European interests. I personally reject both these arguments.

But, he went on to tell his American audience on this later occasion,

> It is quite possible, and I believe sensible, to welcome the possibility of an eventual European defence system while upholding the American record in Europe and elsewhere . . . in defence we Europeans are still very much the junior partners. It is not healthy that this balance should be so uneven. It is not healthy that every American troop movement in or out of Germany should be reported in apocalyptic terms in the European Press. It is not healthy that so many educated Europeans look upon everything to do with nuclear weapons as a complicated and slightly disreputable business with which, thanks to the Americans, they need not soil their minds. It is not healthy that the Americans and Russians, as a natural result of their nuclear pre-eminence, should discuss privately matters such as a non-proliferation treaty which intimately affects the security of Europe.

It was a forthright yet tactful speech, the result of twenty-eight years of examination of the special relationship between America and Britain.

He had long enough to dwell on these impressions, for he was not finally called up until 29 July 1940 when he joined the 70 Sussex Searchlight Regiment, Royal Artillery. It was a beautiful summer, one to which he would refer in his election appearance on television during the crucial 1970 campaign; as he said, it was hard to believe that the fate of the country was being decided in the skies above. At the same time the traditional hold the élite had on politics was being loosened.

One factor that recurs in Heath's life, and that he must have felt more keenly at each stage, in each new environment, was the tendency of people to under-rate him. Over and over again his ability was glimpsed by a few, ignored by more, but eventually, through his utter persistence, it was finally acknowledged if seldom acclaimed. The army was no exception to this, although in so many ways its standards, requirements and hierarchy provided a maze through which he was temperamentally equipped to find the perfect path. He understood its requirements, and he had the necessary qualities.

He was medically declared 'F.E.S.' or fit for every kind of service. Other findings of his medical examination, carried out on 5 April 1939, and very simply coded in war office (now Ministry of Defence) records show:

P	U	L	H	E	E	M	S
2	2	2	1	6	6	2	2

His number was 179215, his national insurance number 2A/92/11/36/C.

What he did not have was the outward appearance of a soldier. 'His chin didn't stick out and his chest didn't stick out, and he always wore his hat rather straight on his head,' remembers Dr J. R. D. Williams, then in the R.A.M.C. 'The rest had chests out, tummies in. But the men liked him. I think you've seen the man in his behaviour.'

As always, his actions and not his personality carried him through. Reactions to his personality were often tepid, and led to a prejudiced reckoning of his worth, and he had to train all the resources of his character to overcome them. It was at the least galling: to someone inwardly so proud it must have seemed intolerable.

At the end of November 1940 he went on an officer's training course. The following March he was posted to 335/107 H.A.A. regiment, where his commanding officer was Major George Chadd, a warm-hearted, no-holds-barred man, who was to become one of his great friends. He attracted Edward by his cheery way of sweeping aside superficialities and reservations with his own bonhomie. At their first meeting he wanted to pick a replacement for his battery, which he was determined should be the best artillery battery in the country.

Second Lieutenant Heath presented himself, saluted, and in reply to the major's questions about his past and his ambitions said he had gained a second-class degree in P.P.E. at Oxford and added, 'I want to go into politics.' Chadd comments now, 'He was the perfectly behaved officer. He didn't volunteer information: he waited until he was asked. The other officer I interviewed was almost sub-standard, and Ted always remembers that I called him back and said, 'I've decided to have you because the other one didn't even salute.'

'I sent him on to Tony Race, who was site commander at Frodsham in Cheshire. Race was a scholar, who had got a First at Oxford. I said, "I am sending you a future Prime Minister of England." '

Tony Race remembers the new recruit as being 'not as portly as he is now, but fairly mature and confident if a little withdrawn. He hadn't a warm personality.' However, two qualities, which he was thankful his new man did possess were stamina and efficiency. 'We had one or two fellows who were charming but utterly incompetent – he was the opposite. We were firing most nights, and exhaustion set in, but he was resilient. We were living fairly roughly, in wooden huts, and moved from site to site, but when we were static we had a discussion on current affairs arranged by the Army Bureau and he was particularly helpful here as his main interest was politics.'

Unlike Chadd, who saw Heath also as 'a scholar – on a par with Race', Race himself says, 'I have no recollection of his being a bookworm', and points out the practical difficulties he would have experienced without a camp library, and constantly on the move or under fire during the defence of Liverpool. Shortly afterwards Race went on a war gunnery course. 'He came top, so he was sent on and I needed a new site commander,' says Chadd. 'We had four guns, heavy ack ack, plus a hundred and twenty men – it was a bit of a responsibility for a chap of twenty-four and I had a sleepless night wondering whether Heath would make a site commander. Then I found out he had sat up all night writing orders for the site – the fire orders, the guard orders, the site standing orders, and so on.

'When we had a concert or the N.A.A.F.I. came and we had to entertain the artists he would go off at 9.30 p.m. – he was a junior officer and behaved as such. There was an element of shyness in him. I felt admiration for him because he came from such a humble background. I never asked about this background, but if you don't know things like that you're not much of a C.O.'

Music was a help to him even in wartime, and continued to act as an entrée socially, taking him to the centre of things. He used to play the piano whenever there was one about (there was one at the permanent H.Q.) and agreed to conduct the battery band, instigated by Chadd. This got them all into trouble the day they borrowed an ambulance to take them to play in Chester, and were overheard rehearsing *en route* within its somewhat confined space by another thunderstruck commanding officer.

'He got a real rocket over that ambulance,' remembers Chadd.

However, when what he considered to be a matter of genuine principle was involved, the purist in him emerged, winning him regard from some and a reputation as too strait-laced from others. Much later in the war an order came round saying that champagne could be ordered for soldiers in the sick bay. 'Someone indented for one dozen bottles, and put them on tables in the officers' mess,' remembers one of the Company. Heath asked where they came from, and somebody explained, 'We haven't got any sick people, so let's drink it.' Heath refused to touch it, and so did his colonel – wisely, as it turned out, for in some other units people were accused of misappropriation.

Light relief was rare but the quartermaster remembered one incident: Captain Heath was carrying out a kit inspection. When he came to his batman's kit, he picked up a pair of boots at arm's length, turned to him and said, 'Those boots badly need repair – get them done.' Gunner Gellatly replied, 'Sorry sir, those are your boots – I have lost my spare pair.'

As an adjutant, from April 1942, he was in his organizational element. 'He churned out reams and reams of paper to make sure everything was done by the book,' remembers a fellow officer. 'Sometimes I thought he overdid it – after all, there was a war on.'

When they were sent down to Sussex for some grimly intensive preparation for D-Day embarkation, the value of his tactics became obvious. Major W. Harrington, the quartermaster (now retired) remembers, 'He was the very soul and model of efficiency, deciding about food, petrol, where to stay – he made the moves as if they were on a chess board. He had a wonderful habit of taking a cat-nap after lunch, for half an hour so so, and woke up feeling like ten men.'

They embarked for France on 3 July 1944 and after landing at Arromanches came under fire in their field role, supporting the sixth airborne division; here they suffered their first major casualties. They moved forward next to take part in the relief of Antwerp, and celebrated afterwards with a dance – music supplied by Heath and his band. Their next task was the defence of a bridge at Nijmegen in Holland, where they spent the winter. On 22 December 1944 it was noted that Captain Heath 'sustained injury of moderate severity (scalp wound) when involved in traffic accident in a forward area. Remains at duty.' This was the only damage, apart from an operation to remove his appendix, that he suffered in the war; and three days later, on Christmas Day 1944, he presented the quartermaster (who loved India and Sussex) with a volume of *Kim*, inscribed with two verses from Kipling's 'Sussex' and a message of his own:

> God gave all men an earth to love
> But since our hearts are small
> Ordained for each one spot should prove
> beloved over all.
>
> Each to his choice and I rejoice
> The lot has fallen to me
> In a fair ground, in a fair ground,
> Yea, Sussex by the sea.

May you long live to enjoy your 'fair ground by the sea', and in the years to come may these tales recall to you, not only your service in the Land of Kim, but also that on the nearby continent:

and remind you of the Regiment in which we serve, and of one who was for three years 'the adj.'

He signed it 'Teddy'.

It is a small example of the thought he gave to individuals as well as to his work, and shows the warmth underlying his coolness and difficulty in communication – the approach may not be very stylish, but it reveals the simplicity of his own motives and affections.

Early in 1945 they moved forward into Germany, and he spent V.E. day at a village called Goch, not far from the town of Kleve (Anne of Cleves home). It was not until 22 September 1945 that he was promoted to acting major, and the next month, as acting lieutenant colonel, appointed commanding officer of the 86 H.A.A. regiment. On 8 November he was mentioned in despatches, but no details were given; during this period they were guarding prisoners-of-war camps around Hanover. He finally embarked for England on 3 June 1946 and was released under Class A (the normal, no priority, category) on 23 August as a captain.

Perhaps it was true, as he said, that nobody would enjoy having such a chunk taken out of their life by a war, but for the army itself he had developed a real affection, very much in line with his patriotism and feeling for hierarchy and order. He wanted to maintain his connection with the army. His desire was rewarded when in March 1947 he was made commanding officer of the 2nd Regiment of the H.A.C. (H.A.A.); and for three years he attended the annual summer territorial army camp. He developed a fierce pride in the H.A.C. which impressed some and bewildered others.

Meanwhile on his demob from the regular army in August 1946 there was an alarming void before him. Edward Heath was thirty, he had no clear prospects or 'connections' and he still owed money to Kent Education Committee. He was eighteen years older than his father had been when he first went out to work, he was nine years older than the Oxford graduates who were now coming down with qualifications equal to his, and who were more attuned to modern conditions. In short, he was at a loss, and the uncertainty of his life at this time reflects his own confusion.

Looking back in recent years over his choice of a career, Heath has been less clear than he was at the time. At one moment it seemed he had been thinking of becoming a barrister, and he remembered that he had got a scholarship worth one hundred pounds, to Gray's Inn awarded on 'testimonial and qualifications'. 'There was a K.C. in Broadstairs who had recommended me to go to the Bar.'[1] The next moment it was music that attracted him: he sought advice from Sir Hugh Allen, Professor of Music at Oxford, who said, 'If you want to go in for music . . . really you ought to become a conductor. But there's no point in trying to become a conductor unless you're prepared to go right to the very top.'[2]

But these are probably retrospective rationalizations for his delay. His replies to Lord Morris and to George Chadd had been clear and consistent; though he may also have felt his true ambition was a little unrealistic. He was too practical to be completely unaware of his own disadvantages – lack of personal projection, followed by lack of background and funds – and not sufficiently confident to discount them. He therefore kept alternatives in mind, but without great enthusiasm. This explains his apparent lack of consistency in these years when replying to questions about his ambitions.

Whatever he wanted to do, it was essential meanwhile that he should earn his living.

[1] Interview with Kenneth Harris in the *Observer Colour Magazine*, 23 January 1966. He told Harris, 'I didn't think of politics very specifically. I think that unless you come from a political family or from a very strong political environment you don't as early as that say to yourself "I'll try to become an M.P.".'

[2] *Edward Heath*, by George Hutchinson, 1970.

7

The Risks of Politics

Edward Heath seemed more confused, more overwhelmed by circumstances, during the immediate post-war period than at any other time in his life. He was not pursuing with great initiative the end that he had stated publicly for at least eleven years now was his goal. Though a man who inclines naturally to extremes of logic and feeling, he is also a man of unusual caution. Looking back on this period he says, 'It didn't seem to me at the time that I could afford the risks of politics, so I went into the Civil Service as a permanent civil servant on the administrative side. But I then found that this didn't really meet what I was trying to achieve . . .'

To get into the Civil Service, he had sat their strict administrative-class examination, and passed out jointly in top place with another man, who later went to work for Shell. The examiners were looking for very different qualities of mind and approach from those that his Oxford examiners had been looking for. An expert on the marks system says, 'The gap between the top and bottom marks was very small – so that really the interview was what placed you. He would have won very high marks on his personality.' Conscientious, reliable, honest, not a risk-taker, not flamboyant: these were the unglamorous assets (or, in the eyes of his critics, the dullness) that made him pre-eminent.

He was next sent to be interviewed by Mr Peter Masefield, now Chairman of the British Airports Authority, who was then head of the Directorate of Long-Term Planning and Projects, in the Ministry of Civil Aviation. Masefield was looking for a number of principals in this division, and was seeing several candidates. He remembers, 'We lunched together off whale-meat in the Aldwych Restaurant below Bush House, next door to Aeriel Joise. There was no dearth of subjects for conversation – Beaverbrook, the Oxford Union, the Attlee Government, Lord Winster, Winston Churchill, affairs in Washington (Masefield had just returned from being Civil Air Attaché there) and, of course, the tasks ahead in Civil Aviation. He was clearly one man for the jobs.' Also picked were J. G. Sims and P. W. Brooks, and then, as Masefield laconically puts it, 'we got down to work'.

'I couldn't have had three more different assistants,' he continues. 'Sims was a civil-service man near retirement, detached and cynical; Brooks was terribly serious, a dyed-in-the-wool professional aviation man, still shyer than Teddy. He had been on the Arctic convoy, which was pretty hairy, on the Swordfish I'd designed. Teddy wanted to learn. We poked our noses into everything.'

Heath took over work on the planning of Empire Air Routes, then being set up for post-war land-plane services; the representation of long-term planning on the Heathrow Planning Committee; the advisory layout panel, and a review of the civil air training and light aircraft requirements. His boss, who liked him and approved of his smartness and his serious interests in the project, realized that though he was shy he was not uncritical of his superiors, and found some of the Heathrow committees maddeningly frustrating and procrastinating.

He wonders whether his decision when he formed his Government to get people in from outside, business experts with practical experience, may have been a result of this period in the Ministry.

Heath was, Masefield believes, imaginative in a practical way. One proof of this, and evidence of that thoroughness and persistence which was by now a trademark, was his examination of the paper plans for the design of the Comet. This was during a transitional phase in aviation: seaplanes, which had been common before the war, were giving way to land-planes, largely because of the existence of a far greater number of runways which had been built for military purposes. However, as Masefield points out, 'the war meant the runways were there but they weren't always very strong'.

De Havillands had designed the Comet with a single wheel on each side, and Heath and his colleagues realized that the bearing strength of runways in Singapore and Rangoon, to name but two, could not take such a concentrated load. Not surprisingly, their criticisms met with a somewhat cold reception from the designers, but Heath was 'like a dog with a bone'. Eventually he and Brooks were able to persuade de Havillands that with multiple wheels the Comet would be a far more viable proposition, world-wide, and the incorporation of this feature meant that B.O.A.C. were able to buy it for their Far East routes.

They were a hardworking group, often staying late in the evening and always working, as was normal then, on Saturday mornings. Teddy liked to go straight off from the office at lunchtime on Saturdays to spend the weekend in Broadstairs. Masefield remembers that it was no good asking him to lunch on that day, or even inviting him to stay for the weekend, because he didn't want to be deterred from his plans for going home.

Although he was fairly reticent about it, one of the attractions there, his colleagues knew, was his girlfriend, Kay. Since it was evidently an established friendship, general expectation was that he would marry her. Yet Masefield, looking back now, says that he was more surprised that other bachelors, still shyer than Teddy, had married rather than that he eventually did not.

The group got to know each other fairly well, and used to have a semi-working lunch twice a week in the restaurant where he had first interviewed Teddy. 'None of us were well off, and it cost us each about 3s. 6d. (17½p),' says Masefield. He quickly realized that Heath was extremely proud of two positions: his past presidency of the Oxford Union, and his present command of the H.A.C. But overriding all else, particularly now he had experienced the shortcomings of officialdom for those who are not making the policy, was his ambition to get into parliament. 'He lives and dreams politics,' Masefield noted in a contemporary report. Heath's chemistry is variable, according to the temperature of those about him. Masefield found '... when you get to know him (which isn't easy) he is a sensitive and warm-hearted chap who has a direct approach and an endearing sense of the ridiculous – which we so often encounter.'

Two incidents stand out from this period which mark a deepening in Heath's own perception of the world about him, with in one case increased confidence and in the other increased anxiety. The first was a lunch at Cricklewood on 13 December 1946 given by Handley Page to discuss the Hermes for the Empire routes. Their host was a tremendous character, described by a friend as 'a cross between an Old Testament prophet and a rough, tough businessman'. The conversation soon left the Hermes behind to discuss the respective merits of Bonar Law and Baldwin as politicians, and whether Gilbert and Sullivan would endure in music. Masefield says, 'Teddy was pro-Baldwin and G. and S., whereas H.P. – to be controversial – gradually worked up the opposite case for the fun of it.' With a great deal more social poise than he might have shown in this situation a few years before, Teddy responded in kind, and it was felt that the old man and the young had got on extremely well together.

The anxiety came one day when, as happened every ten days or so, Masefield had lunch at the Athenaeum with Reggie Winster, the Minister of Civil Aviation. During the lunch Winster, in tears, told him that he was getting the push – and he didn't know why. Masefield says, 'I told Teddy when I got back to the office and I think he was quite affected by it – the fact that a minister could suddenly be fired.'

It was certainly a warning that, though there might be frustrations in his work below, there could be less security if he reached the ranks above. Nevertheless, his frustration at his present powerlessness seems to have spurred him on. He was by this time extremely scathing about Attlee's Government, under which he was, after all, serving in an official capacity: an uncomfortable though not an uncommon position.

So he set about looking for a constituency which would accept him as Conservative candidate. His search started in March 1947, only four months after he had actually entered the Civil Service; but he had three disappointments, spread over the next seven months, before he was successful. The constituencies which turned him down (though in each case he was short-listed) were East Fulham, and – two constituencies in Kent which returned Conservative candidates at the next election – Ashford and Sevenoaks.

Simpler men seem to have had more foresight about Ted Heath's potential. One of these was Edward Dines, whose latent Conservatism only emerged after the election of 1945 when he was shocked by 'the way the nation had slapped Winston Churchill across the face for bringing us through the war – in common parlance what might be called a backhander'. Dines was then about fifty, rather bluff, and worked for Standard Telephones and Cables. As direct in deed as thought, he immediately offered his services to the Bexley Conservative Association. He started by sticking posters on pig-bins, and before long was devoting so much effort to his cause that he was made chairman.

Bexley was a strange constituency to characterize, for it belonged to a type unusual before the war. When Dines first moved there it was almost a country district, with some 6,000 inhabitants spaciously scattered around. By the time he left, about thirty years later, the place was so crowded that in one area 90,000 people were living on less than 5,000 acres and there were some 3,000 people on the council housing list.

'It was the electrification of the line that did it,' says Dines. 'The electric trains came down like a shower of rain, and the houses sprang up like blades of grass.

'In 1933 I bought a corner semi-detached house with three bedrooms, two reception rooms, a large garden, garage space and side entrance and Ideal boiler for £650. The repayments were less than £1 a week, and the rates a few shillings.'

Other houses sold for as little as £395, and, being only thirty-five minutes from Charing Cross, Bexley mushroomed into a dormitory for the vast influx of civil servants, dockers and workers from the industrial areas round the Thames, and from the Vickers factory at Crayford where William Heath had been during the First World War. In the spick-and-span anonymity of thousands of brand-new owner-occupied houses slept new inhabitants who often never spoke to or knew the names of their neighbours; in the 1945 election, when Bexley became for the first time a separate constituency (it was previously part of the Dartford division) they returned Mrs Jennie Adamson as a Labour member to the Labour Government.

Getting the Conservative Association onto its feet in these circumstances represented quite a feat – even the records of pre-war members had been sent for salvage during the war. However Dines soon found and tapped that source of strength which is apparently so much stronger in the Conservative than the Labour movement: the power of its women. Long memories, curiosity, energy, and above all time, were devoted to creating an ever-extending network that turned out a formidable list of names and addresses of real and potential supporters. The records office became a suburban powerhouse, although four agents between 1945 and 1949 and near-bankruptcy showed that much of the potential was dissipated.

Dines was prepared to be dogmatic both about the population and its needs. 'They were modest people of modest means who didn't demand much of life. I understand the British working man,' he declares now, in his seventies. He concluded that Bexley needed a candidate it could readily identify with, and he drew up a blueprint for his ideal candidate on simple lines: in essence, he should be a local boy made good.

Many candidates presented themselves, only to be turned down because they did not fit this blueprint. One was an almost archetypal Tory lady. Dines explains, 'I couldn't fault her. She was intelligent and attractive. Her make-up was immaculate, her fingernails a perfect red.' But, he felt, she was essentially 'too immaculate for the women of Bexley'.

When Dines finally heard of Ted Heath, he did so through keeping his ear to the ground and not through the casting of the Central Office. An acquaintance who had heard of Heath's disappointment at Sevenoaks told Dines about him, adding that he was an ex-service-man. The mention of war service made him prick up his patriotic ears immediately, and further investigation convinced him he was getting warm: to a certain extent because he himself was able to identify with the young man. 'He joined as a private, the same as I did, and rose to be a lieutenant colonel. He had been to a grammar school [so had Dines] and I believe that is the finest method of education there is. More grammar-school boys passed the Indian Civil Service exams than those from anywhere else – the results used to be gazetted in *The Times*. He had made his way on scholarships, which meant he was a wonderful example, and he had no millstones round his neck.'

The final remark in this list of personal preferences was a reference to Heath's bachelordom. At the back of his mind was the thought, echoed today by Mrs Dines, that, 'He travels fastest who travels alone.' He believed that singleness of person was almost as important as singleness of mind in politics. 'At the back of my mind was the thought of another would-be politician, whose wife was always dragging him away; and the end of Eden's first marriage. A sensible chap doesn't get married until he's settled his career.'

Dines's cup was full when he found that his potential candidate was actually in the H.A.C. camp at the time when he decided to summon him: it was to this address that the telegram was despatched. Heath quickly changed from his uniform into his demob suit – a smart single-breasted pinstripe three-piece suit, which was soon to become almost as idiosyncratic throughout the constituency as his smile is now.

He was one of three candidates who on 18 October 1947 came before the selection committee of seven – five women, Dines and another man. Dines's conviction helped to carry the day, and at a later meeting of the executive the vote was three to one for Heath. He had won on his 'ordinariness'.

Dines was still anxious about the reaction to the new candidate of the president of the Bexley Conservative Association, a banker called Martin Holt who worked in the City, lived in Kensington, and spent weekends at his country house in Sussex. Holt was, in Dines's stratified gaze, 'the Squire, a true aristocrat and a true snob', who might disapprove of Heath's humble origin. As it turned out it was Dines himself and not Holt who was the more class-conscious. 'The old man was delighted with him,' he remembers.

Holt was required to show his delight in an entirely old-fashioned financial way. At the Conservative Party Conference, Lord Woolton had declared, 'In the past it has cost a great deal of money to be a Conservative candidate,' adding, 'We cannot afford only to draw our candidates from the people with money.'[1] Bexley had avoided doing this, with a commonsense of which Baldwin would have approved, when, as far back as 1923, after losing the general election, he said, 'Now there has always existed in our party a desire to choose a rich man as a candidate. But if you must have a candidate who can water his constituency with £1,000 a year, you are going to have a choice of about half per cent of the population, and if you are going to fight a party that has the choice of the whole population you will never beat them in this world, and, more than that, you will never deserve to beat them.'

[1] *British Political Parties*, by Robert McKenzie, Heinemann, 1963.

A committee set up under Sir David Maxwell Fyfe recommended changed rules which were adopted at the annual conference in 1948, applying to candidates selected after 31 December 1948, more than a year after Heath's adoption. These said that candidates would not be permitted to contribute more than twenty-five pounds a year to the funds of his or her association, and that M.P.s would not be permitted to contribute more than fifty pounds a year.

Meanwhile Heath was under the conventional pressure – exacerbated by the dire financial straits of his constituency – to produce funds. He persuaded five friends to donate fifty pounds each, and Holt himself presented five hundred.

At his adoption meeting Heath mentioned a few subjects which have since become major and most controversial issues: the need to prove the party's 'genuineness', the need for a 'genuine relationship between employer, employee and the Government', and, ironically in view of Enoch Powell's criticisms years later, a defence of the civil servant who, he said, 'quite naturally has his political opinions but the great majority ignore their opinions in the course of their duty'.

He himself had to resign from the Civil Service on his adoption on Friday, 14 November 1947; and when he left he had worked in the ministry for exactly a year; in spite of the chafing of the red tape, he had basically enjoyed his work.

His next job was very different. He became News Editor of the *Church Times* and the next twenty-one months represent the greatest waste of his life both in terms of the work and of the pleasure he signally failed to derive from this job. Having enjoyed the scope of reporting some of the Oxford Union debates for *Isis*, having contributed also the occasional article on Conservative policy, and having written his dramatic freelance account of his visit to the Spanish Civil War for the *Thanet Advertiser*, he had an illusory idea of the freedom of journalistic life and imagined he would have time to follow his political interests while picking up a steady – and vastly increased salary (by nearly one third) of some £650 a year.

George Hutchinson recounts one anecdote about this period, told to him by John Trevisick, who was also working there and later replaced him. 'Heath shook with laughter like a jelly . . . when he heard of a colleague's misfortunes – like being bitten by a dog when on a fruitless Beevor [editor of the *Church Times*] assignment, or losing oneself in a fog when on the way to a fourth-rate religious play at Walthamstow. The laugh was on him, however, when he altered the report of an annual festival of U.M.C.A. This was his biggest bloomer: he changed the initials U.M.C.A., meaning Universities' Mission to Central Africa, to Y.M.C.A. throughout the copy. You would have thought that he might have heard of the U.M.C.A. or if he wasn't sure he might have asked somebody, but he didn't.'[1]

It was a true journalist's nightmare. Altogether he seemed dispirited in the job, finding it much more demanding of his time and attention than he had realized it would be. His friends knew that he was unhappy during this period, although he managed to joke that he was a 'political fish in holy water'. At one point he tried to get a job with the English Speaking Union instead, and Peter Masefield wrote a glowing testimonial for him, but what impressed the Civil Service was hardly likely to carry weight here, and nothing came of it.

When he turned his attention to the City, however, his luck was in. An introduction from an acquaintance won him an interview with Sir Giles Guthrie, a managing director of Brown, Shipley and Co., a small merchant-banking firm. Heath explained that he wanted to work for the bank for a limited period of one year, to earn his living and to add a practical side to his economic knowledge. Though unusual, this arrangement was agreed after the bank had taken up references from, among others, Martin Holt.

Ion Garnett-Orme, the present chairman, says, 'I think we took him on because we were influenced by his straightforward approach – he told us that he did intend to make politics his career, and to prepare for this he wanted to know something about how one aspect of the country worked. We realized there was nothing in it for the bank.

'He was a different type of chap from most of our trainees – older [he was 31 by now], while most of them are just down from university, with a war record . . .

'We realized very early his mental ability. He is outstanding, extremely quick, and worked very hard. He had an immense capacity for work and was determined to get to the bottom of what he

[1] *Edward Heath*, by George Hutchinson, Longmans, 1970.

was doing and why. He made the fullest possible use of the training. He was shy and reserved at first – possibly one was the product of the other – but once one had established a personal relationship he was a wonderful friend and he made many friends here.'

He passed through the various departments – credit information, cashiers, securities and investment, and, last of all, foreign exchange, where there was most scope. But although he put a great deal of energy and effort into understanding the City and its international dealings, what he regarded as his real work in Bexley was also gradually expanding. When Heath was adopted as the Conservative member for Bexley, the incumbent M.P. was Ashley Bramall, a Labour man who had been up at Oxford at the same time as himself and had replaced Jennie Adamson in a by-election when she resigned. Churchill had consented to help in the by-election campaign and had been driven round Bexley in an open car, then handed an amplifier for an impromptu speech when the car was stuck in a traffic jam, as the organizers had known it would be.

Heath was determined that, whatever stars might or might not appear when a General Election came, he would have prepared the ground thoroughly – that is, street by street and house by house. He started by going out every weekend with an escort of Young Conservatives, literally knocking on doors. It was a form of campaigning that had come in with the new batch of candidates, and to someone of Macmillan's background 'canvassing street by street seemed not merely novel but somewhat distasteful'.[1]

Heath was untroubled by such reservations, just as he had been untroubled by voicing his ambitions as a schoolboy. And his new, American-style, personalized form of canvassing was not just a one-shot burst of energy: it was the pattern he was to follow during each election that fell between his adoption as candidate and his different and more demanding role when, twenty-three years later, as potential Prime Minister, he had to relate to a much wider audience.

Nor was the tour simply undertaken for its public relations effect – or, if it was, he certainly went to extraordinarily subtle and untypical lengths; when a new agent, Reginald Pye, a retired tea-planter from India, came to the constituency in December 1949 it was the

---

[1] *Tides of Fortune*, by Harold Macmillan.

candidate himself who insisted on taking him round the constituency – street by street again, as if by learning the geography he could learn the way to the inhabitants' votes. Agent and candidate were compatible, and in due course they spent nearly every New Year's Eve together (Pye's wife sometimes protested beforehand) making a grand tour of all the Bexley dances, pubs, and potentially fruitful parties. They maintained a remarkable sobriety withal – Heath even in his early days was far too cautious and proud a character to allow any hint of self-indulgence to smudge the edges of his upright image, and if this has lost him enthusiasm from some supporters it has also foiled the armament of some opponents.

This way of celebrating the New Year itself speak volumes. What other man from whatever background, with whatever interests, would have chosen to see nearly every year in like this, instead of being with family, friends, someone they loved? 'Have you nothing better to do on New Year's Eve?' Macmillan asked him once. The sad answer by then was, 'No'. But in 1949 he simply hoped that some future vote might be caught between sips and glances and dances, and stored up for the next General Election.

Heath's first General Election campaign began in February 1950. His family and a few good friends continued to give him unswerving support, which he badly needed – for there were quite a few shocks in store for him in the rough and tumble of real politics. Used as he had been to speaking to the generally attentive and at any rate relatively interested audience in the Oxford Union, and the necessarily quiet audience of his men in the army, he did not find it so easy when it came to facing the mixed views, prejudices, likes and dislikes, belligerence, ignorance and intelligence, of any ordinary everyday uncommitted crowd. He seemed at first in the campaign to lose his public poise, and appear instead as the still shy private individual. Speaking softly, he was soon drowned in the tumult of interruptions and his own discomfiture. When he was introduced as the candidate who 'was born in Kent, bred in Kent and lives in Kent', one heckler put in 'and I hope he bloody well dies in Kent', which was enough to put the unpractised candidate off his stroke. One remembers that, faced with any somewhat similar difficulty, Macmillan used to imagine that his mother was present; Heath's mother, like his father often was there. Quiet as she remained, she struck the local party organizers as a determined character within a very proper exterior. 'She provided the push, and his father agreed,' said one of them.

However poor Heath's delivery, the themes of his speeches contained a solid core of policy which, if not particularly arresting or original, was capable, as time has shown, of providing far-reaching conclusions. He wanted to see both direct taxation and purchase-tax reduced, the cost of food subsidies reduced by wise buying of food, more home-ownership: in a very recognizable phrase, 'Happy and healthy homes are the basis of family life.'

During the campaign he had little to say about either the Labour Party's National Health Act or his own party's 1944 Education Act, the two great reforms of post-war years, except that the first should be better run, and the second better provided for. National service must be retained 'so long as peace is threatened', and, with an interesting sequence of words, he said, 'We believe in closer association with western Europe and America, which Mr Churchill has done so much to foster.' Europe first, America second, ran his ever-logical mind.

Polling day was on 23 February, and the results in the four-cornered contest (Liberal, Conservative, Labour, Communist) were so close that a recount was necessary. Hard work and long hours seldom seem to exhaust Heath – although he is normally early to bed and sleeps soundly for as long as possible. But anxiety and emotional tension fatigue him quickly – perhaps another reason for the colossal defences he has tried to build, like sandbags, round his emotions. Pye, who thought his man was inexhaustible, was troubled to find him completely spent during the 1950 recount. He sat with his head in his hands, awaiting his fate, and apparently tired out. Everything was at stake.

Recovery surged with the result – he had won, by the slender margin of 133 votes, polling 25,854 against Bramall's 25,721, and doubtless helped by the Liberal and Communist diversions.

Supporters from the H.A.C. and from Brown, Shipley had also lent their help. Heath was launched on his twenty-year voyage to the top; and it is safe to say that even of those who were at the ceremony, fewer predicted his eventual success even than usually point out a future leader. There were no warning signs in the happy, thirty-three-year-old Teddy that night of what another Conservative M.P. later called 'the jolly ship that turned into a torpedo'.

8
The Worst Time

The future Conservative Prime Minister had his first taste of the House of Commons as a member under a Labour Government. Attlee had been returned for a second time, but even after five years during which Labour lost not a single by-election, with a devastating majority of only six – a figure that meant tremendously hard work for members on both sides of the floor. 'Only the dying are paired nowadays,' noted Macmillan.[1]

Britain was still in a transitional mood: more so, if anything, than immediately after the war, for a great wave of internal and international changes, unprecedented in peacetime, had changed the social and political landscape, and reactions were volatile. Eire had left the Commonwealth, India the Empire. The railway, coal, and gas and electrical industries had been nationalized, but had not yet settled (or been whittled) down. Clothes rationing had only ended a year before; soap and many foods were still rationed. The national health service was coping magnificently, if not perfectly, and Marshall aid staved off many hardships, but an air of utility and restlessness prevailed. For many who were too young to remember the black spots of pre-war years, and for some who were not, victory had not lived up to its name.

If the old order had gone, and enough were determined that it should not return to hold them back, the new order had not yet had a chance to prove itself. This was true of the country as a whole, and it

---

[1] *Tides of Fortune*, by Harold Macmillan.

was true of the Commons, which was literally being re-built as well as reforming itself with its admixture of new young members. Many might not have stood a chance of being elected a decade previously; but they brought with them a briskness and factual approach that were likely to shape the future positively. The qualities of some older members seemed to rest on their privileged right to a seat – for a few nabobs had survived along with those wise enough to grow even stronger in old age.

Among the new members in 1950 were:

Aitken, W. T. (Bury St Edmunds)
Alport, C. J. M. (Colchester)
Amery, J. (Preston, North)
Arbuthnot, J. S. (Dover)
Ashton, H. (Chelmsford)
Baker, P. (Norfolk, South)
Baldock, J. M. (Harborough)
Banks, Col. C. (Pudsey)
Beach, Maj. W. W. Hicks (Cheltenham)
Bennett, Gordon (Glasgow, Woodside)
Bennett, R. F. B. (Gosport and Fareham)
Bevins, J. R. (Liverpool, Toxteth)
Bishop, F. P. (Harrow, Central)
Black, C. W. (Wimbledon)
Braine, B. (Billericay)
Brown, W. Robson (Esher)
Browne, J. N. (Glasgow, Govan)
Bullus, E. E. (Wembley, North)
Burden, F. A. (Gillingham)
Carr, L. R. (Mitcham)
Clarke, Brig. T. H. (Portsmouth, West)
Clyde, J. L., K.C. (Edinburgh, North)
Cooper, A. E. (Ilford, South)
Craddock, G. B. (Spelthorne)
Cranborne, Viscount (Bournemouth, West)
Crouch, R. F. (Dorset, North)
Crowder, P. (Ruislip, Northwood)
Davies, C. N. B. (Epping)

Deedes, W. F. (Ashford)
Douglas-Hamilton, Lord M. (Inverness)
Evans, H. E. G. (Denbigh) [Nat. L]
Fisher, N. T. L. (Hitchin)
Fort, R. (Clitheroe)
Harris, R. R. (Heston and Isleworth)
Harvey, I. (Harrow, East)
Hay, J. (Henley)
Heald, L. F., K.C. (Chertsey)
Heath, E. R. G. (Bexley)
Higgs, J. M. C. (Bromsgrove)
Hill, Mrs E. (Manchester, Wythenshawe)
Hill, Dr. C. (Luton) [L & C]
Hirst, G. A. N. (Shipley)
Hopkinson, H. (Taunton)
Hornsby-Smith, Miss P. (Chislehurst)
Howard, G. R. (St. Ives) [C & Nat. L]
Howard, S. G. (Cambridgeshire)
Hudson, W. R. A. (Kingston-upon-Hull, North)
Hyde, H. M. (Belfast, North) [UU]
Hylton-Forster, H. B., K.C. (York)
Johnson, H. S. (Brighton, Kemptown)
Jones, Aubrey (Birmingham, Hall Green)
Kaberry, D. (Leeds, North-West)
Leather, E. H. C. (Somerset, North)
Llewellyn, D. (Cardiff, North)
Longden, G. J. M. (Hertfordshire, South-West)
Lucas, P. B. (Brentford and Chiswick)
Macleod, I. (Enfield, West)
MacManaway, Rev. J. G. (Belfast, West) [UU]
Maude, A. E. U. (Ealing, South)
Maudling, R. (Barnet)
McAdden, S. J. (Southend, East)
McKibbin, A. (Belfast, East) [UU]
Nabarro, G. (Kidderminster)
Nicholls, H. (Peterborough)
Nugent, G. R. H. (Guildford)
Oakshott, H. D. (Bebington)

Ormsby-Gore, W. D. (Oswestry)
Orr, Capt. L. P. S. (Down, South) [UU]
Orr-Ewing, C. I. (Hendon, North)
Powell, J. E. (Wolverhampton, South-West)
Price, H. A. (Lewisham, West)
Redmayne, Col. M. (Rushcliffe)
Remnant, P. (Wokingham)
Rodgers, J. (Sevenoaks)
Roper, Sir H. (Cornwall, North)
Russell, R. S. (Wembley, South)
Ryder, Capt. R. E. D., R.N., V.C. (Merton and Morden)
Smith, E. M. (Grantham)
Smithers, P. H. B. (Winchester)
Smyth, Brig. J. G., V.C. (Lambeth, Norwood)
Soames, Capt. C. (Bedford)
Stanley, Capt. R. (North Fylde)
Stevens, G. P. (Portsmouth, Langstone)
Steward, W. A. (Woolwich, West)
Taylor, W. J. (Bradford, North) [C & Nat. L]
Thompson, K. P. (Liverpool, Walton)
Thompson, R. H. M. (Croydon, West)
Tilney, J. D. (Liverpool, Wavertree)
Vaughan-Morgan, J. K. (Reigate)
Vosper, D. F. (Runcorn)
Wakefield, E. B. (Derbyshire, West)
Watkinson, H. (Surrey, Woking)
Wills, G. (Bridgwater)
Wilson, G. (Truro)
Wood, R. (Bridlington) [1]

Nine of the like-minded formed an alliance that was to become one of the breeding grounds of policy and policy makers – the One Nation Group. The nine founder members were Heath himself, Enoch Powell, Iain Macleod, John Rodgers, Cuthbert Alport, Richard Fort, Angus Maude, Gilbert Longden and Robert Carr – and it is interesting to note that Heath has since fallen out, tem-

---

[1] *Times Guide to the House of Commons*, 1950.

porarily or permanently, quietly or loudly, with half of them, the most notable exception being Robert Carr.

Each set out to specialize in some area – Heath himself in finance. A backbone of knowledge, and the organization of ferreting out facts, came from Macleod and Powell who had both worked under Butler in the Conservative Research Department. The group dined together every Wednesday night, and usually got the Whip before anyone else, which meant they were the first to know what the business of the House was. On the basis of this information they prepared questions, and devised a way, led by Macleod, of harrying the Government during question time: having carefully prepared the same ground beforehand, they would all bob up and down, but once one of them was called the others would withdraw leaving him to fire all the ammunition in a single concentrated attack.

'It was the most influential private group ever, extremely effective in its early days,' says one of the founder members. 'We'd had such a thrashing in '45 that our whole mood consisted of looking for new things: the new Toryism was our driving force. I believe that Enoch thought Ted wasn't an intellectual at all – he tended to brush him aside. It was true that Ted oversimplified; he didn't see the light and shade of an argument. He was slap in the middle on policy – for private enterprise and profit, but aware of the need to make the country richer; very much against the Butsekellite approach.'

Young and buoyant, the group brought a new zest into policy-making. They enjoyed wining and dining; any member who made a 'daft' remark was awarded a putty medal and the decoration noted in the minutes; they were eager to learn, and from the best informed sources. 'We thought it quite natural for Eden and Macmillan to come and dine with us,' says one of them. 'Looking back the effrontery was quite something.'

In October 1950 they published a pamphlet called *One Nation – a Tory Approach to Social Problems*. Essentially it was a group approach: each chapter had been written by the specialist in that subject after much discussion, and often re-written after further argument. Maude and Macleod were the final editors. The theme was determined by a post-war electorate – advocating an improved Britain, better housing, education, physical health, reformed industrial relations, protected countryside. As Disraeli had noted as far back as 1872 in his celebrated speech at Crystal Palace when he stressed the need for improvements in many of these same areas, housing, health, 'air, light and water', and the progress already made with the Factory Laws, the people of England would be idiots 'If . . . they should not have long perceived that the time had arrived when social and not political improvement is the object which they ought to pursue.'[1] The people were not idiots, nor, nearly eighty years later, were those who hoped soon to be elected to rule again: yet the majority of them were sincere, as well as calculating, in their policymaking.

In his maiden speech in the House, the young Ted Heath took a stand that Disraeli might, however, have scorned as more befitting the Liberal Party: for in Disraeli's eyes it was the Liberals who were the party of 'Continental' or 'cosmopolitan' ideas, while the Conservatives were the 'national' party, who made the working classes 'proud of belonging to an imperial country'[2] – as Heath's own grandfather had been.

Yet Heath's subject for his nerve-racking maiden speech on 26 June 1950 could not, in view of his subsequent career, have been more aptly chosen, or more of a signpost: he wanted 'to develop Europe and co-ordinate it in the way suggested' by the Schuman Plan. The occasion for his speech was the two-day debate in the Commons on how Britain should have reacted to Robert Schuman's proposal to 'place the whole of the French and German coal and steel output under a common higher authority in an organization open to the participation of the other countries of Europe.'[3] Nobody, of course, thought this was the limit of the planning: the industrial pool was merely to be the first step in a gradual economic and political integration, which would bring with it social and cultural benefits but whose *raison d'être* would be increasingly the independent power of a United States of Europe.

Crucially important was the fact that those who accepted the invitation to participate in the negotiations were expected to accept, in advance, the principle of a supranational European authority, which could overrule their national Governments.

The British Government's first response to the French invitation

---

[1] *Disraeli*, by Robert Blake, Eyre and Spottiswoode, 1966.
[2] Ibid.
[3] *The General Says No*, by Nora Beloff.

expressed willingness to enter 'exploratory' talks with France and Germany; this crossed with a note from the French asking for prior commitment to the principles put forward by Schuman, and the British reply reiterated that they could only take part on the basis of open-ended discussion, without such commitment. To Ernest Bevin's virtual refusal in May was added Attlee's formal statement on 13 June. Taken point by point the Labour Government's attitude seemed natural enough – it is an instinctive thing to refuse to deliver oneself into the power of another before safeguarding terms have been arranged. Britain's economy was stronger than that of her continental neighbours; and freedom, so recently won, seemed too precious to allow even the least hint of outside interference. On the surface this seemed almost a national decision, taken by the Labour Party but with at least the grass roots support of the Conservatives.

But it was a case of not seeing the wood for the trees. The plan could involve the whole security of Europe. The Dutch Government, much more cleverly, had accepted while reserving their 'freedom to go back on the acceptance of these general principles during the negotiations, if, contrary to what is hoped, it should prove in the future that the application of these principles raised serious objection in practice.'[1]

Churchill had given his blessing to the idea of a United States of Europe with England as a sponsor but not a member. Macmillan now began a sustained balancing act between two horses, declaring, 'We will allow no supranational authority to put large masses of our people out of work in Durham, in the Midlands, in South Wales, or in Scotland,'[2] but putting forward alternative proposals at the Strasbourg Assembly a few months later for joint production and development plans. Only a consummate political rider could have ended this act as firmly in one saddle as he was to be thirteen years later, even though he was not placed in the Common Market.

With what now seems to have been an astonishing prescience, as well as with a conviction that Disraeli would have found dubiously Liberal in someone whose character seems so instinctively Tory, the new member for Bexley expressed his view of Europe in unequivocal

---

[1] *Tides of Fortune*, by Harold Macmillan.
[2] *The General Says No*, by Nora Beloff, Penguin, 1963.

terms. He argued for joining the talks primarily, but made it plain that these should lead on to a participation in the development of Europe, on grounds that brought each of Britain's preoccupations into play: the economy, a revitalized Germany, incipient Franco-German strife, the wishes of the United States: all in all, the need for peace and prosperity.

It was, ironically in view of later events, Eden who moved to urge the Government 'in the interests of peace and full employment to accept the invitation to take part in the discussions on the Schuman Plan subject to the same condition as that made by the Netherlands' Government', and he noted that 'the French communique does not include the hideous phrase "supranational"'.[1]

In view of events over the next twenty years, it is worth quoting at some length Heath's own words, the first he spoke in Parliament, which were to become such a cornerstone – if on occasions a stumbling block – of his own policy and career.

Sir Stafford Cripps, the Chancellor, like Bevin, was in ill-health, but nevertheless he had made a most powerful speech in the debate, arguing not only that Britain should not tie herself to terms beforehand, nor take risks with her economy, but also that she should not take any steps which might jeopardize agreement between the other European countries.

Heath, as always, spoke simply, but quite cogently hoping that his views were not too controversial for a maiden speech.[2] 'We on this side of the House feel that by standing aside from the discussion we may be taking a very great risk with our economy in the coming years – a very great risk indeed. [The Chancellor] said it would also be a great risk if we went in and then withdrew. We regard it as a greater risk to stand aside altogether at this stage . . .

'The Chancellor spoke all the time as though this were to be a restrictionist plan. Surely the object of the plan is to be one of expansion . . .'

Heath had recently refreshed his by now considerable knowledge of Germany with another visit, during the Whitsun recess, and went on to speak of that country's motives in terms that illuminated not only her present, but also his own future, belief in the way to strength. Analysing the German Government's action, he said,

[1] *Hansard*, 26 June 1950, col. 1914.   [2] Ibid., cols. 1959–64.

I found that their attitude was governed entirely by political considerations. I believe there is a genuine desire on their part to reach agreement with France and the other countries of Western Europe.

I believe that in that desire the German Government are genuine and I believe, too, that the German Government would be prepared to *make economic sacrifices in order to achieve those political results which they desire. I am convinced that when negotiations take place between the countries about the economic details, the German Government will be prepared to make sacrifices.* [My italics]

A vast expansion of German coal production would result but,

there are sown in those advantages the seeds of conflict with France over this economic basis . . . I submit that there is a very strong reason why we should take part in these discussions – in order that we may balance out the difficulties between France and Germany which are bound to arise on the economic side.

Under the German plan, Germany may very well become once again a major factor in Europe. Anyone going to Europe today is bound to be impressed by the fact that the German dynamics have returned; that Germany *is once again working hard and producing hard and that therefore Germany will become a major factor in Europe.* [My italics]

I suggest that there are only two ways of dealing with that situation: one is to attempt to prolong control, which the Chancellor has already dismissed as being undesirable and impracticable. The only other way is to lead Germany into the one way we want her to go, and I believe that these discussions could give us a chance to do so.

From the United States' point of view, he went on, the capital development of a great area of the world might very well be most important: a reference to the U.S. belief, fostered by Jean Monnet, that European concord was the only means by which they would cease to be a financial burden and political worry to the U.S. The Marshall Plan itself had been made conditional on European co-operation.

Heath ended with some minor attempt at a flourish: 'It was said a long time ago in this House that magnanimity in politics is not seldom the truest wisdom. I appeal tonight to the Government to follow that dictum and to go into the Schuman Plan to develop Europe and to co-ordinate it in the way suggested.'

But it was not this style that won him attentive ears: it was the solidity and apparent open-mindedness of his attitude over Europe that impressed. His view of Europe was no sudden inspiration. It was a deeply held conviction based on a triumvirate of ideas: his love of his country and its independence; springing from this, his sense of the necessity of European unity that would lead to greater economic and political opportunity; and thirdly the need for greater independence of the United States – although on this point he remained discreet. Although he was not yet thirty-four, the conflicts and possible solutions for Europe had preoccupied him since he went to Nuremberg. Thirteen years is a long time to prepare a speech. He would never change his mind, and it was not as open as at first it appeared. Patriotism, and not Liberalism, was what inspired him.

His emphasis on Germany's readiness to make economic sacrifices in order to achieve political gains was significant: this attitude appealed directly to him, and clarified to some extent his own sense of priorities. Equally significant, in a man whose quick and logical intelligence veered towards the simple rather than the subtle, and whose character and mind were becoming increasingly notable for consistency, was his belief that Germany's hard work and production must inevitably lead to increased political status. He was already sketching in his own mind a blueprint that would be presented to the people he governed twenty years later as a guarantee of success.

Heath's political ambitions had been put into still sharper focus at this time by two events in his personal life. The first blow was the disappearance from his life of his good and long-standing friend, Kay Raven. Like most young men, he seems to have assumed that he would one day marry. When Madron Seligman was one day discussing the qualities of his wife Nancy-Joan, he remarked on how extremely capable she was. Teddy said obliquely, 'That's one thing a wife must be – capable.' It might not be the most romantic approach, nor a passionate approach, but neither was it the give-away of a confirmed bachelor. What alternative could there be in his traditional eyes, with his love of family life and closeness, to its continuance in his own life? Marriage, with its concepts of loyalty, fidelity, continuity and exclusiveness could have been made for him – or he for it. But things went wrong, perhaps because in his personal as in his political life he was a long-term planner who did not immediately respond to changed moods around him.

Since Heath has been too guarded to tell the whole story to anyone who can fully explain it, some aspects of the broken friendship remain mysterious: but there are enough clues to support two different theories. The first theory is that, although he wanted to marry Kay, he was both too shy and too proud to ask her outright until he regarded himself as sufficiently eligible, and trusted that more than fifteen years of friendship had forged an unbreakable bond of understanding between them. It almost had: when his brother John married, Kay wrote to the bride-to-be that she was marrying 'into the nicest family in Broadstairs'.[1] That was in 1947, when Kay was herself almost one of the family and was included in most of their outings.

The same year, Madron married Nancy-Joan. He composed the music for his own wedding, and asked Teddy to play it for them at the ceremony. He remembers, 'He had to play the same programme for the chap before as well, and then he had to play it over six or seven times because Nancy-Joan was very late. He showed a touch of that cynicism of his when I said that I had been moved by the address – he said rather sourly that it was exactly the same as he [the clergyman] had given to the people before. He's a great pricker of balloons – can't stand emotional bosh . . .'

One can imagine that this attitude, if maintained when he was alone with Kay, was not exactly the note to strike in an understated love affair. However, it seems that Kay was genuinely very fond of him, as he of her, and she acted as his hostess in the constituency as well as partnering him at home.

Two years later, on 10 June 1949, things seemed outwardly to have progressed little. It was a night when he and Kay together with George Chadd and the girl he later married, Margaret, went to an outdoor ball at the H.A.C. headquarters, Armoury House, in City

[1] *Ted Heath*, by Marian Evans, Kimber, 1970.

Road. Chadd remembers Kay as being 'dark, pleasant'. There was a fair with roundabouts and she said playfully, 'Come on George, let's go off.' Chadd comments on his friend, 'He wasn't sure of himself: he was in no position to get engaged or married.'

Chadd also remembers an incident which shows very clearly the lack of chivalry and imagination Heath sometimes displayed with women in his own age group. 'He drove Margaret home to Bromley, as it was on his way. It was about 4 a.m. and she lived in Stone Road, which lived up to its name – it wasn't made up. At the end of the road she said, "Drop me here," and he took her literally and tipped her out. She had to walk along that rough road in high-heeled shoes and a long dress . . .'

Was Heath obeying her instructions, or thinking of his tyres? Either way it revealed a gauche and ungallant manner with women.

The next year, George and Margaret were going to be married. Summoning more courage than any other friend had done, he asked Heath, who was to be best man and was making the arrangements in May 1950, when he was going to get married too, and received the cryptic answer, 'We can see daylight.'

Too late it seems, or perhaps his thoughts were never communicated, for the news was next broken to the Heath family that Kay was to marry someone else. Mrs Heath, who was closer to her son than anyone else, burst into tears.[1] William Heath, who was always puzzled by his son's self-containment, and could, as a father, hardly have expected to hear of unfulfilled romantic dreams, assessed, 'She was keen on him. He wasn't; or if he was he never showed it. Apparently her family persuaded her to go on holiday with a group of young friends, and that was when she got engaged.'

The second theory of his bachelorhood is that, as time passed and Heath saw what marriage demanded of his friends, he felt unable or unwilling in some way to fulfill the role of ideal husband and therefore faded away as a suitor. There is also the possiblity that he never saw himself in the role of husband.

Women tend to favour the first theory, men the second. Whichever is true, the friendship had been too deep to pass unlamented by both parties, and thirteen years later her picture still stood beside Heath's bed.

[1] *Ted Heath*, by Marian Evans.

Everyone who knew him well enough to know what had happened
– and even those who did not, soon heard some version of the news,
though reports of how upset he was varied – assumed that Heath
would now put, if possible, still more into his career. To a great
extent they were right: no girl was to come so close to him again,
though a few tried; and with his quiet self-knowledge he probably
accepted this truth soon, and with some stoicism.

In the summer of 1950, during the recess, he went away on
holiday with John Rodgers (now Sir John), who was ten years his
senior but like him delighted to be a new boy in Parliament. 'We
motored through France, slowly, to the Riviera, looking at churches
and art galleries, eating good meals,' remembers Sir John. 'We spent
a weekend with Beaverbrook at Cap d'Ail. Ted took several large
books with him – the lives of recent famous politicians, people like
Curzon and F. E. Smith. I took whodunits. Then we drove on to
Spain. We were away three or four weeks. It was quite a powerful
summer. He likes sitting on a beach, reading. He was an agreeable
companion, with an eye for the good things – the interiors and
exteriors of churches.

'But he could go very silent – rather distressingly so on drives.
There would be just a grunt. He was really rather suspicious when
someone else drove.

'He was very keen on keeping fit, and liked to go to bed early –
about ten or eleven at night. He has an iron self-control which is
really almost frightening.'

Whether his silences came from brooding on his past or planning
his future, or, most probably, from both, Heath was still only halfway
through what could later be construed as the most crucial two years
of his life. At one point he said to his companion 'Yes, I owe everything to my mother really.'

In the House he was making a good impression faster than he had
done in any previous field. His maiden speech and his contribution
to the One Nation pamphlet had both had their effect. 'People knew
about him, you know,' remembers the man who was then Conservative Chief Whip, Patrick Buchan-Hepburn (now Lord Hailes),
a man of outstanding integrity and tact, who after two years in the
office was now searching for new assistants. 'The Whips' office was
still rather pre-war in the war there weren't party politics in the

same way. There were a lot of rather senior people. I was looking for new people, and not only those who would want to stay on in the Whips' office.' He decided, after watching him closely for some months, to ask him to join the Whips who are responsible for liaison and discipline within the party. Heath readily agreed, only asking that he might be relieved if after eighteen months, he found it did not suit him – a typically cautious reservation. The other Whips also had to agree to the new man, as of course did the leader himself, but, Lord Hailes remembers, 'Winston left the Whips' office very much to me. Of course I told him who . . . Winston appreciated ability and was very quick to see what people were. Winston was a very classless person, you know.'

Ted Heath thus took up his first Parliamentary office in February 1951, when he had been in the Commons just under one year, and his first duties were to look after M.P.s from Kent, Surrey and Sussex.

The Whip's duties are very heavy, and although his constituency was so close to Westminster he did not spend as much time there as some M.P.s who perhaps went up to their country home and constituency for the weekend. But his care of Bexley was intensive, if not prolonged. Over the years he became president, vice-president or patron of a variety of clubs and societies, some of them dedicated to ends in which he had shown no previous interest whatsoever – the Bexley Rugby Football Club, for example, and the North Kent Budgerigar and Foreign Bird Society. But there were many in which he could take a genuinely deep interest – the Dartford Symphony Orchestra, Bexleyheath and District Club for the Disabled (he has sometimes shown an uncharacteristic radiance when talking to a very ill or disabled person: their difficulty seems to release him from one of his own), Old Bexley Music Society, Bexley Rotary Club and Bexley Light Car Club. A fast driver himself, he had only four cars during the twenty years after Bexley returned him, one of which he drove 'until it was almost in holes', and another of which, a bright yellow Vauxhall Victor, certainly proclaimed a lover of colour and individuality that had hardly been seen in the early years while he plodded through his rigorous programme.

Meanwhile he had extended his original one-year training with Brown, Shipley, and was still with them – though not for very long hours, because of the narrow majority in the Commons. In the summer Heath suggested to the directors that he should make a trip to North America on behalf of the bank, showing again that career push (some outsiders thought it blatant) that went so strangely with his personal reserve. The bank agreed, and he had his first chance to re-examine the social, political and economic climate of the United States since his debating tour in 1939, and also his first sight of a dominion – Canada. It was here, in Ottawa, in September, that he heard the news: weakened still further by the absence through illness of Cripps, the resignation of Bevan (and in sympathy Wilson) in protest against Gaitskell's Budget (which placed half the cost of dentures and spectacles on the patient) and finally Attlee's own illness, the Labour Government had decided to go to the country. A General Election was called for October 1951. Heath sailed leisurely to England to fight for his constituency, but on his return home he had to face news which was the forerunner of the most severe shock of his life.

For about two months his mother had been suffering from abdominal pains. Marian Evans remembers, 'I tried to reassure her and persuade her to go to the doctor, saying perhaps it was appendicitis.'[1] But when eventually Mrs Heath was admitted to Ramsgate Hospital for examination in September the doctors told William Heath that his wife had not long to live: she had cancer. She was allowed to go home, and whenever he was not speaking in Bexley Teddy was driving to or from Broadstairs or sitting with her and the rest of the family. One day 'she asked Teddy to play the piano for her as she lay in bed and he sat at the piano and played for three hours, leaving the doors open so that she could hear.'[2] William Heath remembers, 'She often asked him to play.'

Edith Heath died on 15 October 1951.

For her family and particularly for her elder son, life would never never be the same again. It was the worst moment of Edward Heath's life. As well as being his mother, she had been his champion and his most unselfish friend; and through her spontaneous feelings he had had an outlet for the softer side of his own nature. He could no longer turn to Kay, who on her marriage had moved to another part of Kent. So in two years he had lost the two women who meant

---

[1] *Ted Heath*, by Marian Evans.   [2] Ibid.

most to him, and who had done most to help him both directly and in essence, by openly reflecting his hidden emotions. From now on his emotions would be more heavily chained than ever.

The campaign continued, and, as his mother had wished, Heath fought on, wearing in public the rather wooden gaze that became increasingly characteristic of him over the next twenty years. On 25 October he was returned with an increased majority of 1,639 over the same Labour opponent, Ashley Bramall, as twenty months previously.

Yet in some ways his world was changed completely.

9
Suez and Discretion

Churchill was Prime Minister once more after six years in Opposition but the Conservative majority of only seventeen, far smaller than that predicted by the Gallup Poll, was a disappointment to them. Personal disillusionments were bound to follow as Cabinet posts were announced, and Macmillan, who confessed to finding this procedure 'puzzling',[1] was not altogether prepared for the appointment of Butler (instead of the expected Oliver Lyttleton) as Chancellor, making him in effect the third person in the political hierarchy. Though both Butler and Macmillan had opposed the Right wing of their party in the past, these two were now beginning to diverge in their practised views of power and responsibility. Heath was eventually to be faced with a personal and career choice between them, and his decision would be crucial, but for the moment he was eager to watch and learn from all sources, and according to contemporary witnesses there were moments when he was drawn to each – but more often to Macmillan.

He had quickly settled down as an Assistant Whip, and in November 1951 was designated a Lord Commissioner of the Treasury, one of the traditional titles for Assistant Whips. Lord Hailes remembers, 'I didn't even know how he would turn out when he came in', but already after a few months this was becoming plain.

The Whips' Office, at the nerve-centre of the party, provided an unrivalled watchtower from which to scan both the general trends in the party and the movements of individuals. For someone with

---

[1] *Tides of Fortune*, by Harold Macmillan.

keenness, patience, and perception, it can be a fascinating place, rather like the viewing room of a closed circuit television, and unlike the many Whips who have found the enforced silence depressing (a Whip can never make a speech and is well advised to listen rather than talk around the House), Heath was encouraged in his natural trait of keeping his own counsel except when he was communicating his thoughts to his Chief Whip. Thus to some extent he was both protecting himself from gossip and already potentially contributing to policy, since the Chief Whip is generally closer than anyone to the Prime Minister's business.

Heath's silent watchfulness had a purposeful air about it. 'Soon after he came in I realized he wouldn't stay there – he was very ambitious,' says Lord Hailes. 'But he dedicated himself, as he does to whatever he does, and didn't look miserable the whole time because he couldn't make speeches. We had an awfully quick turnover. An awful lot of Whips retired, and others just wanted to finish their time – they were not interested in seniority; so he was soon made Deputy Chief Whip.' (He held this position jointly, a rare occurrence, the next year, 1952, and alone in 1953.) A possible rival, a man who impressed his colleagues greatly, was Dennis Vosper, another of the 1950 intake, but he indicated that he did not feel in good enough health to take on the duties of Deputy Whip.

Churchill by now was seventy-six, and his age and authority held difficulties as well as advantages, which his Chief Whip was the first to feel. 'With Winston I couldn't get what a Chief Whip usually has – regular appointments in the mornings. But whenever I was called, he could carry on while I was having a long talk with Winston, and I could be absolutely certain everything would be all right. He's absolutely reliable. He's loyal.' His duties were extensive, and full-time, ranging from menial 'pairing', to assisting the Cabinet.

Brown, Shipley had terminated his training with them just after the 1951 election, though they had left the door ajar for future possibilities. So Heath was now financially dependent on his Parliamentary salary. As an M.P. in 1951 he was entitled to £1,000 a year; and as Deputy Chief Whip in 1953 he earned £1,200 a year. The end of his banking training meant that he could give all his time and attention to Parliament, and this, without either professional or even very much personal variety in his life to distract or relax him, he now did. One friend comments, 'I think as soon as he got into the Whips' Office he thought he could make it, and be Prime Minister.'

Certainly he was determined to learn as much as he could and as quickly as he could, but he was patient about actual movement while the groundwork was being perfected, as in his position he could well afford to be. One sharp-minded colleague says, 'I remember him saying, "I think Harold is somebody you can learn a lot from" – it struck me as rather a strange thing to say at the time, but it's true, particularly if your background has been different, you know.'

He was undoubtedly conscious of such differences, but his conviction that his merits outweighed his disadvantages gave him a curiously inscrutable attitude which some people found exasperating. Not so Lord Hailes, though he was, and still is, slightly puzzled by one aspect of his former protegé. He says, 'He is very shy I think; ... *I think* he's very shy. He had more self-assurance as time went on. He was very good as a deputy because he was not pushing himself too much: otherwise I should have known it at once. But he could wait. He wasn't trying to push me, you know . . .

'Many people who don't know it under-rate what the Whips' Office can be – what a lot you can learn about politics and people, particularly if you are not very expansive. He did know about people. He took great trouble to know about them, and their backgrounds, and what they wanted . . . he enjoys people, but I don't know that he needs them – he's extraordinarily self-sufficient.'

He agrees that Heath has never been tremendously popular, but adds that for success in the Commons this was little hindrance: 'Respect is the first thing, and confidence; popularity comes very much second.'

During the Whips' very long working day, which begins about 9.30 or 10 a.m. and carries on at least until the House rises, perhaps in the early hours, Heath had ample time to cull and ponder such truths. Since the Conservative Party, unlike the Labour, does not issue written regulations, the Conservative Whips become if anything still more responsible for the management of party affairs and discipline in the House: a keen Whip could afford to miss nothing.

It was also his first taste of Government. It might have seemed dull to anyone with a less voracious appetite for any task he had chosen. Britain remained an undynamic country, able to maintain high employment but with a still more drastic balance-of-payments deficit than in the worst days of the first term after the war. The Conservatives seemed stale, and were slow to implement the fresh policies of their 1947 Industrial Charter ('to reconcile the need for central direction with the encouragement of individual effort') which had been guided by Butler, as Chairman, with Harold Macmillan, Oliver Stanley, Oliver Lyttleton and David Maxwell Fyfe representing the front bench, and David Clarke, Reginald Maudling and Michael Fraser (now Sir Michael, and Joint Deputy Chairman of the Conservative Party) acting as secretaries. If such senior views could be put aside, what chance had the One Nation Group of a quick response?

The troubles of 1951 had worsened by 1952, when many investment programmes, fuel, power, railways, even water, as well as overseas military expenditure, were reduced. Looking back in his memoirs, Harold Macmillan said, 'Although such a programme was not encouraging for a new Government which had been elected on a policy of expansion, it was no doubt necessary. It might indeed have been better if, instead of taking two or three bites at the poisoned cherry, we had made all the cuts within the first week.'[1] Twenty years later, it would be interesting to compare the fate of the two Conservative administrations, whose problems multiplied during their first two years of office, and to examine how each tried first to tackle its economic dilemma, and second, to simultaneously carry on with the rest of its programme.

Meanwhile there was little cheer elsewhere. The Labour Party, still presided over by Attlee, but weakened by the deaths of Cripps and Ernest Bevin, straddled an uncomfortably widening gap between Gaitskell and Bevan and their legions. King George VI died in February 1952. (A true royalist, like his family, Edward Heath attended the Coronation of Queen Elizabeth II as a member of the Government in 1953 and took his velvet seat home to Broadstairs afterwards.)

Slow progress was however being made towards ending the ubiquitous shortages. A massive building programme obsessed

[1] *Tides of Fortune*, by Harold Macmillan.

Macmillan; in 1954, food rationing finally ended. Foreign Affairs were problematic and Franco-British difficulties were being allowed to grow along with the increasing diplomatic confusion about Britain's attitude towards the Schuman Plan. The decision inherited from Labour remained: there was no real action either way, but a continual and visible hesitation while the European escalator moved on.

Macmillan has said, 'At one moment I began to despair and to wonder whether all this effort was worth while. The Commonwealth and European plans, both then within our grasp, seemed to me worthy and not impracticable.'[1] But in fact participation in the most important plans for Europe slipped through Britain's grasp on 28 November 1951, only a month after the new Government's inception when on the same day Anthony Eden, the Foreign Secretary, and Sir David Maxwell Fyfe, the Home Secretary, had made contradictory statements about this country's intentions.

According to Sir David Maxwell Fyfe, who was speaking to the Council of Europe in Strasbourg, 'His Majesty's Government warmly welcomes the initiative of the French Government in forwarding this imaginative plan.' More guardedly at a Press conference afterwards he merely would not exclude the possibility of Britain's entry; but Eden publicly excluded the possibility when he was speaking the same day at a N.A.T.O. meeting in Rome. It was one of those public discrepancies on foreign policy which the British have often, with good cause, dreaded, and which had led to an apparent liking for greater concentration of responsibility in one person. But worse in the eyes of the strong pro-Europeans, including Heath, than the immediate awkwardness, were the slowly unravelling consequences of exclusion. In time these very difficulties would give him scope to develop talents still hidden from the House. Slow fuses were also being laid, ready for later ignition in Africa, with the inauguration in October 1953 of the Federation of Rhodesia and Nyasaland, and in Egypt with the signing in October 1954 of the Anglo-Egyptian Suez Canal Agreement which entailed the withdrawal of British troops from the Canal Zone. With the formation of policy towards Egypt came the first hints of serious trouble for the Whips.

During the four years from 1951 to 1955, rebellions within the

[1] *Tides of Fortune*, by Harold Macmillan.

Conservative Party came mainly from the Right wing[1] and were usually immediately contained, normally because of Churchill's swift response when he felt that trouble was not worth meeting head-on. The first instance had come on 3 April 1952 when thirty-nine Conservative members signed a motion criticizing the Government's lack of progress towards denationalization of steel and road haulage. In spite of the general Conservative stand against nationalization, it was well known that Churchill was not very much in favour of such action[2] but he soon announced at a meeting of the 1922 Committee (or the Conservative [Private] Members Committee, as it is properly called) which is one of the most influential groups within the party, that they would be denationalized as soon as possible.

Another rebellion, which the mediation of the 1922 Committee could not solve, eventually forced the Government to increase the pay of officers retired from H.M. Forces.

But insurrection sometimes met with greater resistance, as in October and November of 1952, when two motions calling for the restoration of birching made no impression at all on the Government.

Nor could any compromise be reached with the group of Right-wing Conservative back-benchers, the most influential of whom were later known as the 'Suez Group', who, although their most determined efforts were to be reserved for the next Parliament, made a strong showing on 15 December 1953 when forty-one members signed a motion urging '. . . Her Majesty's Government in these circumstances for the time being to suspend negotiations for a revision of the Anglo-Egyptian Treaty forthwith, to withdraw such terms as they may already have offered, and for the present to retain in the Canal Zone sufficient armed forces to discharge our responsibilities for the defence of the Canal.'

Eden had signed the Treaty nevertheless. He might already have taken over as Prime Minister in the summer of 1953, when Churchill was taken ill, had he not himself been recuperating abroad from an operation. A few weeks' later Macmillan's admission to hospital meant that three of the top four were absent through illness, a record to rival the Labour Party's recent physical ills. Macmillan himself wrote later,

[1] *Rebels and Whips*, by Robert J. Jackson, Macmillan, 1968.
[2] *Memoirs*, by Earl of Woolton, Cassell, 1959.

It was in the conduct of economic and home affairs that the trouble lay . . . we felt that in home affairs we were drifting without the formulation of any fixed plan – without a new theme or a new faith. We had almost completed the job of restoration and recovery. We now seemed to need a new programme . . . One of the difficulties was in the Cabinet itself. There were too many elderly Ministers, and new blood was required.[1]

Most of the dissidence in the party had been over home affairs, it is true; in the management of more dangerous foreign issues Macmillan continued, much later, to assert that there had been no great weakness. In October 1954 he himself left housing, having reached his obsessional building target, and became Minister of Defence: there he made a new arrangement which in time would have great repercussions.

One useful agreement during my term of office was in hand for the future of the Simonstown base. This package deal, which would enable us both to use the base in time of war and to sell a considerable quantity of major arms to South Africa, raised some doubts in the Admiralty . . . Although there were certain political dangers, from the Right as 'another surrender' and from the Left as an immoral compact with the 'reactionary' South Africans, this solution stood the test for more than thirteen years . . .[2]

At last in April 1955 when he was eighty, Churchill resigned, leaving a party very much intact.

On several occasions between 1951 and 1955 the Conservative Party faced the possibility of a serious split, but Robert Jackson has pointed out how on each occasion the chasm was avoided by resorting to 'private negotiation and compromise'.[3] He adds, 'In view of these compromises, Patrick Buchan-Hepburn, the Government Chief Whip, did not have to employ harsh methods to keep his party cohesive.'

It was true that no sanctions were being imposed on any of the rebels, but the Chief Whip and his Deputy had perfected their dual

---

[1] *Tides of Fortune*, by Harold Macmillan.   [2] Ibid.
[3] *Rebels and Whips*, by Robert J. Jackson.

roles in dealing with dissidents. Lord Hailes says now, 'A Chief Whip has to take the responsibility and be jolly rude at times, then the Deputy has to pick up the pieces. He became very good at that. He could be very nice to people.' As Deputy too Heath had often replaced the Chief Whip at party meetings, and had managed much of the daily routine in the Whips' Office. 'His organizational skill was very quickly apparent,' one of them remembers. He had also had a large measure of control over the other Whips. Now this period of training and learning was coming to an end.

With the succession of Eden, for fifteen years Churchill's heir apparent, and his confirmation in office in the General Election of May 1955 with an increased majority of sixty, a new and much more turbulent regime was beginning. Seven months later, in December 1955, after Patrick Buchan-Hepburn had been taken into the Cabinet, Edward Heath was Eden's Chief Whip.

It was not a job everyone would have envied, at any time. Even those who have accepted the position sometimes leave it more gratefully than they undertook it. One former Chief Whip said, 'It is a thankless job. You have to be able to play the job dirty and clean. The Chief Whip has to be very tough and the rewards are very few.'[1] Heath himself quickly became known as a very good Chief Whip – which meant, in the absence of the almost magical charm exercised by one or two of his legendary predecessors, that he was a formidable Whip: some said he was the toughest ever. He himself said, 'If I had any above-average influence as Chief Whip, it was not because I was more autocratic but because I was more democratic, than some Chief Whips had been before me.'[2]

It is, of course, possible to construe democratic action in a number of ways. But it is certainly true that while Heath sometimes in the words of Hugh Fraser achieved his ends 'without a harsh word', at other times he carried at least an autocratic manner into his execution of democratic decisions.

He was a stickler for discipline even when Government policy conflicted with his own basic beliefs, for he was no easier on himself than on others. Not long after the election the new member for Norwich South, a young barrister called Geoffrey Rippon, put down

---

[1] *Rebels and Whips*, by Robert J. Jackson.
[2] Interview with Kenneth Harris, the *Observer*, 23 January 1966.

a motion urging Britain's entry to the Common Market. John Rodgers was a co-signatory, and there were several dozen other supporting names. At this point the Government was still far from its eventual decision to seek entry, and was trying instead to establish a European Free Trade Association, in co-ordination with the Common Market, which would maintain greater independence for Britain.

Heath's early commitment to the concept of European integration was well known, and there is no reason to suppose that it was any less dear to him at this moment than at any other time. However he apparently experienced no difficulty in separating his personal from his official line, and his job as Whip took precedence over his own priorities for Europe. He asked the signatories to withdraw. 'I had two ups and downs with Ted on this,' remembers Sir John Rodgers now. 'He said, "For God's sake don't rock the boat" – Maudling was trying to peddle the Free Trade Area. But of course he may have thought this would fall through anyway.' Whatever he thought, his belief in hierarchy was most apparent. With such self-discipline, reinforced by hard work and great efficiency, he was a hard taskmaster for others too.

'He was fratchety as Chief Whip. He and Eden were both bloody bad-tempered,' remembers one member who was not always the first, or even the last, to fall into line. 'He was rather bullying, and would say, "You've bloody well got to obey three-line whips". Peremptory.

'He can be very huffy if you don't agree with him. Afterwards, he doesn't smile, or even notice you: you're sent to Coventry.'

Another witness, himself a former Chief Whip, said, 'Unkind? He doesn't *mean* to be; he's tough, and tough.'

A good Whip can never be universally popular, but Heath varied his tactics according to the situation, and did not conform to any pattern of punishment. In fact, although there were twenty-one revolts during the 1955–9 Parliament, the Whip was not withdrawn from any member. Some chose to resign it, but this was in accordance with Conservative practice for many years, which has been far less strict than in the Labour Party.

Capital punishment was the main cause of contention on the home front during these years. It was an issue on which Heath himself felt many doubts, although he finally, and with cautious admission that he might still be proved wrong, voted against the restoration of the death penalty. Perhaps it was his own doubts in the interim that led to his lenient treatment of those who countered the proposals of the would-be reformers, who were asking that the Death Penalty (Abolition) Bill should be read a second time, with motions suggesting that capital punishment should be allowed for all murders. One of the leading anti-abolitionists was Sir Thomas Moore, who said afterwards that the Whips 'never said a word'[1] to him about his extremely vigorous pursuit of his ends. Yet Heath interviewed almost all the abolitionists individually during the summer recess.

The Capital Punishment issue was finally resolved by allowing a free vote: this again was in line with the increasing tendency in the party to allow questions of conscience to be left to the individual.

Even this freedom brought its own constraints, especially for those whose personal views conflicted, to some minor or major extent, with the views of their constituents. 'All the Abolitionists sat on the fence,' one Conservative says scathingly.

Other domestic crises were also handled in such a way as to largely de-fuse their danger to the party. The sudden ignition of the Suez crisis came five years after Egypt had denounced the 1936 Anglo-Egyptian Treaty in 1951. The blaze, which had been smouldering on the Right wing of the party, was met with equal heat from the Left wing. It was the most serious situation the Conservative Party had faced for decades.

It was a crisis to test the resources of the strongest of Chief Whips; yet Heath's handling of the situation showed no hesitation, and both his discretion and his determination to keep control of the disparate elements earned him respect from most quarters. One perceptive acquaintance guesses, 'I think it may have been the personal high point of his political life. Everybody was coming to him with their troubles.'

However they did not, as they could not, all receive the same treatment. 'With his amazing instinct for detecting the varying degrees of vanity, ambition and public spirit which motivate politicians, Teddy Heath knew exactly whom to be rude to and who to pat on the back,'[2] said one Parliamentary colleague. However, Heath's

[1] *Rebels and Whips*, by Robert J. Jackson.
[2] *Illustrated London News*, 7 August 1965.

vision of his own methods – 'What I tried to do was to make the Whip's Office a co-operative effort and instead of having rigid automatic discipline, I wanted freedom of expression and action from a conviction that what we were doing was the right thing'[1] – certainly appears somewhat strange in the context of Suez. The Right wing particularly felt aggrieved by his attitude. Patrick Maitland, one of the fifteen Right-wingers who had abstained on the vote approving the withdrawal of British forces, spoke of the 'extraordinary and unexampled pressures – some of them altogether underhand – which had been used to force Tories into line.'[2]

The exact nature of these pressures, which presumably were a great deal more subtle than the explosive remark about 'bloody Fascists' with which Heath is widely associated, must have been tailored to fit individual weaknesses, which the sufferers remain understandably unwilling to expose.

Julian Amery, who was one of the Suez cabal, and claims they had had encouragement from Churchill, remembers 'Ted took no personal line', and added about his general attitude as Whip, 'You can't reason with everyone about everything.' But he remembers Heath trying, unsuccessfully, to persuade him and Charles Waterhouse not to put an amendment down which 'put teeth into' an official resolution on Suez at the Conservative Conference at Llandudno a few weeks before the war.

Nigel Nicolson, the first Left-wing Conservative openly to declare his opposition to Eden's policy (which he had first tried privately to change) was one of those who abstained from a vote on Government policy on 8 November. He wrote to Heath that because of the strength of pro-Eden feeling in his constituency, 'I do not expect . . . that I will politically survive.'[3]

Nicolson was, however, deeply impressed by Heath's honesty over the issue, which was evidence of Heath's tendency to treat people as they treated him.

A friend of Nicolson's recalls that the latter related an incident that illustrated Heath's honesty. Pressing the Chief Whip, he asked whether they had yet been told the whole truth? Heath silently and eloquently turned away.

[1] *Illustrated London News*, 7 August, 1965.
[2] *Rebels and Whips*, by Robert J. Jackson.   [3] Ibid.

Eden himself wrote that, 'Though Mr Heath's service in Parliament had been short at that time, I have never known a better-equipped Chief Whip. A ready smile concealed a firm mind.'[1] He told George Hutchinson, 'the rougher the weather, the steadier was his advice'.

Now that Edward Heath is himself Prime Minister he still declines to reveal either what his true feelings about Suez were, whether they ran very deep, or even whether they remain the same today. I asked him whether it had been difficult to convey the variety of very passionate opinions held by the different groups within the party to his own Prime Minister at the time, and he replied that one thing he had never been accused of was failing to put someone's case to Eden in full. When I suggested that his continued silence on Suez could be interpreted as pointless unless it loyally concealed criticism, he said lightly, 'I think you'd better use your discretion about that, don't you?'[2] which in a different sense was certainly the advice he was following himself. Even now certainty about his basic stance on Suez could earn him new enemies.

William Whitelaw, later Heath's own Chief Whip and now Secretary of State for Northern Ireland, had only been in Parliament for a year at the time of Suez. Asked for his assessment of Heath's basic line on Suez, he replied, 'Do you know I have no idea? He does keep his own counsel very much. I have a suspicion but such a tiny suspicion that I couldn't even venture it – but it was a fantastic job of organization to have kept the party together.'

Anthony Kershaw remembers, 'He was never out of the House during that time. He was always tremendously available to all the doubters. I remember going up to him during Suez and saying, "Oh, there's something I want to talk to you about," I forget what it was – and he said, "Oh? What's troubling you?" and then laughed – meaning that everybody was coming up worried and saying I don't like this and I don't like that . . . We were terribly shaken in our morale in the party, but we decided we could be argued out but not shouted out, so that we all rallied round – nearly all, anyway.'

[1] *Full Circle,* by Sir Anthony Eden.
[2] Interview with the author, 1971.

On 10 January 1957, Anthony Eden resigned. The new Prime Minister was not, as had been widely expected R. A. Butler, (who was alleged by some to have led a revolt against Suez and some of whose family claim to have voted Liberal ever since) but Harold Macmillan.

'Quite honestly I don't think he ever thought he would be Prime Minister; but Heath probably knew, from the House,' says Lord Hailes. 'I knew it was going towards Macmillan. I think he liked Heath's reliability.' On Heath's relationship with the various Prime Ministers, he continued: 'Prime Ministers must rely on people. He and his Chief Whip have interlocking jobs, and unless the Old Man is rather difficult to get on with you're so involved in your positions, thinking of your *job*. Prime Ministers are too lonely to be very difficult all the time . . . Heath would take immense trouble. He's very quick to see the point.'

Though Heath was both obedient and loyal in his work for Eden, a Conservative who is closer to him maintains that the relationship was never one of absolute ease. A new note was struck in his dealings with Macmillan; for one thing, 'they entertained each other'.

On 11 January 1957, the evening of his appointment, the new Prime Minister took his Chief Whip to dine at the Turf Club, where they had game pie and a bottle of champagne. The publicity was predictable, as Macmillan realized in retrospect, saying that in the home of his former rival, Butler, there would have been 'plain living and high thinking'.[1]

Unity was of the first importance, more than ever since the recent fissures over Suez would not be closed for some time to come. Butler accepted the post of Home Secretary, but it fell to Heath to satisfy the critics and drive home party priorities among the members. 'Macmillan was a splendid strategist, with great subtlety of mind, whereas Ted was the born tactician who rallied the forces behind Macmillan,' says one of those who found himself being routed out by the Chief Whip rather as a sheepdog brings back a stray.

He made no bones about what had to be done: unpleasant tasks were despatched as crisply as those he relished. The Whip sees men at their best and their worst moments. It was Heath who, having

[1] *Riding the Storm*, by Harold Macmillan, Macmillan, 1971.

seen Macmillan's triumph, had the job of telling Butler.[1] Butler had taken on the load of deputising for both Churchill and Eden, when they were absent through illness, and as the messenger bearing bad news Heath had another close view of the harshness of political life.

Already, the next month, Heath was described with truth, as 'one of the Inner Cabinet'.[2] He was one of the six, the others being Butler, Sandys, Selwyn Lloyd, Lord Salisbury, and the Chancellor himself, Peter Thorneycroft, who spent a weekend with Macmillan drawing up new financial arrangements designed to meet difficulties in the economy. Bank overdrafts were to be easier, the bank rate cut, hire-purchase restrictions easier: the classic treatment for the symptoms, while a cure was sought for the disease. But the treatment had side-effects, and when, in 1958, Macmillan would not cut government expenditure, the Chancellor resigned, together with Nigel Birch and Enoch Powell who were also Ministers in the Treasury.

In the interim there had been a number of less startling, but nevertheless discomforting, situations in the House. In March 1957 it was learned that Heath was mounting a campaign to stop leaks of information and careless talk. There could hardly be a man more security conscious, and the dictum 'Never speak outside the House what you hear in it' took on a new meaning. Right-wing malcontents continued to rumble about Suez. It was in May 1957, four months into the Macmillan administration, that eight members resigned the Whip. It was from the Right too, that rebellions came over defence and N.A.T.O., and the future of Cyprus; but none of the abstentions or statements altered Government policy.

Incipient revolts from the Left wing were equally ignored in the early stages, but usually met with compromise as soon as they swelled to public proportions. One example of this concerned the Rent Act, when 800,000 tenants were to have their rents decontrolled within six months. After private protests to the Minister had failed, the members made their discontent generally known; shortly the Bill was amended so that the houses were not decontrolled for 15 months. (This was not enough to allay all anxiety: some Conservatives still abstained.)

[1] *The Art of the Possible*, by Lord Butler, Hamish Hamilton, 1971.
[2] *Daily Mail*, 25 February 1957.

This greater readiness to meet the Left wing than the Right wing of his party is a reminder of Macmillan's early belief that the party must capture and hold the Left-of-centre audience above all. In his early days as Whip Heath certainly acted very much under orders, though towards the end of his days in office there were strong signs that he was shaping policy as well as carrying it out.

An interesting example of his personal tactics concerned John Rodgers, with whom he had motored through France. In February 1957 Rodgers, who for five years had been P.P.S. to Sir David Eccles, disagreed vociferously with a Bill concerning shop-shutting hours. He remembers Ted coming to see him, his Whip's face sternly on, and saying, 'You can't be a P.P.S. and attack the Government like this: you must make your choice.' Rodgers replied, 'I have', and resigned. Twenty months later, he turned down a job as a Minister. Afterwards, he remembers, 'Ted came to see me. He was very flattering and quite charming – he couldn't have been nicer. He works to an end.' Rodgers became Parliamentary Secretary at the Board of Trade after all.

However well he handled trouble when it arose, he certainly did not always see it coming: nor was he, as the ideal Whip should be, always the first to know everything about his colleagues that might lead them into difficulties. Perhaps his own distaste for gossip meant he was sometimes unaware of things that he should have known; perhaps his own orthodoxy and lack of great warmth discouraged people from coming to him. Ian Harvey resigned as Joint Parliamentary Under-secretary of State at the Foreign Office in 1958. He had known 'Teddy-Tail' as he sometimes liked to call him, teasingly, since their days at Oxford; yet he is sure that when he had to tell the Whips his story, news of his homosexuality came as a complete shock to Heath.

The next year, 1959, William Whitelaw entered the Whips' Office as an Assistant Whip, and he still marvels at the Chief Whip's thoroughness: '. . . the extent of his attention to detail, the way he takes tremendous pains to think through every problem and listen to the views of his Whips.' He remembers the part of Heath's technique that struck him most: his silence. 'We used to have meetings very late at night after the House had adjourned. Quite often there were long silences while he was contemplating the whole situation, which of course again is one of his techniques . . . silences are practical actions, well planned, and they are always happening. Silence is a means of getting the other person to produce more and more of his views so that you know them without getting committed yourself. And sometimes you've got to sit out the silence.'

Heath increasingly thought of himself as a catalyst in policymaking rather than simply as a troubleshooter. In the summer of 1959, Butler reminded a somewhat reluctant Macmillan that they should include provision for reforms of betting, clubs, gambling and the like in their manifesto. 'Macmillan said, "I don't know. We already have the Toby Belch vote. We must not antagonize the Malvolio vote." There were dutiful chuckles round the table. Then the Chief Whip, Ted Heath, ever business-like and forceful, intervened by pointing out that we had committed ourselves to such reforms.'[1] Reforms were on; and the silent Whip had his way with no need for a debate.

One Minister said in 1959, 'Ted Heath is probably the most influential man around the Prime Minister. The P.M. consults him about practically everything – not just on his work as Chief Whip.'[2]

Heath's freedom from family ties meant, as slightly envious married colleagues were quick to point out, that he was free to go to Chequers for a weekend or a night whenever Macmillan wanted him. No doubt he was extremely glad to do so. Not only was he still learning much from the Prime Minister, but it gave him a chance to put forward his own ideas, and to live in an atmosphere for which he felt destined. Julian Amery remembers him playing the piano to Macmillan and himself at Chequers one night; a very different atmosphere from the bachelor flat he lived in at 88 Petty France in Westminster. Even Madron only remembers being invited there once, to change before they went out in evening-dress: 'He had a bed-sitting room with a kitchen and bathroom, a few water-colours, but otherwise impersonal.'

Another friend remembers that Heath used to say goodnight to him at the corner of Parliament Square usually, and as he watched him go home to the bachelor flat he used to think, 'You must be a lonely old bird.'

Undoubtedly, as Heath had since shown himself to be an excellent

[1] *The Art of the Possible,* by Lord Butler.
[2] *Evening Standard,* 20 March 1959.

host, it was anxiety about his habitat that inhibited him from entertaining at home then. Nor was he wholly at ease at other people's gatherings. 'He was very gauche in the early days. He wasn't good at handing round drinks and things like that,' remembers one candid friend. 'He was socially insecure. Nobody was allowed into Petty France.'

When he wanted to entertain, he did so with an attempt at style, but outside his own four walls – usually at Glyndebourne, or a theatre; less frequently, in a restaurant.

However, the fact that he was not *soigné* had its advantages: not only when it came to dealing bluntly with people inside or outside the House, but because his very difference and his appearance of seriousness made people listen to him.

One of those to whose parties he was invited, and through whom he made and renewed many acquaintances, was Duncan Sandys, like himself a strong man for Europe. It was at a birthday party of Sandys that he met, for the second time, two people with whom he was to form a growing friendship: Lord and Lady Aldington, who lived an hour away from his home in Kent, and invited him to Knoll for a bonfire party at Christmas, 1958.

And Churchill himself, like his son-in-law, responded to the younger man's enthusiasm for Europe – he used literally to call him 'young man'—as well as enjoying Heath's obvious admiration for himself. They had, of course, had some contact when Heath was Chief Whip: but Heath told James Margach of the *Sunday Times* that he got to know Churchill better after his retirement. Eventually two paintings signed W.S.C. graced his walls. Occasionally he was invited down to Chertwell, never sure who else he would find. On one occasion he found Churchill engrossed in a game of poker with his secretary, Brown, and Aristotle and Tina Onassis. The stakes were matches. Heath did not realize it at first but they were worth a pound each. Heath, by his own admission not a true gambler, declined to join in; but when Mrs Onassis dropped out he had little choice: to his own surprise he won matches worth seven pounds, and was given a cheque with Churchill's memorable signature. He decided not to cash it, but to keep it. Someone to whom he told the story said, 'I don't think he'd ever been so frightened in his life.'

Heath sometimes revealed a passion for extracting the ultimate pleasure from every moment during his brief escapes abroad. The Seligmans found that if they had agreed to look at churches, Heath would divide, say, Venice into different sections, and they would see fifteen churches in a section each day *before lunch*. Returning to the hotel one day with a piano accordion he had bought, Madron sat down to play it on the jetty near their hotel; Nancy-Joan complained that the noise was too great in the peace of Venice, but Heath insisted meanwhile that it was not loud enough. 'He always likes music played *forte, forte* . . .' In the evening, indefatigable, he would demand a concert, and they would find one.

He was much more boisterous and ebullient than he allowed himself to be at home in England.

Churchill's dictum 'Be indiscreet – it always pays' was the antithesis of Heath's belief. After he had a bad attack of jaundice in February 1959, Onassis invited him to recuperate by taking a trip on his yacht. Heath sadly declined, telling his intimates that Churchill could get away with it, but he could not. He was building a worthy image of himself, which was true enough reflection of the reality, but he lacked dash, the touch of Hotspur for which he evidently yearned but dared not allow himself.

Even so, those who knew a little about Churchill, and more about Heath, wondered whether the young man might not be to some extent modelling himself on the old man when he was late for a party for no apparent reason – having just been sitting in his room upstairs on one occasion – or left his pyjamas thrown on to his bedroom floor after a weekend visit. Was he trying, in small ways, to erase traces of his punctilious upbringing, which clashed in many instances with what he saw of upper-class manners? One of those who has worked with him certainly agrees that if Heath was late, it was usually because he intended to be.

He was very much more conscious of his own social disadvantages in the Conservative Party than he would ever have openly admitted: for instance he advised the parents of one of his god-children (he ended up with seventeen, including eight girls) about which school they should go to: if it was politics the parents had in mind, he indicated, there was no substitute for Eton.

Nine years in the Whips' Office, four of them as Chief Whip, provide a sharp lesson in human nature. The experience of observing

15. December 1965. Conducting the carol concert at Broadstairs.

16. 30 March 1966. The Leader of the Opposition addressing an open-air meeting at Ealing North the day before the General Election.

17. August 1966. Bathing at Le Touquet with five-year-old Amanda Denham.

18. August 1966. In his new motor-boat at Broadstairs.

19. October 1967. At the annual three-day Anglers Club fishing festival at Broadstairs.

20. 21 October 1967. Heath confronts anti-Vietnam war demonstrators outside the party
conference hall at Brighton.

21. 16 October 1971. At the Conservative Party Conference.

22. 28 February 1970. Addressing the twenty-first annual Conservative Local Government Conference, at Church House.

23. 22 May 1970. Addressing a meeting of Tory candidates at the election conference at Church House.

24

25

16 October 1971.

At the Conservative Party Conference.

28. 23 January 1972. Heath signing Britain into the Common Market at Brussels. On his left is Sir Alec Douglas-Home, and on his right Geoffrey Rippon.

other people's weaknesses, and realizing how powerfully these could be played upon had increased the caution and fear of gossip inherent in Heath's slightly defensive, withdrawing nature. He would abjure personal pleasure for the sake of duty, advancement and the public good; and this not only for its own sake, but because he was now convinced that any deeper fulfilment must be along this road.

This was the time when he had least to lose from indulging in a sybaritic way of life: but as usual he chose the spartan.

10

An Advocate for Europe

By March 1960 five months had elapsed since the General Election in October 1959 brought their third successive win with an increased majority of one hundred, for the Conservative Party in general, and of 8,633 for Heath in particular. Five months had also elapsed since Ted Heath ceased to be Chief Whip and, by being appointed Minister of Labour and a member of the Cabinet showed he had won Macmillan's regard. He was free to speak in the House once more. The *Daily Telegraph* had described his first speech for some eight years, on the Local Employment Bill, as genial and pleasant: 'The House welcomed the unsealing of those competent lips; if Mr Heath's tempo was rather too rapid, both for the Opposition and for the Press gallery, it must be excused on account of the extensive ground which he had to cover.'[1] The writer also noted that Mr Butler, Leader of the House, came in during the speech with a formidable portfolio and ruffled through papers which 'might or might not have been relevant to the debate'. More of Heath's speeches were, in the words of a colleague, 'fairly deplorable' in their dullness.

But in March Heath made a speech that was far from genial or dull, and revealed instead a plethora of pent-up frustrations with the House and, much more, its members' ways. Nine years of silent, critical watchfulness found vent before a meeting of the Conservative Political Centre. Having criticized the frequent protraction of the

[1] *Daily Telegraph*, 11 November 1959.

report and even the committee stage of a Bill, and the lengthy debates that followed, he continued, 'Of course you are not in the House all the time. There are the library, the tea room, and the smoking room where you may play chess and draughts but no other game whatsoever. But nobody does anything vehemently. An air of languor pervades the whole place. Listlessness abounds. Members stroll from one room to another, turn over the newspapers, and yawn in each other's faces.

'In the summer from five o'clock to seven the terrace is crowded with fine ladies and country cousins, drinking tea and savouring strawberries. Occasionally some parliamentary person of importance will choose to stalk by, and even – such is the affability of true greatness – have a cup of tea with a party of friends. A poorer way of killing time has not, I think, yet been discovered; but it is a convincing proof of the ennui of parliamentary life.'[1]

It also revealed an impatience with wasteful procedures that were later to harden into a ruthless industriousness that many of his own party would find unpalatable.

As Minister of Labour during a surprisingly calm period he found little opportunity for innovation even along lines he would later keenly pursue. When in January 1960, some M.P.s requested the setting up of a royal commission on trades unions, he replied, 'I think we must first give the T.U.C. the opportunity to deal with its undisciplined minority.'[2] Members avidly noted that this was 'not the 100 per cent complete refusal that Mr Macleod used to give'[3] (the previous Minister of Labour, currently Secretary of State to the Colonies) but recognized that there was 'very little hope that the Government contemplate doing anything'.

His only real chance for action came in February 1960, when a rail strike was threatened. He called the three rail unions in to talks, and three days and one final nine-hour session later, a settlement was announced.

He was, however, only a bird of passage in the job, and had little chance to observe in depth and detail either the intrinsic problems of labour relations, or the potential passions of the leaders, let alone the men, with whom he was dealing. So confident was he that he told

---

[1] *The Times*, 17 March 1960.   [2] Ibid., 4 January 1960.   [3] Ibid.

the Industrial Welfare Society at lunch one day that it was wrong, an 'outmoded idea', to assume that there must be two sides of industry and that they must be in opposition. For someone who did not share the Liberals' belief in profit- and decision-sharing by employees, this was a somewhat unrealistic view.

Meanwhile his continued closeness to Harold Macmillan meant that he was also in a good position to see, and perhaps occasionally to suggest, changes that were fast becoming imperative in Britain's attitude to the Common Market. A former top civil servant sums up the realities that underlay the apparent volte-face: 'One of the things that moved the Macmillan Government in the late '50s and early '60s was a feeling that we had rather come to the end of the road. It had taken very nearly fifteen years from the end of the war for this realization to get into people's minds. Compare the general attitude in Whitehall and in Government in 1958–61 with 1945: it was totally different. A lot of illusions were finally disappearing. There was a negative as well as a positive component – our own role in the present scheme of things was being eroded.'

In the first few post-war years, economic growth had been swiftest in the U.K. and the neutral countries; but ten years later it was notable that the countries which had suffered more in the war were growing faster. 'Between 1954 and 1961, when the distinction between the two groups became most marked, the German Gross Domestic Product grew at the average rate of nearly 6·6 per cent per annum, France's by nearly 4·2 per cent, Italy's by 5·7 per cent . . . By contrast the average rate of growth of the G.D.P. in the United Kingdom was about 2·3 per cent per annum.'[1]

Politically, economically, and even morally, Britain had lost a chance for growth and even leadership when the two Treaties of Rome, one establishing the European Economic Community and the other the European Atomic Energy Community, were signed on 25 March 1957, by France, Germany, Holland, Belgium, Luxembourg and Italy: but without Britain herself. The 'Common Market' or trading area without import duties or quantitative limits on imports, actually came into being on 1 January 1958.

Ernest Bevin's refusal in May 1950 to join the other six countries in

[1] *An Economic History of Western Europe, 1945–64*, by M. M. Postan, Methuen, 1967.

the genesis of the Coal Steel pool under a High (supranational) Authority proposed by Robert Schuman was echoed in opposition by Macmillan, who in spite of his basic pro-European attitudes said 'We would not allow any supranational authority to close down our pits and steel works.' In 1954 Britain formed a council of association with the High Authority, for consultation on coal and steel and for co-ordination where necessary: Duncan Sandys, one of the leaders of the European Movement, said, 'We do not regard this agreement as an end in itself. It provides the machinery to facilitate consultation and co-operation.'[1]

A few months later, in June 1955, the Six, some of them still themselves slightly uncertain about the depth of their involvement with each other, met at Messina in Sicily: their decisions were recorded in a resolution which 'contained the seeds of many of the actual provisions of the treaty (of Rome)'.[2] This was a turning point.

For much of this period the French had been still more concerned with the development of atomic resources than simply with a common market; for this reason they were particularly anxious to work more closely with Britain who had both developed her atomic resources to a greater extent than any of the Six, and had much co-operation from the United States in work on atomic energy. France already blamed Britain for the premature death of plans for a common European army, known as the European Defence Community: in 1952 Churchill had refused to sign the draft for this.

As Anthony Nutting, then still Minister of State at the Foreign Office, put it in simple terms in February 1955, the integration of Europe had been envisaged in three stages: first the coal and steel community, second the European Defence Community, and third the European political community. He emphasized that 'no spokesman of H.M. Government accepted, when in Opposition, supranational control for Britain's basic industry'.[3] Nevertheless Britain continued to seek closer industrial and political co-operation with Europe but without giving anything on the atomic side. Nutting

[1] *Hansard*, 21 February 1955, col. 886.
[2] *Britain and the European Community, 1955–63*, by Miriam Camps, Oxford U.P., 1964.
[3] *Hansard*, 21 February 1955, col. 942.

said, 'The Euratom plan, as it stands, is incompatible with the interests of the U.K.'[1]

Macmillan, speaking as Chancellor on 26 November 1956, said, 'We have turned to some other plan by which we could associate with Europe without injury, and indeed with benefit, to Commonwealth Relationships.'[2] He was speaking of the plans for a European Free Trade Area, which would allow the Six (Common Market countries) to trade with the other eleven members of the O.E.E.C. (Organization for European Economic Co-operation, originally set up to administer Marshall Aid) with gradually reduced tariffs on industrial goods. Since the plan would exclude agricultural products, neither the interests of the Commonwealth, nor Britain's access to cheap world food supplies, would be prejudiced. Reginald Maudling was in charge of the proposals, but had no position in, or great help from, the Foreign Office. As Miriam Camps has pointed out,

> Mr Maudling, himself, was clearly out of sympathy with the objective – and the methods – of the 'Europeans', and this undoubtedly heightened 'European' suspicion of British motives. So, too, did the rather disdainful British attitude towards the European Commission.
>
> British tactics throughout the negotiations were easy to fault: in particular at times they seemed designed to drive into each other's arms the 'Europeans' and the 'protectionists' . . .[3]

France's desire to share Britain's atomic secrets continued to cause a fundamentally widening rift even between the polite surface ice. This was accentuated after de Gaulle returned from retirement to power once more in June 1958, when he realized that the development of joint nuclear research between the Americans and the British was leaving France still further in the dark. Not surprisingly, perhaps, since it could have clashed with the Common Market itself, the talks for a large Free Trade Area failed; but seven of the eleven countries concerned who were not members of the Common Market went on to form a smaller association, E.F.T.A., and their first tariff cuts were implemented in July 1960.

[1] Ibid., 13 June 1956, col. 559 (Oral Answers).
[2] *Hansard*, 26 November 1956, col. 39.
[3] *Britain and the European Community, 1955–63*, by Miriam Camps.

The mutual interdependence of military and political roles was made plainer to Britain herself in 1960 when it was realized that she could not go ahead with the plans for an independent missile, Blue Streak. The cancellation of the rocket meant a shock reappraisal of her role for Britain. It underlined her immediate future dependence on the U.S. and the need to try and balance that with an alternative, which could only be Europe.

The Liberal Party had already declared itself officially in favour of entry to the E.E.C., or Common Market, and the weight of opinion was shifting from 'anti' to 'pro' in Whitehall when, in the summer of 1960, Macmillan decided that he must seriously consider the possibility that entry to the E.E.C. might be in Britain's best interests.

In July 1960 it was announced that Edward Heath was to be Lord Privy Seal with Foreign Office responsibilities. He was forty-four, and in his new position would earn £5,750 a year.

It was an appointment not universally popular, though doubts were based more on political than personal grounds. D. C. Watt writes,

> The appointment of Lord Home as Foreign Secretary, with Mr Edward Heath as his representative, with Cabinet rank, as Lord Privy Seal, in the Commons, and Mr Heath's subsequent appointment as head of the team of negotiators concerned with handling Britain's entry into the Common Market, gave rise to a good deal of public anxiety. Fears were widely voiced lest the arrangement prove inefficient. The bogey of divided control of foreign policy was again raised.[1]

In fact it was the beginning of a very workable association between the two men, who diverged so widely in everything outside their faithfulness to their work. The top two members of the Government, Macmillan and Home, were both old Etonians, both had suffered bad health (Macmillan's originating in a weak heart and from war wounds, Home's from TB of the spine), both had had the clay of their politics fired in the unemployment of the 1920s and 1930s – this was, Home liked to say, 'what really influenced me to go into politics'.[2]

[1] *Personalities and Policies*, by D. C. Watt, Longmans, 1965.
[2] *Sir Alec Douglas-Home*, by Kenneth Young, Dent, 1970.

The appointment of Heath, who was now prominent in the Government although he had no department of his own, was significant. He was so different from Macmillan and Home not only in background, health, lack of paternalism and personal style, but also in the concentration of his ambition, his hard purposefulness, the extremes of his demands of others, and his practical method of working. His appointment showed that the Conservatives felt a new breed of man was needed to help Britain find her new role in the world. There were some who were so conscious of his robot-like efficiency, reserve and toughness that they did not see that, once the job in hand was completed, he would immediately set out to solve harder problems, and satisfy his own inner needs.

Madron Seligman remembers the excitement clearly. 'He was very proud when he was chosen to do the Common Market negotiations. While he was doing them, he was studying de Gaulle as an adversary – reading all his memoirs and speeches.' His choice of the term 'adversary' is revealing. However Heath's attitude was not simply xenophobic nor was it that of someone steeped in inherited prejudice against the French. He admired de Gaulle and his assessment of him as an adversary stemmed from his realization that to the General, French dominance in Europe was a *sine qua non*. He also realized that de Gaulle was more than capable of wrecking exploratory negotiations for Britain's conjunction with the Common Market as he had done for an enlarged Free Trade Area. Added information about de Gaulle came from Macmillan, who had worked closely under him as the Minister resident at Allied Headquarters in North West Africa from 1942 to 1945.

There were many tightropes to walk before the final attempt to bridge the huge gap between de Gaulle's ambition for France and his concept of how this might be achieved with Britain participating in the Common Market.

Political and public opinion in Britain was still, and would perhaps always continue to be, divided about the wisdom of joining or even forming a close association with the Common Market. The Liberals had pre-empted the increasingly favourable view that some top Conservatives now held, together with some far-sighted civil servants (particularly Sir Frank Lee, the Permanent Secretary to the Treasury, who was chairman of the Economic Steering Committee responsible for re-examining the various possibilities for Britain in her relations with the Six). The Cabinet itself was, however, far from united: Butler was conspicuously less than enthusiastic, but finally and astutely Macmillan put him in charge of the committee that supported the negotiating team. A hardening of the Labour Party against the idea of entry to the Common Market, led by Hugh Gaitskell but notably without the support of Roy Jenkins, briefly aligned the centre and Far Left of the Labour Party with the Far Right of the Conservatives: it was the latter who retreated and became less vociferous in their criticisms of their own leadership. If the experts were divided, the people were equally so, although at this stage they had less information to fuel their feelings, apart from a certainty that more weight on the European side of the scales must mean less on the Commonwealth side, which must in turn mean more expensive loyalties and food.

Another anxiety was the effect entry to the Common Market might have on Britain's relations with the U.S.: Macmillan hoped these might be strengthened if the U.S. saw Britain as a leading company in a consortium ready for partnerships rather than as a shrinking subsidiary; but this possibility had still to be tested.

The delicacy and the strength of the pose that Macmillan had to strike – and hold – against this variegated and shifting background can hardly be over-estimated. Small wonder that when, on 31 July 1961, Macmillan at last announced the Government's decision to open formal negotiations with the Governments of the Six, he emphasized that, although application for membership under article 237 of the Treaty of Rome was a prerequisite of more useful discussion, any decision to join or not to join would not be made until *after* the negotiations had been concluded; for the moment the House was merely being asked to approve talks, not treaties. Such an inventive position was the daughter of necessity; but Heath's own mastery of it, and his continuation of the same position ten years later during his own term of office, show a natural aptitude both for balancing on the edge of difficulties and for letting time remove obstacles in its own way. This may have been an outlet for a sense of intrigue he could not ordinarily allow himself; at any rate, he was learning skills now from not just one but two consummate masters, Macmillan and de Gaulle, and a pupil of lesser self-discipline

and integrity might have been overwhelmed, or tempted to drama-
tize even at the expense of progress. Heath's discretion, and a growing love of challenge, that helped to replace the gaps in emotional
excitement in his own life, were two great assets in handling the
friendly but untamed Six.

The awkwardness of his position becomes still clearer when it is
remembered that almost half of the exploratory talks had taken place
before Britain's application for membership was announced: up to
that point he could offer nothing in return for the promise of concessions.

In September 1960, the Commonwealth Finance Ministers had
met in London and aired their worries. A communiqué issued
afterwards said that they 'recognized the importance of political and
economic unity on Western Europe', and noted that in negotiations
'the essential interests of Commonwealth countries should be safe-
guarded'. In the same month, General de Gaulle had given a Press
conference where he summed up his hopes for further organization
of the Six and re-organizing N.A.T.O.: he was still hoping to implement ideas he had expressed in a letter to President Eisenhower and
Mr Macmillan in September 1958, for extending the overall
coverage of N.A.T.O. but to concentrate the decision-making in the
hands of the Americans, British and French.[1] (The response to this
suggestion, which would have also increased problems regarding
German armaments, had been one of the causes for the breakdown
of Maudling's Free Trade Area talks two years before – this time
de Gaulle's timing could not have been plainer.) The Germans would
probably have supported the British in the quest for a wider customs
union, but for the French this smacked of allowing Britain to benefit
economically from the Six without giving sufficient political
returns.

Meanwhile hopes for political integration of the Six continued:
but although talks were held by the Six in the first few months of
1960, little actual progress was made. It may have been this very
fact, which meant that politically there was still a chance for Britain
to contribute equally to any solution virtually from the beginning
(whereas economically if Britain should join the Six she would
suffer from the drawbacks of being a late-comer) that hardened

[1] *Britain and the European Community, 1955–63*, by Miriam Camps.

opinion in London. In February 1961 Heath made a most important statement to the Council of the Western European Union (the Six plus Britain) in which it was clearly revealed that there was movement among decision-makers in the United Kingdom. Britain could not expect to take part in political discussions on the future of the Common Market countries, said Mr Heath, 'unless or until they had joined, or formed some association with, the community'. He also gave an indication of what had transpired in exploratory talks with the Germans and Italians and (currently as it happened) the French: he made it plain that the British were now prepared to make various concessions, the most crucial of which would be to accept the common external tariff, which would eventually mean the end of preference both for Commonwealth industrial goods in Britain and for British goods in the Commonwealth. He was evidently authorized to concede less on tropical and agricultural products, for which he simply said that the British Government 'visualized special arrangements'.

More than compensating for this toe-in-the-water test for these particular products came the sweeping change of attitude towards common institutions that must presumably be supranational. The Government fully recognized that, 'common institutions would be necessary to control a common . . . tariff', and, most pointedly, they were 'not afraid of any such institutions'.

Two months after this, in April 1961, Mr Macmillan had a chance to ascertain the attitude of the new administration in the U.S. when he visited President Kennedy in Washington: evidently the President provided reassurance, and even encouragement, about the effect that Britain's joining the Common Market would have on her trans-Atlantic links.[1]

In May 1961 a strong hint of hardening policy was given by Mr Heath in the House of Commons, when he listed the various possibilities for Britain in her dealings with the Six, ranging from 'a form of association' to 'full membership, provided that proper arrangements are made for Commonwealth trade and for our agricultural system . . . and proper arrangements for our E.F.T.A. partners.'

In June, Macmillan told the House of Commons that three ministers were going to capitals of Commonwealth countries for

[1] *Britain and the European Community, 1955–63,* by Miriam Camps.

talks; but he was by no means ready for a declaration of intent. When Jennie Lee said she had heard from business interests outside the House of more guarantees and information than would seem to be indicated by the Prime Minister, and wondered whether they might be informed by the end of July that the Government had decided to enter the Common Market, Macmillan coolly replied, to ministerial laughter, 'If the honourable lady believes that I can only say the famous words of the Duke of Wellington: "She can believe anything." '[1]

The next month, Butler declared, 'It is impossible to say at this stage whether there will be negotiations or whether there will not.'[2]

By this time five ministers were in or *en route* to various parts of the Commonwealth: Mr Sandys, the Minister for Commonwealth Relations, a convinced European, and to some extent a patron of Heath's, was given the hardest job, visiting New Zealand, Canada and Australia; another very difficult task went to Mr Thorneycroft, then Minister of Aviation, who visited India, Pakistan, Malaya and Ceylon. Among the less strenuous and demanding journeys, was Heath's own: he went to Cyprus, Macmillan perhaps feeling that this negotiator should save his energy and his ammunition for the battle ahead.

The feelings of most of those 'consulted' were best perhaps expressed in a communiqué released by the Australians, which noted that 'the absence of objection should not in the circumstances be interpreted as implying approval'.

Macmillan's announcement of formal application for Britain's entry was followed by debates – one lasting thirteen hours – in which some small but significant clues to hopes of the future path of the negotiations were planted. On the question of loss of sovereignty, Heath, an ardent royalist himself at heart, argued that it was rather a pooling of sovereignty similar to that we already ratified in our N.A.T.O. arrangements. On the subject of Federalism, as Miriam Camps at once noted, 'Mr Heath was noticeably silent.'[3]

Lord Chandos invoked the historical perspective that was often missing from the economic discussions themselves when he said, 'We may be taking a step here of far greater importance in the

[1] *The Times*, 14 June 1961.   [2] *Sunday Express*, 9 July 1961.
[3] *Britain and the European Community, 1955–63*, by Miriam Camps.

national life than any single measure of which I can readily think, even the repeal of the Corn Laws.' And a similar fanfare was suggested by Heath's opening speech to the Six in Paris on 10 October 1961, which contrasted greatly with his rather tight exposition in the Commons. He said the Six must recognize that Britain had reached 'a major turning point in its history', and admitted that the 'negotiations will affect profoundly the way of life, the political thought, and even the character of each of our peoples'.

In time, the necessity of making the same set of facts and figures sound acceptable to the British but ungenerous to the Six would take its toll of energy and confidence even from the exceptional negotiating team (Sir Pierson Dixon, head of the delegation, who was also H.M. Ambassador to Paris, and his deputy, Sir Eric Roll, Vienna-born, trilingual, with an engagingly sympathetic personality to project crystalline conclusions, were backed up by other experienced and strong 'Europeans'). But for the moment, as Miriam Camps in her unparalleled sketch of Mr Heath put it, 'The Lord Privy Seal skated with great confidence on very thin ice . . . Somehow he managed to make it seem plausible to say, on the one hand, that the British had already made a major decision on principle but, on the other, that the decision must be conditional on the outcome of the negotiations.'[1] Miss Camps's metaphor, and the combination of discipline and gambling in Heath's approach, remind one of Sir Henry Raeburn's painting of *The Reverend Robert Walker, D.D., skating on Duddingston Loch*. The aura of Heath's faith, and therefore effectiveness in allaying criticism, was as impressive as the clergyman's. Scepticism about the truth of Britain's intentions was really on the wane. A Belgian official, speaking of his commitment, remarked, 'If this is not so, then Heath is a truly marvellous actor.'[2]

Mr Macmillan appears to have had something of the same success in convincing a much more cynical audience, General de Gaulle, that Britain's willingness to adapt her policies in the interests of uniting Europe was really genuine, when the two met at the Chateau de Champs on 1 and 2 June 1962.

But overshadowing all the arguments about the economy, agriculture and the Commonwealth (where Britain, as a late seeker after

---

[1] *Britain and the European Community, 1955–63*, by Miriam Camps.
[2] *Time*, 13 July 1962.

membership, inevitably but none too quickly, had to make many concessions to meet the sometimes generous, sometimes rigorous demands of the Six) there still loomed the larger question of defence.

Only a month after Macmillan's cordial meeting with the General at Champs, Heath was having to explain to his constituency that if Britain entered the Common Market it would not mean giving away her atomic secrets. Any such report, deriving from Britain's readiness to accept the substantive provisions of the Euratom treaty was, he said, 'completely untrue and unjustified'.[1] Euratom existed for peaceful purposes, and its use of the atom excluded the military anyway.

On the economic side the British team had not started to make concessions a substantial reality until the spring of 1962: in spite of this they hoped to make a great deal of progress before the Commonwealth Prime Ministers' Conference in the autumn. However the Six, and notably the French, did not feel outstandingly anxious to spend August, the traditional holiday month, continuing negotiations which no doubt in their view could well have been given extra time at the beginning rather than now. The British delayed conceding, even though it was obvious that, being in the weakest position, this was inevitable; this may have had a crucial effect in allowing de Gaulle later to re-present the case for British recalcitrance. Patience, apparent stolidity, near-intransigence, were good qualities for Heath to show: but perhaps he made a mistake in showing them for too long.

The political pressures in Britain were great, and his own timetable was so gruelling that he may well not have seen time slipping past in Brussels as the General did in the Elysée Palace. For a time he travelled back to London every weekend to keep up a course on rapid reading. The course lasted for twelve weeks and cost three guineas. He replied personally to a large anti-Common Market mail with letters running to two or even three pages.[2] Lunches in Brussels were often working lunches in the back room of a modest but gastronomically excellent restaurant which he dubbed 'The Club', and which held a table permanently reserved for himself, Sir Pierson Dixon and Sir Eric Roll.[3] Oysters or not, a working lunch

[1] *The Times*, 6 July 1962.   [2] *Sunday Times*, 9 September 1962.
[3] *Daily Telegraph*, 19 November 1962.

means more work than relaxation. By the end of July 1962 the delegates were looking rather weary and depressed, and the Foreign Office took the unusual step of denying a report that Heath had said at a *private* meeting of the Tory Foreign Affairs Committee that he doubted Britain was 'ever going to get in' to the Common Market.[1]

And this was only the periphery. The meetings of the ministers of the Six themselves and Britain often went on until three or four in the morning, and sometimes lasted all night. Part of this time was taken up with discussions, by the Six among themselves, to determine attitudes to each point before it was put to Heath and his team, who meanwhile had been excluded. As Nora Beloff said, 'A less resilient personality than the Lord Privy Seal would have been driven to distraction by the long hours he was to spend pacing in ante-rooms.'[2]

Often Heath sought to untie particularly difficult knots with the individual country or countries most concerned – efforts that earned him extra criticism from the Beaverbrook Press, which was determined to keep Britain out.

A not untypical slice of his programme in August (1962) started with a continuous eighteen-hour discussion in Brussels immediately followed by a flight to London and instant journey to Chequers to report to Macmillan on Friday night, an emergency meeting at Admiralty House on Saturday, and a Press briefing at the Foreign Office on Saturday afternoon.[3]

In February 1963 it was calculated that Heath, in eighteen months, had made twenty-seven trips to Brussels, eleven to Paris, and twenty-two to other countries, covering 50,000 miles. The cost to Britain of the talks so far was estimated at a million pounds.[4] The cost in terms of energy and anxiety is incalculable: yet for someone whose temperament, beneath the self-discipline, is volatile and even touchy, Heath maintained an impressive outward composure in his dealings with the Six. With his own team it was sometimes different: any slight reluctance or inability to meet his most searching standards might be met by an instant explosion of rage, which was not forgotten by those few who witnessed it.

The autumn of 1962 was a time for introspection for the British

---

[1] *Daily Express*, 25 July 1962.   [2] *The General Says No*, Penguin, 1963 p. 114.
[3] *Evening Standard*, 6 August 1962. [4] *Sunday Express*, 17 February 1963.

Government: but its analysis of progress had to be made public, both in the House and at the Party Conference. Macmillan fore-stalled speculation by broadcasting about the Common Market on television on 20 September. There were, he said, two reasons why Britain should join the Common Market: one political, the other economic. He was enthusiastic about the progress made by the negotiating team on two areas – 'now for the Asian countries we have got on the whole very good terms, very good; for the African and Caribbean countries we have got wonderful terms, just wonder-ful terms, if they choose to take them.'[1] But he had to admit the great difficulties that still existed about corn, meat and dairy produce.

It was a fair assessment. Much progress had been made towards reducing tariffs important in Commonwealth trade, ensuring that Commonwealth countries in Africa and the West Indies should be offered associated status on the same terms as former French terri-tories, and promising to seek to negotiate individual trade treaties between the enlarged Common Market and India, Pakistan and Ceylon by 1966. However the British demand for 'comparable outlets' for her Commonwealth food producers clashed with the French desire to expand her agricultural exports. Britain had actually been preparing to make concessions when on 5 August at 3 a.m. the French had produced a text on farm financing (largely benefiting themselves) and demanded that Heath, who had agreed to its provisions verbally, should sign it. His refusal to do so without taking legal advice meant that this crucial question would not be discussed again until October, after the recess. Nor had much pro-gress been made on the transition period for Britain's own agricul-ture, although doubtless the team realized there was little hope of actually achieving their first objective of an adjustment period of twelve to fifteen years.

On 11 October Heath told the Commons, 'Europe is incomplete without Britain, we in Britain are incomplete without Europe.' Later he told the House, 'We have achieved about two-thirds of the outline over the whole field . . . there are bound to be formidable negotiations ahead. We shall pursue them with patience and deter-mination.' He made his case at the Conservative Party Conference in Brighton with a ratiocination worthy of any lawyer: Gaitskell had

[1] *The Times*, 21 September 1962.

asked himself if Britain would inevitably become stronger and more prosperous by entering the Common Market, and had given himself the answer, 'No.' Heath declared that Gaitskell had asked himself the wrong question, and so, 'he really must not be surprised if he gives himself the wrong answer'. What Mr Gaitskell should have asked himself was: whether the opportunities created by going in would enable us to become stronger and therefore would we become weaker by staying out. The answer to that question was, 'Yes.' He added that we were not being asked to go into a Federation. Fewer than a score of hands were raised in opposition to a vote of confidence on the negotiations.

Heath's mastery of the intricacies of his brief, of which he made the most dramatic use in a quiet fashion, blinding his audiences with technicalities and putting them under the spell of his own enthusiasm for them, made a great impression on the House, large sections of the Party and the Press alike. Lord Hill said he knew so much about it that the Opposition was 'always slightly unconvincing'. Frank Giles wrote in the *Sunday Times* that entry was now very nearly a certainty, and added, 'If the Archangel Gabriel himself were conducting these negotiations he could (assuming of course that he was British) scarcely do better than Mr Heath.' 'His skill, patience, knowledge and general amiability' had evoked extraordinary warmth in European circles.[1]

After Macmillan's statement, much more was at stake than previously for the British delegation when a fresh round of negotiations started. On 25 October the Six set out their principles for adapting British agriculture to the Common Market: the transitional period should end in December 1969, and deficiency payments to farmers were to end the day Britain acceded to the Community. Heath condemned these proposals, and the next weeks were spent mainly on these points – which gave General de Gaulle more ammunition for his later allegation that the negotiations had been 'going round in circles'.

The two Governments were preoccupied by totally different problems and there was little affinity between them.

Progress was minimal, and Woodrow Wyatt suggested after

---

[1] *Sunday Times*, 30 October 1962.

visiting Brussels that the team was going into too much detail over, for example, kangaroo-meat, the importation of must for the British wine-producing industry, and special Asian rice for sailors in the Port of London.[1]

The crux of the negotiations, when it came, was not instantly recognized. Afterwards, it seemed clear to many that the most important meeting took place not in Brussels, but at Rambouillet; not between Heath and the Six but between Macmillan and de Gaulle; it was not about British agriculture but about French exclusion from the Anglo-American nuclear cabal.

The meeting at Rambouillet took place on 15 and 16 December soon after it was known that the U.S. would probably soon withdraw its support for the Skybolt missile (on which the British had been relying since the cancellation of the independent Blue Streak) and only a few days before Macmillan was due to meet President Kennedy at Nassau. Miriam Camps writes, 'The available evidence indicates that Mr Macmillan told General de Gaulle that he expected to discuss this matter with President Kennedy and that he would probably accept Polaris missiles in substitution for the Skybolt missiles.'[2] Polaris missiles could only be fired from the appropriate submarine launchers or war-heads: the mere mention of them must have been an aggravation to the General after his twice-repeated appeal to become an equal in a nuclear triumvirate. An official statement said that Macmillan and de Gaulle had found themselves in close agreement about Western policy and Western defence, and that Skybolt was not mentioned specifically.

But just over three years later, Heath told a different story: 'President de Gaulle himself told me in November last year that Mr Macmillan had given him the relevant facts about Skybolt and Polaris at Rambouillet.'[3] The easy relationship between Macmillan and Heath was bound to come under strain as a result of the Rambouillet talks, for Heath, with foresight, realized the likely effect on the General of Britain's impending agreement with the U.S., and felt that Macmillan was not fully aware of the psychological implications for France.

[1] *Sunday Times*, 9 December 1962.
[2] *Britain and the European Community, 1955–63*, by Miriam Camps.
[3] Edward Heath quoted in the *Guardian*, 29 March 1966.

Outwardly, however, all was calm, if not warm. The General still doubted that Britain would or perhaps even could make the necessary mental adjustments for joining the Common Market.

The day after Rambouillet, Macmillan set out for the Bahamas. On the same day, 17 December, *The Times* correspondent in Paris quoted *Le Monde:* 'writing as if the General had created the Common Market', and ominously declaring that 'it is for Britain to buy her subscription and not for the Six to buy British membership'.

Four days later Kennedy's offer of Polaris missiles to Britain, to form part of a multi-lateral N.A.T.O. force, was published. Next he offered the missiles on the same basis to France but without submarines; it was of course an empty offer. Nora Beloff wrote that, 'Gaullist circles . . . are castigating the Polaris offer as, among other things, a trap, a nonsense, an insult, and a joke.'[1]

Henry Kissinger has put the *casus belli* most acutely.

The Nassau agreement could not have been timed more disastrously for Britain's application for membership in the Common Market. If Britain over-estimated its special ties with the U.S. de Gaulle took them at face value. He had never forgotten Churchill's statement that if Britain were forced to choose between Europe and the open sea it would unhesitatingly choose the latter. The difference between the tenacity with which Britain had argued about the economic conditions of its entry into Europe and its willingness to settle its nuclear future in a three-day conference with the U.S. seemed to reflect British priorities. Britain's special relationship with the U.S. in the nuclear field could have two meanings: it was either a challenge to de Gaulle's contention that a united Europe required its own defence; or else it seemed designed to assure Britain a preeminent place in a united Europe. Neither contingency was attractive to de Gaulle.[2]

Nor was the recurring thought that perhaps Britain was playing the Trojan Horse for the U.S.

The guillotine rattled ominously before it fell. Rumours of de Gaulle's increasing displeasure about Britain's determination to

---

[1] *The Observer*, 30 December 1962.
[2] *The Troubled Partnership*, by Henry Kissinger, p. 84, McGraw-Hill, 1965.

come into Europe reached the ears of the British team in Brussels and shocked them into immediate action. The three top men, Heath, Dixon and Roll, flew to Paris on Friday, 11 January 1963 and lunched at the British Embassy. The French Foreign Minister, M. Couve de Murville, was invited. Finally Heath put the question: 'Are there any insuperable political obstacles that would, in the absence of any final technical difficulty, prevent us [from joining]?' Twice the question was put, and twice the answer came from Couve de Murville, 'No.'

In view of later events, a member of the British team comments, 'I believe that these people were not telling us an untruth: I think they didn't know. Obviously if you serve a man like the General you never quite know what he's going to do.'

Only three days later, on 14 January General de Gaulle gave another of his remarkable Press Conferences, in which he described the supposed incompatibilities between the Six, with their economic, commercial and social similarities, and England, which he described as 'insular, maritime', with 'original customs and traditions'. 'In short, the nature, structure and economic context of England differ profoundly from those of the other States of Europe.' She might one one day, he suggested, be willing to change her ways to the point of accepting the conditions practised by the Six: but 'it is also possible that England is not yet prepared to do this, and that indeed appears to be the outcome of the long, long Brussels talks.'

Threats however, even as unveiled as this, did not visibly shake Heath, who was rather the man to assume still greater outward stolidity when his security was threatened: one remembers Eden's words about him as the Suez crisis worsened. 'He was stalwart, but I don't know how he was feeling inside,' says another of the British team. British strategy was now entirely at the mercy of de Gaulle: but Heath's tactics, checked beforehand on the telephone with Macmillan, were nerveless and flawless. It was only three months since the Cuban missile crisis had been coolly de-fused when President Kennedy, taking advice from his brother Robert, the Attorney-General, had replied to the more friendly of two letters from Khruschev and ignored the more aggressive one, with satisfactory results. Perhaps it was the success of this half-bluff, as well as his own instinct for the deadpan when emotions were charged, that enabled

Heath to carry on with the normal routine of talks and concessions in what was after all a safe, if uncomfortable, situation, as if de Gaulle had never spoken. Nor did any comment come immediately from the British Government.

On Thursday, 17 January, three days after the General's declaration, the Five listened to an icy recapitulation of his views from M. Couve de Murville, and were presented with a demand for the suspension of the talks. Afterwards, Nicholas Carroll had a brief glimpse of a vulnerable negotiator who was seeing his table snatched from him:

> At the end of Black Thursday just after midnight I saw Mr Heath by chance as he went up in the lift to his hotel bedroom. For the first time for fifteen months the Lord Privy Seal, normally cheerful and tireless and the best-liked negotiator here, seemed frozen into profound depression; his cheeks grey, his eyes glazed with fatigue. In trying to shut Britain out of Europe General de Gaulle has struck Mr Heath a cruel personal blow. But by Friday when the fight continued British morale had improved.[1]

Heath's physical resilience – as long as he got enough sleep which had not been a guaranteed commodity throughout – and his impassivity, were both greatly helpful in hiding the turmoil he must have endured during the suspense of the next twelve days before the final severance. The admiration other members of the British team generally felt for him was certainly unanimous at this time; and the majority of the British Press reacted the same way. He had enjoyed the company of the world's newspapermen as much as he ever enjoys being with strangers, both because they were specialists and because they kept him informed. 'What did they tell?' I asked. 'They told me what people were telling the Press.'

The *coup de grâce*, the French veto, was finally delivered by M. Couve de Murville on 29 January 1963, after two weeks of attempts by the other Five to salvage the negotiations. Speaking after him, Heath delivered a speech to which several members of his delegation had contributed. It came with added force from the lips of one of the most English of Englishmen who had truly wished to embrace European unity. If nothing else, he wished to extract from the finale

[1] *Sunday Times*, 20 January 1963.

the moral advantage for Britain: she had not, on this occasion, held back from Europe; she had been kept out.

On his appearance in the House of Commons on 12 February he was greeted 'peaceably by the Opposition and with a warm personal cheer from his own party'.[1]

But inevitably the post-mortems followed, one of the prime charges being that Britain had laid herself open to charges of intransigence from the General by taking too strong a stand during the first months of the negotiations, and making concessions which were too late to allow for any impetus to be built up within the timetable of the Six. Was the accusation justified?

'I've often asked myself that question,' says Sir Eric Roll, ten years later. 'It's not so much a question of whether we made the concessions in time but whether we came up to the crunch quickly enough. Some people say that we should never have stopped around the 4th or 5th of August 1962 and had this long interval when we were in full spate – perfectly true, but the fact of the matter is that the other side didn't want to carry on. The Commission were determined to have their holidays then – they said, "We must have a break now." I don't know whether we could have persuaded the ministers to override the Commission – I doubt whether even if we had pressed terribly hard we would have succeeded in keeping them there.'

Sir Eric, a close friend of the leader of the delegation, Sir Pierson Dixon, who has since died, outlined their different opinions of de Gaulle's intentions: 'I think if I might refer to his [Sir Pierson's] views he would probably have said in retrospect that de Gaulle never intended to let us in, that he was always going to veto . . . I'm not so sure. I think de Gaulle was on two options: negotiate very toughly and maybe say yes, but don't forgo the chance of saying no. Some of my French friends tell me that if it hadn't been for the Nassau meeting he wouldn't have vetoed – I don't know if this is just being apologetic after the event.'

The drama of the outcome, and Heath's dignity in defeat, made him the hero of the hour. Now, after the 1971 negotiations, it is possible to say that his method of handling these first negotiations was finally fruitful. But in the aftermath of depression that followed

[1] *The Times*, 21 January 1963.

in the 1960s, there were some different opinions. On the question of his mastery of his subject, one spectator says, 'It is perfectly true that he had the ability, which isn't uncommon among ministers – happily – of absorbing a technical brief very quickly: but I wouldn't, without any disrespect to him in any way, regard him as exceptional. Cripps, for example, was quite outstanding in that regard.' In the House, particularly, Heath was helped by the boredom and ignorance that afflicted some of his own and the Opposition Party on the subject.

But at least one man wonders whether Heath's concentration on the brief was altogether advantageous to himself. 'Perhaps he was inclined to centralize things too much in his own hands: not *vis-à-vis* his officials but *vis-à-vis* his Ministerial colleagues. Some of his colleagues would have felt a bit happier, and he'd have had a little more room for manoeuvre, if he hadn't always been in the front line. Then the negotiations could have been more subtle and more technically flexible – and it is just conceivable, for instance, that better progress might have been made in agriculture if those particular negotiations could have been delegated at an early stage. There was a certain tendency to bunch.'

Leaving hypotheses aside, it is true that Heath impressed his own team – one of them remembers that Heath loved 'going into battle and fraternizing with the other side', and many observers formed the impression that he was more relaxed, in spite of his lack of languages, in the social context abroad than at home. He also – a point which was to be invaluable in the future – deeply impressed the other side, chiefly by the depth of his commitment to Europe.

'He didn't have the cold impassivity of Couve, or the ebullience of Luns, or the great technical detail of Mansholt on agriculture, but I think he impressed with his seriousness, his determination and his sincerity of purpose,' says an experienced European observer. 'He's very English: I mean English rather than British; without an ounce of racialism; a somewhat reserved person – but not like Couve. The only time I've known Couve really relaxed was when he talked about Claret and ran down Burgundy.'

The remark about him seeming English rather than British was inspired: Heath, when filling in forms (as for instance when giving details for army records) fills in his nationality as English, not British.

Later in the year, Heath's efforts were rewarded from abroad by the award of the Charlemagne prize, carrying with it £446 for 'encouraging international understanding and co-operation in the European sphere'.

In Europe, Heath's name was well known, if not a household word; he was acquiring a reputation as a statesman. At home, the view of him was as different as the British and continental views of Byron – we considered him a clever rhymer, they a genius – had been a hundred and fifty years previously: here he was acknowledged to have thoroughly quashed the Opposition allegation that he was 'negotiating from his knees'; but apart from marks for 'trying', acclaim tended to rebound upon him somewhat awkwardly: he became known as a technocrat.

As most men would, he responded to the different atmospheres at home and abroad with different nuances of his personality: even he did not have the self-control, or perhaps the wish, to present a uniformly flat and impenetrable surface to his entire circle of acquaintances, although this is his instinctive reaction whenever he feels uneasy with someone. In Europe those sympathetic to him found him more relaxed and genial than he seemed against the hierarchical English background. His poor ability as a linguist was if anything an indirect advantage to him: his lack of verbal brilliance was disguised by his dependence on translators but the aura of his whole-hearted belief in Europe was overwhelmingly endearing. His love of music too appealed to people who valued the cultural more than the social. He carried the score of Britten's 'War Requiem' with him almost throughout the negotiations, and at one stage during the talks cheered himself up by going to St Stephen's Cathedral in Vienna and playing a Bach toccata and fugue.[1] He even played specifically for one or two of the European negotiators. On the Continent, English and Europeans alike found him burgeoning more than commonly at home.

Some of the secretaries, however, never saw anything beyond their man's impeccable front – it worried one, in particular, who felt Heath's self-control in the face of his bitter disappointment at the breakdown of talks was almost sinister.

He was however more responsive to suggestion than they guessed.

[1] *Illustrated London News*, 7 August 1965.

He spent some weeks holidaying at home in Broadstairs in the summer of 1962, and read six C. P. Snow novels in a row, straight off – 'all the angry young men kept telling me I ought to read him so I did.' And that, it seems, was that.

His social life in England, meanwhile, had suffered considerably during his time in Brussels. He made the trip back to London every weekend during his rapid-reading course, but none of his personal commitments seemed as compelling. Partly because of times and distances it was often left to his secretaries at the Foreign Office to arrange part of his social life, and in particular to contact his few women friends, none of them now particularly close, whenever he wanted to take one to the opera or a concert. Speculation about his private life, which seemed to most people extraordinarily empty, was inevitable. One well-born, charming, and beautiful young woman with naïve ambitions to become the Prime Minister's wife, asked someone, 'I'm a Liberal: do you think it matters?'

The girl who claimed that he had put his arm round her – but added that then she must have said something wrong, perhaps about the Common Market, because the mood was broken – was eagerly questioned by all those who were inevitably and naturally curious about a man who was beginning to emerge more strongly but enigmatically every minute. In the summer of 1962 Sir Gerald Nabarro had voiced the thoughts of more than a few when he called Ted Heath 'the best future Prime Minister we've got,' but added, 'there is only one bar to Mr Heath – he has no wife. The British people would never stomach a bachelor at No. 10 Downing Street.'[1]

With the greater credibility that a Foreign Correspondent sometimes achieves, hitting on truths because of greater detachment, *Time Magazine* made no bones about Heath's own hopes in July 1962. 'Heath's friends have no doubt that some day Heath hopes to go to Chequers on his own – as Prime Minister. His long-range chances look good.'[2]

Only six months later de Gaulle's veto gave quite a different appearance to his chances. Suddenly, the immediate future looked empty. It was a triple disappointment: for Heath as a minister, for his own personal ideas about Europe, and, so it seemed at the time, for his progress towards No. 10.

[1] *Sunday Telegraph*, 12 August 1962.   [2] *Time*, 13 July 1962.

11

The Innovator

For all the anguish involved, the Brussels negotiations had at least kept Heath at a safe distance from the political dangers at home, which came to the first of its hydra heads on Friday, 13 July 1962, on the 'Night of the Long Knives', when seven Cabinet resignations were announced. But the Conservative Party remained in difficulties. Macmillan, so implacable once a dislike was formed, had continued to hold his European negotiator in high esteem throughout the tortuous technical talks: indeed in December 1962 Lady Dorothy Macmillan said, 'I do not suppose anyone realizes the overwhelming regard and affection my husband has for Mr Heath.'

The veto the next month did not arouse the opposite response in the Prime Minister, but he seemed to have felt that his Minister for Europe might safely graze for a while. Butler, now Deputy Prime Minister (a title which he later deduced should be neither conferred nor accepted, since it carried neither power nor rights but only responsibilities) began some of the salvage work with the Six,[1] while Heath concentrated more on restoring Britain in her E.F.T.A. frame.

Heath was only later able to talk about his 'bitter disappointment' over the veto, but his few fairly close friends spotted the disease without the help of symptoms, and did much to try and restore his morale. It was they rather than himself who wondered aloud if his whole career had not now been put in jeopardy, and worried about Macmillan's opinion of him.

[1] *Daily Telegraph*, 29 October 1963.

'I've done better than any of our contemporaries, you know,' he would say. If the remark showed a mixture of smarting disappointment and understandable sense of having been thwarted, it also revealed that familiar pride. It was almost true: none of his contemporaries from Oxford had a place in the firmament, and of the 1950 Parliamentary intake only Iain Macleod, who was Leader of the House of Commons from 1961 to 1963, Enoch Powell, who had followed Macleod as Minister of Health, and Reginald Maudling, now Chancellor of the Exchequer, had in their various ways achieved as much or more than he. In the eyes of the party in 1963 Heath was something of a has-been. The other three enjoyed a brief advantage in having previously been closer to Butler than to Macmillan: yet their own difficulties were also embryonically recognizable. Maudling's attempts to fight rising unemployment by purchase-tax cuts were unsuccessful: by February 1963 the number out of work was 873,000, and his reflationary Budget, which led to the danger of overheating the economy, combined with an easiness of manner and swiftness of mind that led many to misjudge him as lazy. Macleod and Powell both had great gifts of oratory, backed by exceedingly strong and individual political faiths, and extraordinary personalities: but Macleod's Liberal policies when he was Secretary of State for the Colonies had blackened him in the eyes of the Right wing of the Party, just as Powell's opposition to the Common Market had lowered him in the eyes of the opposite quarter of the party. So if Heath was not ahead, no longer regarded as a highly probable leader, he was not behind either.

The continuing respect for him in Europe must have made him feel schizophrenic. At any rate with the confidence and energy born of at least some personal success and satisfaction he turned his attentions to a realizable goal: an elegant home of his own. At the end of 1962 he had received notice to vacate his bachelor flat in Petty France, and had found another nearby but regarded this as very temporary. He was as demanding as usual when pursuing an objective; friends were pressed into the search as soon as he returned from Brussels.

With his usual methodical casting, Heath picked a woman as chief co-hunter: but the choice was logical rather than inspired since Nancy-Joan Seligman admits to having eventually tired of finding a lovely flat in Roebuck House, which he didn't like; then a modern flat in Bayswater, which he turned his thumbs down on as 'not special enough', and not near the House of Commons . . . Finally he found one he liked well enough, but friends remember his secretary, the resourceful and impeccably efficient Rosemary Bushe, stepping in firmly: 'You can't afford it,' she said – the rent was about £1,100 – and that was that. (The number of people whose advice on such matters Heath would take just like that is probably limited to two – his father is the other.)

Meanwhile one of his long-term contingency plans had paid off: the fact that it had been made in the mid 'fifties is another pointer to his far-sightedness and ambition. It also says much about the style to which he hoped to become accustomed as time passed. He had had his name down with Peterhouse College, Cambridge, in the hope that he might be able to rent a set of their chambers in Albany, Piccadilly. One day he got the news that a tenant, Arnold Bax, had died, and that his accommodation was vacant. On inspection, these particular rooms turned out to be extremely dilapidated behind the façade, but the proportions of the rooms, and the ambience – between Savile Row and Piccadilly, without a murmur of traffic inside the castle-thick walls – made them a must for him. Nor were they expensive: together with quarters for a housekeeper and a cellar the rent was six hundred and seventy seven pounds per annum for a seven years' lease.[1]

An interior decorator, Mrs Jo Pattrick, was engaged, and her ideas were so effective that he was later to seek her help again when he moved to No. 10 Downing Street. But waiting for the finished product was more than he could bear. George Chadd remembers that he and Dr Williams were taken back there late one evening. Heath was nearly forty-seven yet 'he was just like a child – like a little boy with a rabbit hutch. He was so natural – that's what I liked about him – saying, "Come and see it" while everything was still covered in builders' dust and we had to grope round in the dark lighting matches.'

Finally on 15 July 1963 he was installed, and sent out his new address: F2, Albany, Piccadilly, W.1. His choice may partly have been directed, as one observer believes, by 'one-upmanship', but his

[1] *The Sunday Times*, 28 January 1968.

delight was entirely spontaneous. 'He was tickled pink,' admits the same observer.

A few old favourites, mainly paintings, went with him; his Coronation chair stood behind a new pine-and-black desk in the study, overlooked by a portrait of the younger Pitt. But most things were new, and diligently selected. A long search – carried out by himself and hard-pressed friends – failed to produce a dining-table he liked, so he ordered one to be made. 'He is meticulous, and very patient when he wants something. He will wait for the right thing,' says one of those involved in the hunt.

Stereophonic equipment fit for a musician was installed in the drawing-room, and here Heath who by this time had a stupendous collection of records, fastidiously selected, indulged in his still favourite recreation of listening to music: sometimes alone, sometimes with friends.

According to R. A. Pye, his agent, he had a distinct policy about entertaining: no husband should be invited without his wife, or vice versa. (The housekeeper was also a good cook, but drinks were often offered, meals rarely.) This rule was sometimes broken with long-standing friends, but many wives saw Heath's own habitat for the first time. Among them was Margaret Chadd, George's wife, who noticed that the flat was wonderfully equipped with everything down to an egg-rack.

For many years she had wrapped up a parcel of home-grown asparagus for George to take to Teddy when they met at their annual H.A.C. reunion at the beginning of May. If the asparagus was given to Teddy on Saturday, Margaret would receive a hand-written letter on the Monday thanking her. But an invitation to his home was an honour indeed.

He was also becoming, as even the critical were beginning to admit, a more thoughtful host. But he could be easily embarrassed by his guests. One out-going American woman friend, leaving for home, bade him goodbye for a year or so and firmly kissed him in front of several others. One of the assembled company remembers, 'He blushed as red as my wife's skirt.'

Sometimes it was the guests who might feel embarrassed.

Madron remembers taking a party of Americans round to Albany early one morning to meet him (he had acted as short-term host to numbers of transatlantic visitors over the years, from a number of sources, and most of them had found him agreeable). Since there had been a crisis the night before, Madron was aware that Heath might not be completely relaxed, and went so far as to warn the guests of the dangers of their situation. Heath is never at his most alert early in the morning anyway; he likes to potter and read, and even do some work, in his dressing-gown before girding himself to meet the day. They sat waiting for him. Suddenly Heath entered, and without saying a word to the assembled guests strode across to where all the papers were laid out waiting for him. He scanned them all, and then, finally, turned to bid the strangers, and his friend, good morning.

If this behaviour was unconscious, or in his own eyes correct (he hates to be kept waiting but keeps other people waiting at all but the most important functions, which leads someone to conclude, 'He must feel he's worth waiting for') he showed also a tendency to assert his 'difference' in a number of tiny ways. One of these was a decision to grow roses in a window-box at Albany: 'People told me you could not grow roses in a London window-box, so I turned awkward and did,' he said frankly.[1] A more obvious example of instinctive aggressiveness at the simplest level it would be hard to find, though the admission of it was doubtless tongue in cheek. (The roses were a gift from a musical woman friend.)

Another idiosyncratic choice was shown in his choice of photographs. He had seven, on a low shelf in his drawing-room: one each of Churchill, Eden and Macmillan, all signed, one of himself conducting a choir, and three of him with V.I.P.s – the Queen, Khruschev and the Pope. The reaction of visitors to this artful yet naïve biographical display varied with the degree of their own sophistication. A Frenchman, aghast, asked a friend, 'Does he always have the same pictures there?'

In the bedroom were some family photographs, though not, surprisingly, one of his mother. When he first moved in, a photograph of Kay Raven, now married for some thirteen years, stood beside his bed; but now that visitors were being admitted to his residence he had to edit even his memories, and before very long it was hidden from view.

[1] Andrew Alexander, interview with Heath, *Daily Telegraph* Magazine.

His own very keen sense of the importance of reputation, which he had guarded so zealously and so effectively, even at the cost of denying himself some of the harmless pleasure he desired, was confirmed by external events that rocked the Government on its heels in the summer of 1963: the Profumo Affair. Following the admission by John Profumo, Minister of War, that he had lied in a personal statement to the House of Commons when he denied having had an intimate relationship with Christine Keeler, who was also sexually involved with a Russian Embassy intelligence officer, Captain Evyeni Ivanov, several members of the Conservative Government suggested that Macmillan should resign. The Liberal leader, Jo Grimond, accused Macmillan either of knowing what had been going on and having ignored it, or of not bothering to find out in spite of the rumours that had been circulating widely since February.

Heath himself had been told of the rumours some time before, but had refused to believe that a Minister of the Crown – and in this case not only British but Conservative – would involve himself in any scandalous situation. After Profumo's statement in the House he was triumphant, believing it utterly and convinced of his vindication. The admission came as a great shock to him, and seems also to have aroused a hesitant curiosity about the power of the sexual drive: the facts were one thing, the feelings quite another, and to him apparently inexplicable.

Those who found him over-innocent in this respect, including some M.P.s and journalists who had heard of the rumours some time before, often in fact had to have aspects of the situation explained to them in turn when they realized they were not so wise as at first they thought. Heath's good friends tended to be wholesome, straightforward, usually happily married, a little conventional in the discussion of the personal, and consciously reticent with him in discussing even their own private lives; it is easy to understand how he 'missed out' (rather happily in one sense) on the psychology of those who were less fortunate in their lives, whether continually or in an occasional aberration. He seemed to one perhaps over-sophisticated onlooker rather child-like in his attitude to sexual matters: he seemed to know in theory more than he really understood.

Because he was unmarried, which is an admitted disadvantage for a politician (except perhaps for the advantage of independence) there had been the occasional rumour about his own sex life, as others tried to imagine it. In the eyes of the simplistic, homosexuality was the obvious reason for not marrying. One admitted homosexual who knows him well says firmly, 'I am sure Ted Heath is not a homosexual.' This observation provides no proof since Heath seldom reveals any sexual side of his nature. But his tendency to be so shy with strange women suggests an almost adolescent fear of them. It seems likely that he is a heterosexual but in this area emotionally immature, and that he has never felt a strong need for direct sexual expression, or has sublimated any needs he has felt.

In a speech at Liverpool during the aftermath of the Profumo period Heath made a pronouncement that was surely heartfelt, with a sense of delivery due to the self-containment of his own nature, and almost a pledge of his own honour in these particular terms. 'It is idle', he said, 'to pretend that any of us in public life should think we can afford standards of conduct – either in public or in private – which do not bear looking into.'[1]

His view of the leaders of men was that they should lead morally, as well as politically: a view that can lead to intolerance through incomprehension, which is why many others have said, as Richard Crossman has on occasion, that those picked to represent the people should not be too far removed from them, in the sense of being above them.

But while Heath holds most of his own moral views firmly – certainly once he has solved the question to his own satisfaction – he has largely either lost or hidden the tendency he had as a schoolboy to narrow censoriousness.

The difficulties of the Government in general at least diverted attention from Heath's own becalmed situation. The breakdown of the Common Market negotiations necessarily meant that he carried less weight in the Cabinet, and as number two in his department was certainly awkwardly placed. Sir Alec Douglas-Home was a very sympathetic number one in the Foreign Office, but at that time was not as convinced as Macmillan had been of the short-term advantages

[1] *Sunday Express*, 22 August 1965.

of joining the Common Market – to shake the country out of a lethargy – or the long-term advantages that both Macmillan and Heath hoped for from economic and political integration. Therefore his view of how seriously things had gone wrong was probably slightly modified. In the Commons, Heath, who had concentrated so much on European affairs, had nothing like the same weight of authority and knowledge when it came to discussing the rest of the world, in which events were taking place that were to affect his own future.

Home and Heath together signed the partial test-ban treaty of which John Kennedy was so proud: America, Russia and Britain were the signatories in Moscow, General de Gaulle having declined to participate.

Although Macmillan's days seemed clearly numbered – twenty-seven Conservatives had abstained in the debate asking for a vote of confidence in the Government after Profumo's admission – it did not occur to anyone, least of all Heath, that he might become the next Prime Minister. One man seemed still less likely: Sir Alec Douglas-Home.[1] He had recently 'reluctantly' talked to the Prime Minister, who had been dispirited by his feeling – shared by some Cabinet colleagues – that he would never recover the lost ground. But by now, in September, Macmillan seemed renascent: 'He talked about himself and his desire to stay, not desire to go. He just told me that he wanted to stay, and that was that.'[2]

Illness, however, so often the unexpected arbiter in politics, intervened on the eve of the Conservative Party Conference. On 8 October the delegates gathering in Blackpool were given the news that Macmillan had been taken to hospital. It was Macleod who was called to the telephone to receive the news of his illness: resignation was not yet mentioned. Butler, who was acting head of the Government, moved into the suite of rooms reserved for the Prime Minister in Blackpool.[3] Hailsham received the loudest applause when he entered the conference hall on 9 October.[4] The third man who looked like a possible successor, should Macmillan retire, was Maudling: but he was only forty-six.

[1] *Sir Alec Douglas-Home*, by Kenneth Young.
[2] Ibid.
[3] *The Fight for the Tory Leadership*, by Randolph Churchill, Heinemann, 1964.
[4] Ibid.

The Gallup Poll asked a hypothetical question, and the answers were published in the *Telegraph*: 'If Mr Macmillan were to retire, who would you like to see take his place?'

The answers, given in percentages of votes, were:

	Con	Lab	Lib	Rest	Total (Average)
Lord Hailsham	18	7	11	1	10
Mr Butler	15	15	16	5	14
Mr Maudling	11	8	16	7	10
Mr Heath	9	4	3	6	6
Mr Macleod	6	3	6	4	5
Mr Selwyn Lloyd	5	4	5	4	4
The Earl of Home	3	1	2	1	2
Don't know	33	53	38	64	45

Lord Home was virtually unknown, and both he and Hailsham seemed to suffer a handicap from being titled in the eyes of Labour voters. Liberals had a higher regard for Maudling apparently and also slightly for Butler than did his own party; the Liberals were noticeably unenthusiastic about Heath, who came next to bottom in their rating. In view of his commitment to Europe, this is interesting: for, after all, the Liberals had been the first to advocate entry to the E.E.C. However, many people feel that, whatever liberal decisions he takes, Heath is not at heart a liberal – and this may have affected many belonging to a party which truly puts its conscience first and its public image second.

Macmillan's resignation was announced on 10 October. It was because of dissatisfaction with the way in which his successor was chosen that a radical change was made in procedure for subsequent cases; again, this was later to be of the utmost significance for Heath. The Cabinet, Conservative members of both houses of Parliament and of the party organizations were questioned for several days about the succession: the final verdict was not for either of the favourites, Butler and Hailsham, nor for Maudling, but for Home. On the morning the Queen sent for Home *The Times* carried the headline: 'The Queen may send for Mr Butler today.'

Iain Macleod revealed the ground-swell of dissatisfaction with the motives and methods of selection in his review of Randolph

Churchill's book, *The Fight for the Tory Leadership*, in the *Spectator*. He suggested that Macmillan, determined that whatever happened Butler should not succeed him, nevertheless thought that none of the younger and brighter potential successors had a decisive lead; so he turned to Hailsham. 'Only Hailsham could stop Butler, and when Hailsham failed to gather enough support then Macmillan still refused to accept Butler. Almost in desperation now he turned to Home.'[1] Macleod was not convinced by the subsequent claim by Martin Redmayne (Heath's successor as Chief Whip) that Home had a small lead on Tory M.P.s' 'First Preferences'. But after the fifteen Whips had worked hard for a week, it was not surprising that he should have a lead of one or two.

Julian Amery adds, 'It looked impossible to win a fourth election, but Macmillan thought Quintin was the only man who could do it if he didn't do it himself.'

It was a long drawn-out and testing time for all concerned. One of those closest to Heath, and particularly impressed by him at this time, was his P.P.S., Anthony Kershaw. 'He would never do anything underhand – this was terribly clear when Alec was elected leader of the party and it was possible for younger members to further their ambitions,' he says. 'A number of people declared themselves, or let it be known that they would be available; someone like Quintin completely openly as one would expect, others more discreetly. The one person who was in that category who didn't move or do anything at all was Ted.'

Ambition in fact, some believe, was holding him back at the moment rather than urging him forward: *reculer pour mieux sauter*. One astute analyst says, 'He coldly assessed that this was not the moment to move and that it would be very unwise to make the slightest move if it wasn't going to be acceptable. He was riding in a hard race but he never moved in the saddle at all during that time – he made no attempt to ride out. I think it was absolutely right to keep himself for the next opportunity and I thought that showed intense personal control because there were doubts up to the last moment about whether Alec would take on that burden – he didn't want to particularly and there were obvious difficulties. The others were more or less smoked out – people would come to them and say,

---

[1] The *Spectator*.

"Will you stand if things go your way?" and they could hardly say, "No, I won't." But he'd so arranged things that no one even asked him the question – he just looked at them with a cold, cod-like eye and the subject was hastily dropped.'

Heath in fact himself supported Home, it was thought, partly for selfish reasons: a younger man would obviously have provided a more likely impediment in the future. And as usual once his decision was made his loyalty was absolute.

One man did have the courage to ask him outright why he wasn't trying for the leadership, and remembers Heath replying, 'It's not my time yet.'

Meanwhile, his good friend Lord Aldington, together with Maudling, Macleod, and Frederick Erroll, President of the Board of Trade, had been with Enoch Powell at his home at No. 33 South Eaton Place, talking in a desperate attempt to find an alternative to Home[1] – who himself, in his first audience with the Queen, had postponed kissing her hand until he was sure he could form a Government.

Macleod and Powell were so entrenched in their feelings that they refused to serve under him. Heath commented on this situation on television on 24 October making it very plain that they had not been vetoed. It was a 'matter of great regret' to him that they had refused to take part in the new administration, but 'the important thing is that they were offered office'. He went on to point out 'they knew what the Prime Minister's views were through serving with him as colleagues. From the point of view of policy I do not think they should have had reservations . . . I believe this Government under the present Prime Minister is going to pursue exactly the same principles we faced in One Nation and have adhered to ever since.'[2] Heath now, in fact, because of the two resignations, was the only one of the nine founder members of the One Nation Group still in office.

People were now beginning to get a rather better look at the political Heath, the 'torpedo': at about this time Lord Hill was writing his memoirs, extracts of which were published a few months later in the *Sunday Times*. Heath was, he wrote, 'a fascinating man . . . superficially so friendly and approachable . . . but the reality is

[1] *The Fight for the Tory Leadership*, by Randolph Churchill.
[2] *The Times*, 25 October 1963.

rather different.' In his simple summing up, Heath was 'probably the toughest politician on either side of the House.'[1]

Heath's job in the new Cabinet was more straightforward than it sounded: he was to be Secretary of State for Industry, Trade and Regional Development and President of the Board of Trade. In fact he was to look ahead, and reorganize both policy and its application. Straightforward perhaps, but not easy; and he was soon to need all his toughness.

For his next battle, though it was on ground he chose himself, was fought almost alone. It was the battle to abolish resale price maintenance, a device designed to protect producers and shopkeepers against the potential price-cutting of department stores, multiples, etc. R.P.M. had been introduced in the nineteenth century to fix the price of books, and in 1896 was applied to chemists' goods. Since then it had spread: producers now fixed or recommended prices for articles ranging from consumer goods and office equipment to building materials. Various committees had reported on it: in 1920 in favour, although one man pointed out that 'retailers who are able to do with a trading margin lower than the average are precluded from doing so',[2] in 1931 with greater awareness of the disadvantages, but no attempt to change matters; and in 1949, when the Lloyd Jacobs committee was firmly against it. The Labour Government proposed reforms, but were voted out of office before these became law.

Other Presidents of the Board of Trade had started out with good intentions of reforming the legislation, but the tremendous antagonism to the idea expressed by small shopkeepers, as well as some larger ones, and the fear of losing such a large section of the middle-class vote had been voiced loudly in the party and apparently coincided with amnesia on the part of the past presidents.

In the autumn of 1963 Heath had to fly up to Scotland. Sitting beside him in the plane was Anthony Kershaw. 'That was the first time he showed me the R.P.M. thing', remembers Kershaw. 'He said, "What do you think of that?" I said, "It's fine, but there'll be a hell of a row." He wouldn't reply to that sort of observation – he

---

[1] *Sunday Times*, 7 June 1964.
[2] *Resale Price Maintenance – Studies*, edited by B. S. Yamey, Weidenfeld & Nicholson, 1966.

never would, he just docketed it away in his mind. Then he worked on it and didn't give an inch. The document which I saw in the aeroplane two or three months before it was introduced was substantially the law which he backed through. He is completely inflexible: he wouldn't take anything from the Cabinet or anyone. When he's made up his mind to do something he really is completely inflexible – he takes a long time to make it up and he talks to an awful lot of people, but after he's made it up you might as well talk to yourself – you can pack it up because he won't change.'

Coming from Kershaw, himself a barrister and son of a judge, used to persuading people to change their minds or to see things in a different light, this is an outstanding assertion: and it is no exaggeration. However, what Kershaw did not know was the anguish that Heath was actually going through as the result of that determination. A person's strength can sometimes come as close to breaking him as his weakness.

Heath's motives in wanting to bring in the reforms were three-fold, the main one being that he thought it was right. It would obviously also make people remember him at the Board of Trade (especially as others had failed to do likewise); and it became a matter of pride not to back down however hard he was pressed.

Shortly before Heath introduced his Bill, Mr John Stonehouse, a Labour member, introduced a Private Member's Bill seeking to abolish R.P.M. except where the Restrictive Practices Court found it not against the public interest. The Bill did not survive a second reading: but it may have been partly responsible both for precipitating Heath's action, and arousing Tory resentment.

When Heath's Bill was published in January, it met a generally favourable response: however, small shopkeepers were, as expected, loud in their complaints, and were backed up in a full-scale campaign by the *Express*. The next three months were fraught with a full-scale backbench rebellion. It was to friends outside the House that Heath now had to turn for an unbiased opinion of what devastating effects his pursuit of reform might have on his own career: he wanted to persist, but he asked someone whose judgment he greatly trusted if he was right to persist. 'Yes,' said the friend, 'if you want to make a name in politics you must be steadfast.'

The name he was making, meanwhile, was not altogether desirable, although it was extremely useful for a politician to have such a reputation for toughness. Some thought he was being hardest on the very class he came from. A member of the Cabinet says, 'That's right, and that's why he's got this affinity with the successful young manager and very little sympathy for the rather unsuccessful who've had opportunities and haven't taken them. Of the unsuccessful small shopkeeper, he said, " *Why* can't they succeed?" He had no sympathy for them at all. Yet he's a lot of time for those who've had no chance at all – Ted wants to help them.'

On 10 March Heath came out in the House with a quite unintentional pun: 'It is now apparent that there is no halfway house. We can permit resale price maintenance to go on in every case, with all that it entails in the way of higher costs, a less efficient distribution supply, and less opportunity for consumers' preferences to influence supply, or we can provide for price competition, and facilitate the introduction of new and improved methods of distribution by ending resale price maintenance, except where it can be shown that it helps the consumer and is not contrary to the public interest.'

The next day, twenty-one Conservatives voted against the Government and seventeen more abstained: the Government majority fell to a single vote. It was the greatest internal revolt the Conservative Party had faced in post-war years: and what worried many members, including even some of those who had voted for abolition, was the fact that Heath had not apparently given a jot for party unity.

He was showing himself as a hard man: not naturally hard, but consciously hard. 'He was very ambitious, but never unfairly,' says Anthony Kershaw. 'Both with himself and others he was hard but just: and convinced he could do the job. It was a worthy ambition.'

In the past when he wanted something he had been hard on family and friends. Now, increasingly, he was hard on colleagues, hard on the party, and hard on himself. 'After the R.P.M. fight he was emotionally exhausted. You can see it from a photograph: his eyes are all screwed up,' remembers Madron Seligman. 'But he said that three or four Presidents of the Board of Trade had funked it and it had to be done.'

Done it was, and, very important to his later psychology, he had done it virtually alone – many who voted with him did so because they thought that though it would lose them votes in the next election it was 'right in the long term'; others wanted to avoid a still wider split. Personally Heath might be in a small wilderness, without the enforced (if probably welcome) camaraderie he had enjoyed with his team in Brussels: now, in his isolation, he had nevertheless enforced his own view on his party, largely against its will. The strenuous demands Heath made of the British team at the UNCTAD conference at Geneva in the same year, convinced some of them that he was determined to crown his reputation with an international success, and that this aim was a greater spur to him than his care for the under-developed nations. Those who did not fight back against his tirades fared worse than those who argued. But, if not happy, the team was successful and Heath made this another mark in the limited time left to this Government. He returned to England very anxious to know what publicity the conference had received.

Sir Alec could stave off the election until the last possible moment, in the autumn, or he could go to the country in the spring. Heath, together with many senior Conservatives, counselled the later date, and public opinion polls in the intervening months suggested that this was right. However, on 16 October Labour won the General Election with a majority of five seats.

Heath's own election plans were slightly put out by his father's wedding to his third and present wife, Mary. 'William insisted in having it on Mary's birthday, 10 October', remembers a friend, 'and he had to go down for it. His father is the only person who can speak to him now.'

Surprisingly, Heath seemed to take the 1964 defeat rather philosophically. Madron and Nancy-Joan Seligman remember inviting him to spend the following weekend with them, slightly anxious in case he should feel terribly deflated after thirteen years in Government and five in the Cabinet. Instead, browsing round bookshops he declared, 'Isn't it lovely to be free.' Perhaps he saw it as a chance to recharge. But a seat alone was not enough for him now, and he was very soon approached again by his old firm of merchant bankers, Brown, Shipley and Co. Ltd. On 23 October, exactly one week after the Conservatives had lost power, Heath became a director of Brown, Shipley; he resigned on 9 August the following year, after he had been made leader of the Opposition. There were five directors at the time. His European contacts and friendships with foreign bankers were considered particularly useful, and he made a number of trips to France and Switzerland for the firm. His secretary, Joyce Hill, remembers, 'He was more dynamic than most people in banking. He knew exactly what he wanted: he put a few comments on the side of the page and then left it to you to construct a letter and he signed it. He didn't know how hard you worked. He had so many phone calls. He had lunch in the City most days, and he was always running behind schedule.'

Jack Higgins, a manager and Chief Foreign Exchange dealer, remembers, 'He spent two days with me when he came back and just let me talk – he mastered every subject that I expounded on literally without question. He understood it all: it takes some people years. He had the ability to extract information from you, and had deep insights into the thinking of various Treasury Ministers abroad. If everyone had fallen down dead he could have run the bank and controlled it.'

He also made good use of his contacts and knowledge to improve his own financial position: his investment in Brown, Shipley Holding Ltd., registered at Companies House, consisted of 3,125 shares worth about £7,000. Part of this was a bonus issue. He had obviously saved and invested hard, particularly no doubt while in Brussels.

While never mean – in fact while most generous in entertaining and giving presents to his family, friends and god-children – Heath had a quality extolled in the One Nation document as a particularly Conservative virtue: thrift. Unless it was a special occasion, he usually 'went Dutch' on evenings out with friends, and when he visited Bexley it was on the understanding that in the constituency, Reginald Pye footed the bills, while in London Heath did so.

He also loves receiving presents. 'He can be rather like Queen Mary in his way of admiring things,' says one friend drily. And he 'loves bargains': he returned from Singapore triumphant about two china plates, having beaten the seller down twice and got them for what he considered to be far less than their real value. In his carefulness one can see the home influence, his careful costing of eggs for breakfast at Balliol, his economic training, and the natural aptitude for financial detail that must have made the Brussels negotiations intrinsically interesting.

He maintained his interest in financial minutiae after he became Prime Minister. Because wet weather had meant the cancellation of a garden party in Bexley in June 1970, and the Conservative Association was short of ready cash, they planned to sell £1,000 of investments. 'Within three days Heath rang up and said why not get a bank overdraft – and this among all his business as Prime Minister!' recounts Pye. In the end, neither proved necessary.

But this attention to detail of all kinds perhaps suggested to the unimaginative that he had no resources capable of shaping a grand design.

That Heath had no great grip on the imagination of his party was shown in December 1964, when the Young Conservatives chose Macleod in preference to himself as their next President. What was happening during these nine and a half months to launch him as the next leader of the Opposition?

The Labour Government, with its difficult financial inheritance, was in desperate straits for some fifteen months – they were faced with the deficit of eight hundred million pounds along with their victory. Heath has always been a man to get some enjoyment out of other people's problems (unless they are people of whom he is truly fond, or possess the seeds of true tragedy in them). On the battle for the pound he was, remembers one man, 'cynical and humorous'.

Heath's attitude and his position were to his advantage: on 7 February 1965, he became Shadow Chancellor of the Exchequer, in a position to attack and not to have to prove the workability of his own policies.

The Labour Party's 1965 Finance Bill, the longest Bill presented to the House for many years, gave him an ideal opportunity for a spot assault.

His experience in the Common Market negotiations had convinced him that a small, highly specialized team, each man concentrating on an area of specific responsibility and constantly reporting to the centre, was the best way of combating an elusive opponent. He began by cancelling a long-arranged trip of his own to the Konigswinter Conference in Germany, and sat down with his chosen few to plan their strategy: tactics were largely left to the individuals. Etonians and others were quick to spot that the inner core, consisting of Peter Walker (Douglas-Home's choice as a Front Bench spokesman on the

Economy), William Clark, Peter Emery, John Hall and Anthony Barber, were not the products of the traditional Tory schools. Most had made their way in business, and Walker, a grocer's son, had left school at sixteen, done extremely well as a broker, brilliantly in Unit Trusts (he was a millionaire about the time he was thirty) and by 1964 was Deputy Chairman of Slater Walker Securities. Three better known and very astute minds were also involved: Sir Edward Boyle (now Lord Boyle), Keith Joseph and Martin Redmayne. Then there were three legal experts, Mr van Straubenzee, Mr Patrick Jenkin and Mr Stratton Mills, who concentrated on the clauses concerned with close companies.

Maudling, guiding through his two Budgets in 1963 and 1964, had been happy to accommodate the Opposition in small ways in return for like help: but Heath made it plain that not even minor bargains were on.

There were more than a hundred divisions on the Bill, which Heath described as 'the longest and most complicated Finance Bill for over fifty years'. Heath's group met daily whenever the Finance Bill was due for discussion, often for breakfast at Albany, sometimes in the House at noon.

'He had a strong grip on parliamentary tactics. There was a good debate when the notable Press were there, and divisions when the Conservatives needed them – that was his Whip's training,' remembers Peter Walker, now Secretary of State for the Environment. 'He knew when to have a major row, and when not. It was the first time a Finance Bill had really been tackled in detail.

'Tony Barber worked on corporation tax, myself on capital gains, and Boyle handled the overseas side. We each worked with one other. You went to him with suggestions . . . One major change concerned life assurance – originally the proceeds would have been subject to capital gains tax.

'He saw earlier than most the changing commercial concept of Britain. Early on I put the boom in Europe down to post-war recovery. It wasn't, and I now see no alternative to joining the Common Market. He had a personal faith in Europe.'

It was also Heath's personal faith in honesty that won a somewhat critical Walker over to become one of Heath's staunchest supporters. 'Someone', he said, 'made an effective dishonest speech attacking the Finance Bill. Ted was absolutely furious and said, "We can't argue against legislation like this." Then he went over to the man and said, "That was a thoroughly dishonest speech and I hope you'll abstain from making them in future." '

On 3 June, *The Times* carried the headline 'Equal Votes on Corporation Tax: Government saved by Chairman's casting vote.' There were cries of 'Resign', and Heath said, 'It is quite apparent that the Government are no longer in a position to carry on with their business': a fully political remark in view of his narrow scrape with R.P.M. a year before.

On the night of 6–7 July the Government was twice defeated: Heath again pressed his accusation.

The marathon achieved less in terms of changing the Bill than in changing the Conservatives' view of Heath. He had proved that he could not only go it alone as he had done on R.P.M. – with a strength in isolation that perhaps gave some colleagues a nagging feeling of unease at not really being needed – but that he could co-ordinate and direct a pressure group, thus exerting a leverage on the whole Parliamentary system that was, in internal terms, highly successful and satisfying. Essentially a loner, he had proved beyond any shadow of doubt that his Whip's knowledge of tactics, allied to his own instinct for channelled aggression, enabled him to work well in a team.

Against all their own prejudices, resentments, even dislikes of him, a majority of people in the party were being slowly forced to recognize that he had these two ingredients of leadership, even though he lacked the charm, magnetism, and, as yet, the stature that emotionally people often also seek in a man they choose to put at their head.

Altogether 211 hours of Parliamentary time were taken up by the Finance Bill, largely of course because of the Opposition tactics. Some amendments were carried – for instance Scotland benefited from the relief from import duties on goods brought to a registered shipbuilding yard, and many private citizens from the exemption from capital gains tax of chattels sold for £1,000 or less. Most important for firms trading abroad was a concession extending transitional relief from corporation tax for them from five to seven years.

It was an expensive battle in terms of time, and with a few exceptions not very productive in financial terms. But politically it was a notable and markedly successful onslaught.

The Prime Minister, Mr Wilson, commented, 'It was rather like marching your troops through a long deep valley with the enemy ranged on the mountain-tops on either side. We were fighting them on their own ground in the worst possible conditions but we won through.'

Sir Alec Douglas-Home was no longer acceptable to the whole of the party. While Heath was busy on the financial swings, in July 1965 some of his less subtle supporters were working up a good speed on the roundabouts. Rumours were strong that Sir Alec Douglas-Home was going to retire. Ian Waller wrote in the *Sunday Telegraph* on 18 July 1965: 'Heath's standing as a possible successor as leader of the Conservatives had been severely damaged as the result of the collapse of the coup designed to oust Sir Alec in his favour which has just been attempted at Westminster.' He said that three weeks previously lobby correspondents had been approached by some of the younger M.P.s belonging to the pro-Heath under thirty-six group, and been told that a major revolt was imminent, with a hundred people supporting Heath. Waller said, 'I could find no evidence to back this.'

It was at a meeting of the Back Benchers' 1922 Committee on Thursday, 22 July, that Sir Alec made an unexpected announcement: he would resign. No one had suggested it to him, he said, 'but there are those who, perfectly properly, feel that a change of leadership might be for the best'.[1]

In February Sir Alec Douglas-Home had announced the method by which future leaders of the Conservative Party were to be chosen. Like the Labour Party, they were now to hold a ballot. If someone emerged with an overall majority of not less than 15 per cent, that would suffice. If not, there would be a second and possibly a third ballot.

This system was evidently more likely to favour Heath than the old 'magic circle' had done, at least in his own eyes. He was still, in spite of his denials, extremely conscious of the old Etonian underpinning of the party – many of his friends with hardly any interest in pure politics can reel off the number of old Etonians who have been in the House at any one time, and there is only one likely source of their information, only one likely reason for the impression

[1] *Sir Alec Douglas-Home*, by Kenneth Young.

it made on them: Heath's fervency in the face of an intangible opposition that he could not see how to fight.

Leaving his own henchmen to add what they could to the crop of his own past labours, he went down to Glyndebourne after the night of Sir Alec's resignation, as he had already planned, to see Verdi's *Macbeth*. There were those who saw a Macbeth in Heath himself at this time: but afterwards Sir Alec absolutely acquitted his successor of any charges that he had made moves against him. In fact there was no need for him to: he was the froth on the wave of younger members who were surging forward at this time; anyway political assassination is not in his nature, with his fervent belief in the strength of the British hierarchy.

To the surprise and deep disappointment of many, Iain Macleod decided not to enter the lists. The nominations on Monday, 26 July were predictably: Maudling – the favourite – and Heath, but also a surprise third: Enoch Powell. The results of the first ballot, announced the next afternoon, were: Heath – 150 votes; Maudling – 133 votes; Powell – 15 votes. This meant, since Heath did not have a 15 per cent overall majority, there should have been a second ballot; but Maudling and Powell announced that they would withdraw. It was an uncomfortably narrow victory for Heath.

His father has long since ceased trying to talk to Teddy about the intricacies of political issues and parliamentary life. It has hurt him to be excluded when he would like to learn what it is all about, but he says, 'When all the answer you get to questions is "Yes", "No", or "I don't know", you soon give up asking.' But on the human level the narrowness of Heath's win, and the dangerous implications of it, could not be hidden from him. It is these internal politics that still cause him to sit and think, brooding on his son's difficulties. 'When it's a hundred and fifty on one side, and a hundred and thirty-three on the other . . .' he says, dangling the implication; and the impression the figures made on him was so strong that seven years have done little to erase his anxiety.

It was not, especially at first, ill-founded worry. Victory carried its own backlash. 'Teddy is socially shy, and the snob element in the party said he was too common, having elected him on the basis of "wouldn't it be nice to have somebody who was more a man of the people",' observes one M.P. 'One thing they always used to pick on was that he didn't take any exercise – and this is regarded as dreadful in the Tory Party.'

If he was chosen as a man of the people, it was an amazing misconception. Few men have come, through recognizing if not understanding their own unpopularity, to hold popularity in such low esteem as Heath does; when he used the term it is almost a term of abuse.[1] (One wonders whether Maudling's personal popularity, which far exceeded his own, may also have been a final proof to Heath that respect was worth far more in political terms.) And it is true that he has never tried hard to share the everyday tastes or interests, or enter into the daily personal battles, of the majority of men and women. He cares more for people's potential than for their actual or individual happiness: the stoic in him holds the scales of judgment.

Some people chose him as the best opponent for Wilson: of the same age, comparable class, education, both specializing in economics, both developing new ways of wielding power. Again it was at best a half-valid comparison: few men can be by temperament and conviction so much at odds: and to Heath especially the comparison seemed odious.

For the moment however all was submerged in the joy of the moment. With his father, step-mother and the Seligmans Heath took a holiday at Villefranche, not far from Nice. He is a man who has increasingly learned to hide his pleasure as well as his pain: however, Mary Heath remembers a moment of real delight breaking through when they arrived. It was his first visit to the French Riviera. 'He said to Nancy-Joan, "Isn't this marvellous – just think, a fortnight of this," ' his step-mother recalls, 'I've never seen him so excited – have you, darling?' William thinks probably not. In his high-spirited mood, he turned to a typical outlet: playing a practical joke. The recipient was Moura Lympany, whom he had met at a party some time before, and who occasionally accompanied him to the theatre or to Glyndebourne when she was not working hard in practice for a concert of her own. Apparently she was staying on the coast not far away. 'He rang her up pretending to be Sir Malcolm Sargent and asking if she could play in a very special concert. He got her all worked up,' says Madron.

[1] See his use of the term in *Old World, New Horizons*.

A true friend to him (as Heath indeed is to her in any real misfortune) Miss Lympany herself omitted to mention this story. But she did admit to having been teased by Heath at a concert given by Arthur Rubinstein – 'Ah, there's a *great brain* playing.' She makes it plain that theirs is no deep relationship. 'He will probably come round and drink some champagne, eat a little smoked salmon, before we go to a performance. He never rings up to cry on my shoulder.'

Another friend remembers Heath becoming quite flustered with embarrassment when Moura was teasing him at Glyndebourne. It is hard to understand how a man who is intensely open to chagrin and pain himself can relish, even momentarily, inflicting them on his friends – one can only guess that to him it is an indirect way of expressing affection, however hard this seems on those he is fond of.

Though he was photographed looking purposeful at the tiller of a yacht for the *Telegraph* weekend magazine,[1] Heath in fact was an inexperienced sailor at this time. 'He used to sail with us in a little boat in Brittany,' remembers Madron, 'but in Villefranche he didn't know what to do with a tiller – we nearly went on the rocks.'

One day Madron, his son Lincoln and Heath entered a dinghy race. 'Teddy had never been in a race before. We came last by miles,' recounts Madron. 'We were both rather over-weight, and Lincoln said, "If Daddy and Uncle Teddy hadn't been so fat we might have won the race."'

Many of Heath's political friends dropped by to talk about the future. Among them were David Howell and Edward du Cann, both languorous-looking individuals, and photographs of the three, looking rather indolent, gathered some unfair comment back in Britain.

There was a sharp comment on the spot, too. Eating a peach at lunch one day Heath was horrified to discover a maggot in it. Always squeamish, he handed it to Madron who extracted the maggot for him. This incident was watched with furiously scornful eyes by one of the women present (the wife of someone later to become one of Heath's ministers) who asked bitingly, 'How can you expect to become Prime Minister if you can't get a maggot out of a peach?'

How, indeed?

Back in England, Heath was being described as 'the most elusive

1 Picture published 31 December 1965.

politician since Curzon'.[1] On his return he was subjected to a deluge of interviews, most of which left him as elusive as they found him. But James Margach elicited some revealing answers – particularly interesting as a reflection of him at this time, when he was resting in his tent between battles.

Characteristically he claimed that he had modelled himself on nobody. But he admitted, 'I think I was attracted to Pitt because as a young man he showed great courage and had remarkable achievements throughout some of the most important and tempestuous days of nineteenth-century history.'[2] (It is interesting that he said 'history' and not 'life'.)

'I do enjoy a good argument,' he said, but was careful to balance the picture of aggression with his relaxation – 'the refreshment of mind and spirit such as only music can bring.'[3]

Three months later, Kenneth Harris probed still further. Some of the answers were different in detail but proved the same point. Instead of Pitt, he now cited Disraeli, again plainly identifying with him: 'I admired him because he didn't come from the top men of the politicians of his day and indeed was opposed by them in his early political life.'[4] To me, he added that Disraeli 'did have a vision'; and that 'an unimaginative approach can grip people.'

He talked about his religious life – not an easy subject even for a less private man. He believed in an after-life, he said, and, 'I believe in prayer and I pray . . . One should approach one's political problems in the setting of one's beliefs about God, man, and society.'[5]

The tricky question of marriage he dealt with notably well: he was asked whether he would make a better Prime Minister if he were married, and replied, 'I don't know. It would depend to some extent on the woman, wouldn't it? What I do know is that a man who got married in order to be a better Prime Minister wouldn't be either a good Prime Minister or a good husband.'[6]

These answers were direct and in line with his own beliefs and behaviour. But on the question of the leadership of the Tory Party, he gave a reply that was hardly recognizable as his own: 'Convince

[1] *Observer*, 1 August 1965.   [2] *Sunday Times*, 3 October 1965.
[3] Ibid.   [4] *Observer Colour Magazine*, 16 January 1966.
[5] Ibid.   [6] Ibid.

them you are really taking them into your confidence because you believe in doing it.'[1]

Taking people into his confidence was exactly what Heath was not doing – for the very good reason that, as he confided to Madron, he was no longer sure exactly who his friends in politics were. 'People didn't like working with him because he didn't tell them how his mind was working,' says someone who is now a minister.

Promotion often brings suspicion in its train, as Heath was now finding to his cost. And he was quite unable to hide the fact even from people who were not in the House with him. 'He seemed to tighten up and withdraw after he got the leadership,' remarked someone from abroad who saw him only a few times each year. Even the officials of the Conservative Party felt the difference, and wondered how their party, as well as their man, would fare.

Heath continued to insist that you could not build an image for a politician: he must eventually emerge simply as the man he is. But Heath, like most intelligent people, was not a static individual. A moody man, already in his life he had passed through different phases, felt triumphant and defeated, known sorrow and elation; and, at each stage of his life, he had been – for all his extraordinary consistency of thought and fidelity of purpose – a slightly different man, evolving, developing, advancing, withdrawing: changing. Therefore, while his statement was in a sense true, it remained to be seen exactly what man would in time emerge.

At once however he began to shape his image to what he deemed necessary and compatible with the best of the varying facets of his own nature.

'Ted paid minimum attention to the public practically till he was leader himself. Before that he only took trouble with the Government machine and party in the House of Commons,' says a minister. 'He was largely unknown to the public – he could have walked down the main street of Birmingham unrecognized yet he was prominent in Westminster and Whitehall. He found the public part of it difficult.'

It was true that he was not a figure who attracted much public attention, in spite of all the spadework he had done both in his constituency and throughout the country, particularly during his tenure

[1] *Observer Colour Magazine*, 16 January 1966.

of the post which included regional development. 'I don't know any member who had spent so much time travelling round the country, and given so many weekends to speaking to local associations,' says one M.P.

However, his tactics with people were far from faultless. A staunch woman Conservative who had looked forward to meeting the new leader with an impatience bordering on hero-worship was confused when he chatted to a group including herself to find 'it was as though there was a glass wall between him and you'. On another occasion he was sitting next to Sylvia Constantine, wife of Theo Constantine, the Chairman of the National Union of the Conservative and Unionist Associations. As so often with women he does not know well, he was almost completely silent. 'She was having a terrible time and not getting any distance – then she reminded him they'd met and who she was and he changed completely,' says another guest.

Sometimes he simply could not bother to make any effort at all, particularly if he felt there was little to gain. 'Sometimes it's so funny to see him at a dinner between two ladies who've been dying to meet him, and he simply closes his eyes and takes off for a nap,' admits one aide. Another adds, 'They don't know what's expected of them. In fact all that's expected of them is that they should be entertaining. This is why he likes people like Lady Aldington and Lady Adeane. The same applies to those who work for him – they must either be entertaining, or know how to introduce other people who are. Otherwise it ends in tears.'

He was learning to be more *soigné* in the party, however. 'When he was on the up-and-up he used to talk about how he'd seen Monty and what Winston had said to him . . . the sort of thing you'd have expected him to impress his local association with, not us,' says an M.P. 'He stopped doing that after he became leader.'

Occasionally when he made a great effort his good intentions went awry. There was the occasion when he went down to Lowestoft to stay with his new P.P.S., James Prior (now Joint Deputy Chairman of the Conservative Party), and his wife Jane for a weekend. They live not far from Heath's old friend George Chadd and his wife Margaret, whom they also saw. Back in London after the weekend, Heath sat down to write his hostess, Jane, a charming thank-you letter. 'Dear Margaret . . .' it began.

The same weekend, someone who called at the house mentioned to Heath that he had taken his sons to see the figure of him at Madame Tussaud's. 'What did I look like?' enquired the leader. 'Awful – far too fat,' was the frank reply. Heath who was on a diet anyway, swung round to Prior. 'Get that altered,' he said.

The politician was emerging as he intended to be.

12

Opposition Compounded

Edward Heath was the first leader of the Conservative Party to be chosen in Opposition since Bonar Law; and, at the age of forty-nine, he was a relatively youthful leader. It is plainly more difficult to step into the breach in a time of relative inactivity; for whereas a new Prime Minister inherits an automatic aura and immediate power a new leader inherits almost inevitable dissension and restraints on his influence. In a country which has successfully relied on a two-party system for centuries, British politics have nevertheless very frequently provided a tragi-comic sideshow when a party which has held power for some time is left like Punch and Judy in Opposition. If the Labour Party has open squabbles and, sometimes, a curious and ignominious retreat from its own best policies, the Conservative Party, behind an apparently more united front, probably hides more true bitchiness and has to try to find the common denominator across a far more disparate range of views. But it is less hampered, as well as helped, by idealism; and under Heath 'realism' became a watchword.

The Tory Party was changing and would continue to change, Heath announced: but without yet giving very many hints as to what these changes were to be. At first his words sounded rather like the advertising man's 'new'. The promise of change was the rainmaker's chant while in fact new policies – not always progressive, though often radical – were being formulated to fertilize the stale soil of the past.

'At the end of the thirteen years of Conservative Government people got bored with us and they thought that we'd rather run out of steam. In 1963 I think this was true . . .' he said.[1]

[1] B.B.C. *Panorama*, interview with Heath, 24 June 1969.

His Shadow Cabinet looked sound enough for revival: Reginald Maudling was to be Deputy Leader, Iain Macleod (who, in spite of some personal antagonism to Heath, supported him and took his own camp over to Heath's in the leadership fight) was to be Shadow Chancellor, and Enoch Powell was made spokesman on Defence. The notion of appointing shadow specialists was relatively new to the party, but had worked on the Finance Bill. 'It was a smaller party in '45 and briefs were wide-ranging. I ran the Opposition differently in 1965,' he says.

In January Sir Alec had made the future leader Chairman of the Advisory Committee on Policy. One of those closely involved in the restructuring of policy says, 'the first phase, till July '65, was a new policy in a hurry. Heath had shown determination for the party to have a new policy, but had not examined every aspect of it too critically. He had no complete policy of his own at that time, but a great desire to change, modernize and get rid of the old and fuddy-duddy. He had a desire for change more than a particular line of policy. The result was his in terms of energy, but often others' policy.'

It could hardly be otherwise: thirty-six separate groups consisting largely of M.P.s, businessmen, professional men and university teachers, had each concentrated and reported on a specific area.[1]

But during September, many alterations were made: Heath showed some determination not to antagonize his Shadow Cabinet by imposing too much on them, but his beliefs were recognizably central. In particular his own European flame still burned.

'Putting Britain Right Ahead' concentrated on four main areas: all of them now to some extent implemented. It alleged that existing taxation oppressed 'the very people . . . upon whose vigour and initiative' Britain's future depended: new incentives should be created for them. There was a strong statement of intent on Europe: of joining the Community at 'the first favourable opportunity'. Trade union reforms envisaged included greater bargaining related to productivity, and more industrial courts.

In welfare, the document advocated the concentration of resources on those most in need (this, by implication, meant less for others),

[1] *The British General Election of 1966*, by D. E. Butler and Anthony King, Macmillan, 1966.

the extension of occupational pensions schemes to cover the whole of the working population, and a detailed housing programme.

But in a fifth area Heath was prepared to coerce his colleagues: on the question of an incomes policy. Macleod, Shadow Chancellor, was strongly in favour of one; so were most of his colleagues in the Shadow Cabinet. And in fact a year previously the party manifesto had said outright that an effective incomes policy was 'crucial to the achievement of sustained growth without inflation'.

Now, apparently without any consultation or even notification of his Shadow Chancellor, Heath virtually decided to reverse this decision under outward cover of almost ignoring the question.

One of those present at the discussion says, 'I think he'd pretty well made up his mind, but there were at least two people in the Shadow Cabinet who at that time were not in favour of his policy. Edward Boyle [who had served both as Economic and Financial Secretary to the Treasury] was a very outspoken opponent of a free policy, and Reggie Maudling was very much tarred with his own brush as Chancellor of the Exchequer. Enoch carried the opposite point of view to ridiculous extents.

'Ted's view was much closer to Enoch's than to Boyle's. But the more extreme Enoch became the more difficult the whole thing became. Enoch thought that any idea of incomes policy whether it was voluntary or just guidelines or compulsory was just absolute nonsense. Most of the Shadow Cabinet thought you must have an incomes policy.'

Heath would not revert to earlier policy. But in personal as well as political terms it was plainly a delicate situation. Almost miraculously, it seems, there was no row with Maudling – 'great credit to Reggie,' says one of his friends, 'and Ted had gone out of his way to avoid giving cause for confrontations. Many people felt "how happy I would be with either". They had the same approach, background and broad political philosophy. The difference has emerged since, with the amount of new drive from Ted Heath's energetic leadership; there would have been a slower pace from Maudling.'

But although signs of change were in themselves enough to please many, as Lord Blakenham put it 're-forming under fire' – the decisions arrived at were by no means pleasing to many more progressive Conservatives. One young woman who had arrived to work for

Heath ready to sink herself in her job found the pragmatic stance, and the 'realism' chorus so far from the deep strides she felt her party should really be taking that she quickly left again. 'He wasn't idealistic enough,' she complained; and it does seem that it was during this formative period of leadership that the battle between the elemental romantic in Edward Heath and the critical Classicist finally died: romance could now be kept as a pleasurable pastime, as an emotional release, for instance still in music, 'one can say that music has a deepening effect', he agreed,[1] but romance had no place in his formal priorities. One remembers his words about his mother: 'She had the spiritual sense of her Christian faith. Not that she was at all ethereal about it – she kept our feet on the ground,' and sees how he was managing to justify his aims and beliefs with hard practice.

The most obviously controversial part of the policy document was concerned with the proposed trade union reforms, and the next month, November 1965, Heath spelt out on all three television channels – B.B.C. 1 and 2, and I.T.V. – exactly what he planned to do about the unions, and how he proposed to make agreements enforceable at law on both sides.

One might have expected some trouble over this from the main body of Conservative opinion particularly in view of the absence of a statutory prices and incomes policy, but, perhaps in order to circumvent opposition at this fairly early stage, no votes were taken on the document at the conference in Brighton in October 1965 – where, incidentally, Heath broke tradition by attending every day. But there were strong hints of rifts to come on other subjects. Enoch Powell, always delighting in the provocative, made a speech which suggested that Britain should revise and withdraw from her role in Southern Asia. Conservative M.P. Aidan Crawley demanded his resignation from the Shadow Cabinet, and Denis Healey wrote tellingly of the ensuing squabble adding, 'only Mr Heath keeps mum'.

It was the first of an increasingly explosive series of issues that was to be utilized by Powell, who plainly felt increasingly dissatisfied and frustrated in a team where his intellect, outstanding if idiosyncratic, seemed to produce no proportionate response. Running his one-man guerilla war, Powell placed his personal dynamite against the fissures

[1] Interview at Chequers, May 1972.

in the rock of party unity twice more within the next three months: first in January, when he clashed with Maudling over the connection between the trade unions and inflation; and then he began his attack on coloured immigration, indirectly, by denouncing the 'unreal convention' in British politics banning attacks on the Commonwealth.

This was the dart that stuck. Within these three months race became a raging issue inside the Conservative Party, and it was one that, more than anything else, impaled Heath on his two tenets of patriotism and justice. Pragmatism was a pale shadow here, with all its defects revealed.

The racial issue was lightly veiled in the guise of the Rhodesian problem to those who chose to overlook it at the conference in 1965. 'Ted wanted above everything to create and keep national unity; he thought the public wouldn't understand splits or one party as it were operating against the constitution when the constitution was under pressure. But he found himself being goaded along to the Right,' says a colleague.

'Ted was accused of failing to give leadership – he started to come across as a weak man who didn't know his mind,' says one of those close to him. 'All those who knew him well knew how utterly false this was – but the impression stuck for nearly the next five years, and it all started from those three months over Rhodesia'.

Negotiations between the Wilson Government and Mr Ian Smith had broken down; smoke signals of a unilateral declaration of independence – which was actually declared three weeks later – hung thick in the air. The Shadow Cabinet issued a statement that such a U.D.I. would have no validity. Lord Salisbury talked of friends in Rhodesia and suggested that the conference should declare itself against 'stabbing them to the heart', but no vote against the possibility of sanctions was taken – and on this question the Conservative Party was soon to be split in three sections.

In his speech, Heath spoke in general terms of the need for 'freedom and independence to stand on our own feet', and of the conference's 'mood of realism'. On the question of Rhodesia itself, he said, 'As an Opposition we shall concentrate all our efforts on securing a solution by negotiation.' He sent a message to Smith and his colleagues with a hint of Macmillan in the phraseology: 'We believe that a middle way must be found. If there are still thoughts of unilateral action, then turn back from the brink.'

On 11 November 1965, Rhodesia declared herself independent: illegally so, since her requests for independence had been met with refusals from the present Labour Government and the previous Conservative administration. In 1964 Duncan Sandys had explained the basis of the refusal of independence – in Rhodesia the franchise remained 'incomparably more restricted' than in any country given independence in the last fifty years. In spite of their own desire for freedom, the ruling class in Rhodesia had emerged determined to resist for as long as possible the concept of progress towards majority rule, which Ian Smith later described on television as 'the counting of heads like the counting of sheep'.

Britain declared the regime illegal and introduced economic sanctions; nine days later the U.N. Security Council urged all states to sever economic relations with Rhodesia, and urged an embargo on oil. The position of the Conservatives was largely determined by their policy towards Rhodesia when they were in power; but on sanctions, which they had declined to condemn at the Party Conference, there were deep divisions.

On Saturday, 20 November 1965, Heath was addressing party members in Newcastle. It was now ten days since U.D.I. and he recognized that there was a depth of emotion cutting across party lines. (It is doubtful in fact whether the majority of the electorate knew or cared very much about the details of the issue, but the main principle was one that could have had explosive repercussions.) 'A heavy responsibility rested upon me as your leader,' Heath said, '. . . Throughout these difficult days my desire has been that we should maintain national unity – that has been our objective, that has been achieved. We have succeeded because we have maintained our party unity. Despite individual differences of view we have maintained a consistent policy in Government and in Opposition of condemnation of U.D.I. The Government has received our support. The Enabling Bill giving the Government the wider powers since the Second World War was passed through both Houses in a sitting without a division. We have followed this course because we have believed it to be right.'

But supporting the Government in general, if not in every particular, was soon to prove a most uncomfortable role, and whereas party dissidence had not greatly concerned Heath at the time of his battle over R.P.M. now, as leader, it was like a chasm that might open beneath his feet at any minute. Very soon the illusion of 'national unity' was discovered in its superficiality.

At the beginning of December, Heath tried to mark out separate territory for the Conservatives by asking for an assurance that British forces would not invade Rhodesia. He was under heavy attack from the 1922 Conservative Back Bench Committee, particularly the Right wing of the party, and perhaps some premonitions of the ignominy to come oppressed him, and added to the aura of intro-version that often surrounded him in times of difficulty. The moment of horror and mortification for Heath, and danger for the party, came on 21 December (1965) when, after the debate on the Government's proposal to embargo oil supplies to Rhodesia, there was a three-way split among the Conservatives. Heath had tried to retain a dignified balance by counselling abstention: but 80 Conservative M.P.s defied him and his Whips. Of these 30 voted for the embargo and 50 against; the rest, whatever their feelings, were meek enough to follow their leader.

From this moment on Rhodesia was a bedevilled question. Wherever Heath positioned himself, opposition sprang up somewhere else in the party.

From now on Heath's recurrent failure to give his party even a token semblance of unity on Rhodesia was to provide Wilson with a beautifully bright sword to use against him. As a man who likes to deal with certainties, and usually does, he was now a space-walker because the issues were not crystal clear in his own mind: therefore he could not project his view or communicate with the party on the basis of entrenched beliefs, but only of commonsense, a poor crusader against prejudice. Not until 'race' entered the English landscape would he be absolutely sure of his position: not until he was sure could he communicate it.

In the seven years since then, Heath has become much more sophisticated, and can now radiate energy to cover more than one contingency: though he is still happier when dealing with black and white issues. But his own uncertainty then was pervasive, and the feelings of his party towards him over the question of Rhodesia were probably only an extension of what was felt about him in the narrower, every-day context of the party.

James Prior remembers the conference at which the issue of Rhodesia was first raised. 'He had his constituents into lunch. My wife had to sit next to him. She'd met him three or four times by that time, but he sat through nearly the whole of lunch without saying a word to anyone – to his constituents, to my wife, to anyone. He seemed incapable of radiating any warmth at all, at that time. He had to learn how to do that.'

He was in the position of the general who does not yet have the heartfelt acclaim of his men.

After the conference, criticism of him continued like a groundswell: he was called cold and weak. Only the core closest to him were in a position to see the truth, as it slowly began to emerge.

Among them was James Prior, whose admiration for his leader increased with virtually every crisis – 'he comes through it all with tremendous courage. He is absolutely determined to do things well.' But, since that luncheon, he had been only too aware of the difficulties they had to face, and of the interpretative role he himself would have to play until Heath's true personality had been fully impressed on the party.

'I joined him the day after he became leader of the party,' he continued. He had left a four months old appointment as vice-chairman of the party to become his P.P.S. 'It was a tremendous shock to me to be moved so quickly, but they were looking for someone who could advise him and keep contacts with that part of the party which had not voted for him and by whom he was regarded with a certain amount of suspicion. I was a bridge to the people who had voted for Maudling and to the rural side of the party. But I had voted for him myself.' (Prior, a good humoured and straightforward man, is a farmer with pronounced cricketing and sailing interests.)

He found his new boss not altogether easy at first. 'It takes a good many years to get a really close relationship with him – much longer than with most men. And he was never really happy while working with the Shadow Cabinet in 1965 and 1966 – he was determined to try and cut the size because he always felt much happier working with a small group.'

Anthony Kershaw knew his man much better when he became

leader, as he had already been his P.P.S. for some time. He says, 'We had some quarrels when I was looking after him about his lateness – he started off making bad impressions.

'One gets the impression that he's not always alert to what's going on about him – on the contrary, he's got an extraordinarily quick eye. I remember one day he had his hair cut in a slightly different way. I looked him up and down as usual and turned away slightly – and he said, "Too short?" I didn't think I had given anything away at all.

'His command of his immediate environment can be very disconcerting – he's got an unsettling habit of reading and signing letters while he talks to you, and you can't believe that he's concentrating on what you're saying: yet he is really doing the two things at the same time. It's an amazing trick.'

Kershaw, with his professional training and practice in the use of words, also gives a most interesting analysis of Heath's style of speech. He believes its deficiencies, whatever their origin, are not due to lack of industry or concentration. 'He takes extraordinary care when he's drafting – he drafts and drafts and drafts and drafts, takes out a comma and puts it back in, crosses out a phrase and puts it back. He's not sensitive to words in the musical or rhythmic sense but very sensitive to their meaning – the political overtones. What they sound like is the last thing he thinks of but he's determined that they should mean what he thinks they should mean.'

However, oratorical inspiration was not there for him to cross out or put back. A member of the Cabinet today remembers his own embarrassment when he had persuaded him to make a more colourful speech: it was an experiment he would never encourage him to repeat. The only outlet from this spartan verbal prison in which he placed himself came not in a set speech, but on the odd occasion when he spoke without notes but with the banked-down fires of emotion: at the funeral of his friend Timothy Bligh, at the centenary dinner for Baldwin (and, later, after the signing of the treaty of accession to the Common Market). They are few and far between, but they go far towards explaining the essential reason for the trust his closest followers have in him.

As Kershaw himself says, 'I don't know anybody who is more obviously honest than he is. Although he would always be tough and even unfeeling in the way he dealt with people if he considered it necessary, it would always be done with perfect honesty, and if he says he'll do a thing he always does it.

'He doesn't enter into any commitments that he doesn't intend to keep. To use the old cliché, there's nobody I'd rather go tiger-hunting with.'

(It was a cliché Macmillan had also ascribed to him.)

His demands of his staff were enormous and unapologetic. 'I had no personal life at all for two years,' says someone who was attached to him for that time. 'At first I found the demands overwhelming,' says another. Wives of Heath's staff had to be still more unselfish than their husbands – they had not even the excitement of being part of the team.

Sometimes the demands seemed less than reasonable. One man entered Heath's room with a cold, and apologised for having it. 'He said, "Well, that's all right, but don't get another one, it's quite unnecessary." He told me to go and get injections – he has them all the time, the slightest thing that's wrong with him he's off to the doctor's.'

Another aide understands Heath's emphasis on health: 'He has a fine constitution and regards it as part of his duty to keep it so. He could be most astonishing when we were going round the country on a tour. We would go to bed with a lot of work to do at about 2 a.m. and perhaps have a bottle of champagne with a newspaper editor just before going to bed, then make an eight o'clock start – well, you were lucky if you saw him off before 8.20 – but off you would go then on a whistle-stop tour. After three or four days of this you would have thought he would be collapsed – everybody else was – but he was as fresh as a daisy.'

While making huge demands of himself and his team and establishing himself in their confidence, Heath was for a long while as leader apparently unable to give back to the party what it needed if it was going to continue its support for him and perhaps add enthusiasm to its token acceptance of him.

Conservatives who had voted to make Heath leader because they thought he was the man to beat Wilson with were dismayed to find that, at this stage, he came off very much the worse in House of Commons exchanges during Question Time. His few staunch supporters begged him not to go into encounters they could see in advance he would lose; and, slowly, and with some difficulty when he was really angry, he learned to take their advice. Meanwhile those Conservatives without any special fondness for him began to doubt whether he in fact possessed the basic qualities of toughness and incisiveness with which he had been credited, and had persuaded some to vote for him, or even the potential as a technocrat that had held some attraction for others.

'When the Conservative Party get the jitters in opposition, the bitchiness can hardly be believed,' remembers one close spectator. 'There were endless attempts to get rid of Ted.'

The effect of this was not to make him lose his basic grip, but to shield himself still more from the buffets of his own supposed supporters by retreating as far as he could into himself. There, in inward retreat and contemplation, he seemed for a while slightly sour, though he was too philosophical to become bitter. Concentrating on himself and his inner resources, summoning all his will and morale, trusting only a few, he deliberately developed himself, forced himself into a new inner self-resilience and independence. Party administrators sensed in him a new strength: not all of them liked it. Looking back on this period, and Heath's own personality in opposition, many observers find a single word: it was at this time that he became tempered, in the sense that steel is tempered.

This became publicly obvious in the New Year (January 1966), when Heath visited the Far East, accompanied by Anthony Barber (who had been Parliamentary Private Secretary to Macmillan while Heath was still Chief Whip) and Christopher Chataway.

On the day of his return, he had to face some criticism that, in his current mood, was too bitter to swallow. Angus Maude, the front-bench spokesman on the Colonies, had published an article in the *Spectator*, alleging that to the majority of the electorate the Opposition had become a 'meaningless irrelevance', and that the party had 'completely lost effective political initiative'. Singling out the Rhodesian policy for particular blame, Maude said that his own party's official line was doubly mortifying to those who believed the Government's policy was wrong.

Heath's reply was simple: 'I do not accept that from anybody.' Maude was sacked from the front bench. James Prior comments, 'He wouldn't behave in the same way now: he is so much immeasurably stronger now, he can put up with more criticism. But at that time it was disgraceful and I don't think he had any alternative. We had a weekend in Bolton and Penrith as soon as he got back from the Far East, and on the Monday went over to Stratford [Maude's constituency] to look at a factory. The Press were trying to get a picture of Angus and Ted together – I was having to walk between them the whole time.'

Heath's internal and external depression deepened the next month, February, when the Conservatives lost the Hull North by-election and Heath's own standing in the Gallup Poll was lower than Sir Alec's had been fourteen months previously. 'This was a terrible time,' remembers a colleague. 'Whatever he did, however hard he tried, he could not get through – people were hammering away with their doubts – and of course after a time you do begin to lose self-confidence. There were at least three periods when even he, a man of enormous resilience, did lose his self-confidence. The first time was after the Hull by-election, when he was very despondent.'

The Government were taking advantage of their moral superiority to make up for the vulnerability of their minute majority. Wilson continually and effectively knocked Heath about with words on the floor of the House; Crossman, more seriously, said that the Conservatives wanted to abolish all-in social security and go back to the days of means testing.

This was the setting for the General Election of 31 March 1966. Although it was generally agreed that Heath had failed to come across to the electorate, particularly on television, where even many of his own side found him 'wooden and unimpressive – awful', he was in fact making some points about this country which strongly reflected his personal attitudes to what he regarded as its severe plight.

In Newcastle, he said, he had seen a man who had been fined fifteen pounds for working too hard. He asked simply, 'I ask you how can this country get on its feet again . . . when people are fined for working too hard.'

He analysed the British character, and with one significant exception the character was remarkably like his own: 'The British are a very remarkable people. They are level-headed, and very tough, but they are slow to see danger and slower still to change. It is that resistance to change which puts the British people in so much danger now . . . In the long run we shall not survive if for some reason, for some failure of will, we let ourselves drift slowly backwards into industrial failure and out-of-date technology.'

The big difference between the general British character, as he saw it, and his own, was in his very high sensitivity to danger of any kind, whether political, social or personal. As someone who is very fond of him unthinkingly said, 'He reminds me of a very intelligent animal, always on guard.' I myself noticed this at the beginning of each interview, when he seemed suspicious of my early questions, then gradually relaxed and expanded.

The way out now was straightforward. He reminded people of Dean Acheson's brilliant summary, that the British had 'lost an Empire without finding a role'. It had caused great offence; but when dealing with impersonal criticism Heath retains an objective balance. 'It didn't offend me: it seemed to me to be true,' he admitted. Now Europe could provide that role, and we should go in at the first opportunity.

His ineffectiveness in delivering these really heart-felt beliefs through the medium of his own lack of overt emotion, physical magnetism, oratorical magic, was such that Labour won the election by ninety-seven votes: it was the greatest Labour landslide since 1945.

Someone who was with Heath on election night thought he seemed close to tears: even in exhaustion, whatever his disappointment, it seems unlikely that such a physical manifestation was in fact imminent.

If it had been the loss might not have been so severe. Not only would a more extrovert emotionalism have relieved Heath's own feelings: it might also have convinced an electorate who saw him largely, in the words of Robert Carvel, of the *Evening Standard*, as a 'cardboard politician' that he was not when seen in three-dimensions stuffed with sawdust. In fact he has at least his fair share of the mediaeval humours: blood, melancholy, phlegm and choler.

He had given vent to the full force of his feelings in public on one occasion only during the campaign, and that was in front of Nicholas Tomalin at Roose Airport when he was given details of a speech Wilson had just made about him. Tomalin's piece, entitled 'Heath's One Flash of Passion', caught immeasurably more of this aspect of Heath's character than any Press or television cameraman had been able to record. 'This is too sordid for words . . . what a poisonous speech . . . "I lie on my back like a spaniel?" What a revolting bit . . . This is a lie . . . Wilson must be out of his mind . . . Abuse like this is unforgivable when you're dealing with international relations.'[1] The sense of personal, and still more of public, outrage forced the words out pell-mell. Heath's belief in the sanctity of political *politesse*, of the dignity of ordered democracy, left him mentally gawping behind his protests.

Only two weeks previously he had done fairly well with abuse himself, describing Wilson as 'a man whose power has gone to his head, whose Left wing is impotent, whose colleagues are incompetent, and who feels he can sit astride his party like a pygmy.'[2]

This was excellent vituperation indeed, and absolutely genuine: in the House, spectators were amazed to see him stalk past Wilson without a word, quite ignoring the usual niceties between the leaders of parties. Yet in his own mind there seems to have remained a fine distinction between the grandeur of genuine appalling rudeness and the pettiness of tongue-out spiteful abuse: when someone in Broadstairs showed him some beer-mats poking fun at Wilson he did not even smile, but dismissed them as 'in bad taste'.

Though he did not always keep to them, and when really angry did not want to, he had standards that were, according to view, high or priggish, but in either case were by now instinctive. The same reaction seized him after he was taken, as a birthday treat, to see *Hair*. As the curtain came down at the end, he turned to his friends and said, 'What a way to have to earn a living.'

It was this appreciation of what he considered dignified and proper that came to his aid the day after the 1966 election results were announced: he was most graceful in conceding defeat, and perhaps not truly *bouleversé*. Most friends claim to have told him that he had no chance at all in 1966: that he must wait for the next time.

There were immediate benefits from the election: one or two members of the Shadow Cabinet were removed, which left him with the smaller team he always preferred, and he knew he could now settle down to a long period in Opposition, to make long-term policy plans in depth.

---

[1] *Sunday Times*, 20 March 1966.   [2] Ibid., 6 March 1966.

The policy group's first report, which had been shaped into 'Putting Britain Right Ahead', was also the basis of the 1966 manifesto. Not surprisingly, Heath decided that the material had to be gone over once more – although, as one of the team remarked, 'he hates thinking *again*'. Now he decided to cut down the policy groups, reconstruct them, ask them to consider once more, and to report again in 1968. With two years to mull over their decisions, some different shades of thoughts emerged, which once again were sifted. The final results were incorporated in another document, Make Life Better. One most important change concerned the farmers, and the change of support system from subsidies to levies, which would make entry into the Common Market easier to negotiate. But many crucial points – like whether or not to introduce Value Added Tax – were not seriously on the agenda for another two years. In other words, policy at this time was consistently emerging and changing, in a more natural manner, and not being manufactured simply for the sake of change.

While this was more likely to produce a policy to meet the real needs of the moment, and match the stated aims of the party, it fell far short of the demands of some intellectuals in the wings. 'Rather than having a philosophy that he wanted to see translated, he seemed to want things to be administratively tidy and well-organized,' complained one of these. 'Therefore he was only radical if you could get him at a formative moment. And there was some evident insecurity: he had not the divine right of aristocrats.'

Even so, there were deceptive moments soon after the 1966 election when the worst seemed to be over.

Derek Brierley, who had got to know Heath when he was his adjutant at the H.A.C. and through a common interest in music had become one of his friends, remembers going to see a trilogy by Noel Coward with him about this time. 'We arrived just before the curtain went up, and the audience stood up and applauded,' he remembers. Heath was understandably gratified, particularly as he apparently got a bigger hand than another member of the audience – Princess Margaret.

And in October 1966 the Gallup Poll published in the *Telegraph* showed that for the first time Heath was ahead of Wilson.

Three months later, in January 1967, Heath was inwardly at a low ebb again. Rhodesia continued to loom in Parliament. The Labour Budget raised family allowances. And in May Wilson made a formal application to join the Common Market.

During this period Heath's relationship with Edward du Cann, who had risen under Home to become party chairman, had come under increasing strain. Du Cann had hoped that when Home finally had to go he would be replaced by Maudling. Heath's narrow victory did little to change his mind, and he did not take great trouble to conceal his critical feelings, or to avert the criticism of the leader by others. Suffering from the after-effects of several attempts to oust him, Heath finally decided that the party chairman must go.

This was more easily said than effected. Du Cann enlisted the firm support of many Conservative area chairmen, and tenaciously held his position for a further year. Finally, in September 1967, du Cann went, after vain attempts within the party to reconcile the two. 'Edward was too smooth for Ted: they didn't bring out the best in each other,' was the bland verdict of someone who had had a ringside view of the mutual antagonism and had tried to act as a go-between.

Du Cann was replaced by a man who admired the leader greatly and who had a background in many respects similar to Heath's own: Anthony Barber.

In Glasgow in September (1967) Heath faced cries of 'shame' from women attending a conference of Conservative Associations in Glasgow when he refused to promise to reintroduce hanging or corporal punishment. 'As long as I am leader I am not going to lay down a party line on these matters,'[1] he said; but for all the importance of the decision, negative moments like these were irksome.

Capital punishment was an issue that continued to haunt the party, and Heath's own position on this question for some years reflected a genuine ambivalence of his own, as well as responding to the needs of his audience. However, it happened to be an area where he felt his own experiences had some validity, and he had a growing assurance in answering questions here that had quite eluded him in his other area of uncertainty, Rhodesia. Robin Day pressed him on the issue twice in eight months, and received a slightly stronger

[1] *The Times*, 9 September 1967.

answer the second time than the first; however, he was plainly reserving the right to change his position on both occasions.

Day asked, 'Do you think that hanging should be restored for certain kinds of murder?' Heath replied, '. . . I was a soldier during the war and one realized that at times it was necessary to take life. There are others who believe that capital punishment may be a deterrent . . . I myself want to see whether or not it is a deterrent. I would very much like to see it abolished . . . I would much prefer that it should not be restored, but if it is proved against my wishes that it is essential as a deterrent in modern society then I would accept that that was the case but I would very much regret it.'

More succinctly and daringly but no less ambiguously, he said eight months later, 'My position is perfectly well-known, I voted against the restoration of capital punishment.'[1]

He had done so late in 1969, after what a colleague remembers as 'a week of agonizing'. By this time his ambivalence was more of a cloak than a deep uncertainty, for he had slowly come to the conclusion that capital punishment was wrong. One of those to whom he turned for advice remembers, 'He wanted very strongly to vote against restoration, but he was under enormous pressure from large sections of the party. The pressure that was put on him in every single public meeting that I went to with him, in question time it was always "Will you bring back the death penalty?"' Such experiences were neither enjoyable nor intellectually stimulating for him.

The conflict between conscience and his anxiety about losing the support of the Right wing of the party does not show him in a glorious light, but finally he did do what he felt was right. In doing so he doubtless lost some more of the waning Right wing Conservative support, but, ironically, a member of the Labour Party declared that for the first time he admired Ted Heath.

In the first of these interviews, he also seemed in a slight logical tangle about the different claims of freedom and order. 'You can't have true freedom in a country unless you've got order,' he said '. . . it's freedom to do right and to do evil.'[2] One would have thought that in his view, as a prerequisite of true freedom, order might have eliminated the freedom to do evil – but these philosophical areas really do not engage him deeply, even now.

[1] *Panorama*, 2 February 1970.   [2] Ibid., 24 June 1969.

'He didn't enjoy the day-to-day drudgery of being leader of the Opposition. There were some facets he was frankly disinterested in,' remembers a colleague. 'He is a big man in every sense of the word, and concentrated on what he was interested in.'

'He thinks that things are more important than people. He's never wasting his time – he's thinking, not reading the papers; or if he is reading the papers or a magazine it's because he *intends* to be late. He is a rather contrived person.

'He may be late for people but he's never late for an engagement of importance. If he were coming to see me for some reason or other I would have been very surprised if he were on time.'

Heath has a natural inclination to augment his own self-sufficiency, which, though considerable, is not infallible. It was during this period in Opposition that he assembled his network of carefully assessed friends and acquaintances. His political team and friends alike learned to read his moods as soon as they entered his presence, and would advise others as they do still, on how to judge the situation: 'Look at his eyes: they tell you how he is feeling,' says one. 'He is very romantic: and extremely annoyed when things are not done as well as they could be,' says another. 'You'd know at once what the temperature was,' says a third.

He was more often seeking information than overt backing during the endless hours of interrogation to which his formal and informal team were subjected, but although most of those close to him agree that then, as now, he was unmoved by any but the most outstanding argument, it was generally recognized that tact was a useful accessory to knowledge. 'In arguments he didn't mind if you were right; if you were right he would change his mind very quickly. But it was very important not to disagree with him the whole time even if you did disagree. It was better to confine your observations to when you knew you were right *and* thought it was important – both together.'

Not all the interviews took place face to face: the telephone is a favourite instrument of Heath's. 'He loves to disconcert you by starting off with an unexpected question of a startling remark. But he's very brief', says someone who has been frequently disconcerted by having to analyse, extempore, some surprise development at the ring of the telephone.

'He has long telephone lists and he rings around his enormous number of friends and chats. He rings up with a purpose, but he rings a lot of people, an awful lot of people ... In Albany when the papers weren't heavy he would quite often ring half a dozen people while he was having the bath run.'

An observer whose admiration for Heath is combined with a most perceptive honesty knows how to gauge his moods: 'He's up and down. It depends who rings who on the telephone. He uses friends as other people use their wives, only he happens to have about eight wives. When he's down he does the ringing.'

But his self-control, will, supreme sense of logic, and own deflating wit combined with his native resilience to ensure that he never spent an inordinate length of time in the doldrums. Heath's sense of humour, once nicely observed by *Isis* as being used as a weapon rather than as an ornament can be unpleasant for his victims when his mood is harsh, but has a certain panache at subtler moments.

Geoffrey Tucker, an advertising man who has put his talents to the Conservatives' use, remembers being in the House of Commons after a meeting of the Shadow Cabinet, and exchanging a formal 'Goodnight, Mr Heath', 'Goodnight, Mr Tucker', with the leader. Going down the stairs he passed Wilson and Jenkins, and a moment later, from above, 'Goodnight, Tucker' boomed out in regimental tones. 'I drew myself to attention and said "Goodnight, Sir." Jenkins looked round amazed. Heath kept a deadpan face.'

Jenkins had replaced Callaghan as Chancellor on 29 November 1967, after the devaluation of the pound. And, on the opposite side of the House, he was the one man Heath ever privately showed real regard for. Madron Seligman, who chose Heath to be god-father to one of his sons, chose Jenkins to be god-father of another, and recalls that Heath has sometimes dropped a remark like 'Roy's the one Labour man you can invite'.

The two do have a lot in common: political integrity, as well as their shared belief in the Common Market; a certain defensiveness of manner with strangers, and comparable, if not similar, social backgrounds – Jenkins's father had been a miner as a young man. They had known each other at Balliol, they had observed each other's testing and tactics in the House.

But early in 1968 while the Labour Government was struggling to recover from its devastating economic setback, Heath was faced with another problem of dealing with that man of not dissimilar extraction: Enoch Powell, largely Welsh (though he was born in Birmingham) also had miners among his ancestors: but in his case it was a great-grandfather who had last hewed coal; his father was a schoolmaster.

For the past two years, since his speech at the 1965 Conference undercutting the Conservatives' own East of Suez policy (like the Labour Party, he advocated withdrawal) and his first venture into potential racialism, with a speech at Birmingham University on 20 November (1965) suggesting that admission for aliens and Commonwealth immigrants should be on the same basis, and that there should be a scheme for voluntary repatriation, Powell had been increasingly acting as a deliberate irritant to his leader. 'I think it may have been the old-age syndrome – that one day he woke up, looked in the mirror, and thought, I'm four years older than the leader,' says one of the senior men in the party. Whatever his personal motivation, Powell seems to have convinced himself utterly of the rectitude of his views, and of their assured palatability to the majority of his fellow countrymen. His tactics with Heath would seem to have been that, having had no success in stinging him through the almost impermeably hardened hide of his opinions, he decided to attack the vulnerable trunk – Heath's sense of personal security. It was a logical and disastrous error.

Race, by this time because of Rhodesia a poisoned thorn in the flesh of the party, which looked as if it might work itself straight into the bloodstream in spite of the decision in the 1966 election to eschew its harmful potential, was again his chosen ground. In 1963 when the Conservatives were in office – and Powell himself in the Cabinet, as Minister of Health – the Kenya Independence Act had left a loophole for the quarter of a million Asians living in Kenya to come to Britain should they wish. At the conference in 1967 Powell called this loophole 'quite monstrous'.

The Shadow Cabinet's view was still not quite decided: but it was firm enough for Quintin Hogg, the Conservative spokesman, to make a speech on 15 November 1967 aiming at a consensus between the two Front Benches and criticizing exploitation of 'disagreeable racial over-tones' in 'what is potentially an emotionally charged atmosphere'.

In January 1968, new laws were introduced in Kenya concerning employment of non-citizens: work permits could be issued for a maximum of two years, after which the non-citizens were expected to leave. Their choice was normally to return to India or come to Britain: about 1,000 a month were choosing the latter.

On 9 February 1968, Powell made a speech specifically attacking the loophole that allowed the Kenyan Asians absolute right of entry to the U.K. (an advantage over Commonwealth citizens), and of the flow of immigration in general saying that, 'it is hard to describe such a policy, or lack of policy, as otherwise than crazy'.

On 20 February Duncan Sandys asked the Government to introduce legislation to deal with the influx. At a Shadow Cabinet meeting a few days later the Conservatives decided to press the Government for the phasing of the entry of the Asians so that they would only be allowed to enter the country in small numbers at a time. Some Labour M.P.s also pressed their own party for new action.[1]

On 22 February 1968 the Cabinet decided to introduce legislation which would, among other things, prevent the Kenya Asians who had British passports from being allowed to use them as a right of entry to the U.K. Among those Conservatives opposed to the policy of the Government and their own Shadow Cabinet were Iain Macleod, Edward Boyle and Reginald Maudling. They all felt that Britain should honour the passports she had issued.

The passing of the Bill on 1 March did not end the debate about either the Asians in particular or the flow of immigrants in general, although discussions now took place with less sense of pressure. Heath's own position is easy to chart from the Shadow Cabinet's pressure on the Government to introduce legislation. He had visited the cynosures of immigration, talked to social workers, learned of the problems of the immigrants and the still greater problems both they and the community often faced if they could not bring in their families to join them: in terms of personal hardship, and, more important in his view, an unhealthy imbalance in society.

A member of the Shadow Cabinet remembers, 'I don't think Ted wanted any more immigrants to come in than Enoch did. But I think he felt as a good many others of us did that once you have allowed these people to come, for good reasons or for bad but usually

[1] *No Entry*, by David Steele, C. Hurst, 1969.

because it suited our convenience that they should come, one was in honour bound to treat them as normal citizens and not to see them harassed. This meant trouble with the Right wing, on the question of dependants – Ted stuck rigidly to the view that we must allow the dependants of those here to join them. We got away with that – even in a place like Bournemouth not renowned for its liberality we managed to hold the line quite well. We met local councillors from Birmingham, Wolverhampton, Smethwick . . . he knew more about the problems at the end of the time than anybody else. Ted in his usual way knew the facts rather better than the party.'

There was special significance to the date of Powell's speech on 9 February. It was a Friday, and Shadow Cabinet meetings took place on Monday and Wednesdays. The previous Wednesday, 7 February (1968), they had had a preliminary discussion on immigration, and had agreed to continue with it on the following Monday. Although the meeting was not conclusive, the guidelines of the policy Heath was to set out were already plain. While not going as far as Macleod, Maudling and Boyle in wishing to honour the liberality of the law, Heath was absolutely against a blanket lock-out – hence the statement two weeks later asking for phased entry, which would also allow families to be reunited.

A member of the Cabinet remembers, 'Enoch's speech at the weekend undermined the whole of our position right in the middle of the policy discussions. The Shadow Cabinet meeting on Monday is certainly the only Cabinet in which I can remember that there was a good deal of ill-feeling. Enoch sat there absolutely like a sphinx and never blinked an eye.'

Heath did not act yet: but he was wound up and set like a trap to go off when Powell made his next move, for which he also chose a weekend setting – Saturday, 21 April – when he addressed the West Midlands Area Conservatives in Birmingham. Powell's speech was a carefully prepared challenge to the leadership. He avoided the central Conservative channels (they were also avoiding him) for relaying speeches, and made his own elaborate and very successful arrangements for television and Press coverage. In fifteen or twenty years, he declared, there would be three and a half million Commonwealth immigrants and their descendants. 'We must be mad, literally mad,' he continued, and went on to claim that as well as virtually stopping further inflow, the official policy of the Conservatives was also to encourage re-emigration. After giving some unsavoury details of alleged local intimidation by immigrants, Powell produced the sentences that prophesied doom for others, but spelt it immediately for himself: 'As I look ahead I am filled with foreboding. I seem to see "the River Tiber foaming with much blood".'

The Sunday papers splashed the speech. Heath was spending the weekend in Broadstairs, and immediately rang a few people to inform them of his intentions about Powell. 'He had no hesitation – his mind was clear,' says one of those he spoke to. Another colleague says, 'I think he had *absolutely* made up his mind to sack him – firstly because this was the second occasion on which Enoch had spoken right outside the party line; secondly this next speech showed a marked disloyalty and contempt for his Shadow Cabinet colleagues – it was impossible to get on as a team, and thirdly the language which was used was language we had studiously tried to avoid using; fourthly it was certainly using immigration as a great political issue, something that in the 1966 election we had deliberately eschewed. Then on top of that he just felt that he couldn't work with Powell any longer – there was this constant business on the front bench of Healey, Callaghan, Jenkins and Wilson saying, "What is the policy of the Opposition? On the one hand the leader of the Opposition says such-and-such a thing, and on the other hand the Right Honourable Gentleman for Wolverhampton is saying another..." '

On his way back from Broadstairs Heath called in to see his agent in Bexley. It was about half past five, about an hour earlier than he would usually call if he were passing, and Pye was working in his garden without a shirt when Heath's car drew up. 'We spent about an hour talking about Powell,' he remembers. 'I thought he was over-rating it, and had to ring and admit I was wrong the next evening.'

Heath had left a message with Powell's agent that he should ring him that evening at Albany. When Powell telephoned, he found that an assertion he had recently made to Nicholas Tomalin of the *Sunday Times*, that provided he kept a power base going in the Conservative Party 'Ted Heath can never sack me from the Shadow Cabinet'[1] was a complete and utter miscalculation. He was out with a vengeance. Heath condemned the speech in a word – 'racialist'.

[1] *Enoch Powell: Tory Tribune*, Andrew Roth, 1970.

Powell in his letter to Heath the next day denied the charge, and continued, 'I believe you will be Prime Minister of this country and that you will be an outstandingly able Prime Minister – perhaps even a great one.'

The brinkmanship involved was greater than was at first apparent. 'Enoch was trying in his Dear Ted letter to put himself right with the few, the *very few*, who at that time supported Ted,' confessed one intimate.

Heath's action, apparently precipitate, had in fact been well prepared as a contingency. And its speed was essential: the next day might have been too late. 'The month after this happened was a very, very difficult month,' says one of the team. 'I can't remember how many thousands of letters we received. One was ashamed in many respects to allow the girls in the office to open them. I would guess that ninety-eight per cent of them were anti-immigrant. It took enormous character to get through.'

True enough; but, as *The Times* gently expressed it in a leader, 'in dismissing Mr Powell, Mr Heath takes the known risk of having Mr Powell as an enemy; that, fortunately, is less grave than the risk of having Mr Powell as a colleague.'[1]

Where did this leave Heath on the question of race, which had plagued the Conservative Party for so long? While condemning Powell as a racialist, he was certainly far less liberal than Boyle and Macleod in his basic attitudes. The issue perhaps shows more clearly than most partly why he was to become Prime Minister: he reflected very accurately, one would guess, the middle-of-the-road attitude of the normal, insular Englishman who would not enjoy overt emotional attachment to a cause but nevertheless would stand by to see at least elemental justice done.

One of his colleagues says, 'Emotionally committed? Yes, he was to a certain extent but not so much as most people. It takes a great deal to make him emotionally committed; but part of that was obviously the fact that Enoch stirred him up so much – he became more emotionally committed.'

Political caution may have made him veil his feelings even in the Shadow Cabinet meetings. Madron Seligman indicates a much stronger understated passion; when he returned from a visit to South

[1] *The Times*, 22 April 1968.

Africa, he asked Heath, 'Why not give apartheid a chance?' He received the terse rebuke, 'I can't talk to you any more. You're becoming Right wing.'

Such passion does not, however, have much in common with compassion; rather it is a hard hatred of injustice and of the defiance of Christian rights, combined with the deepest contempt for those who would try to profit personally from a worsening of the situation. It could be argued that Heath must have deliberately truncated his own compassion, perhaps fearing that it might be exploited, and this explanation would certainly make sense in view of his personal history. But whatever the reason behind Heath's withdrawal from the softer emotions, the withdrawal has been taken to great lengths. It is indeed fortunate that he is an exemplarily fair-minded man.

He is also a man who understands completely the priceless value of a reputation for ruthlessness: the man who has such a reputation seldom has to give proof of it; occasional verbal reminders of it are generally sufficient to act effectively upon the nervous systems of others, with equivalent rest for his own peace of mind. Few ruthless people are *totally* without ruth.

Thus the sacking of Powell and Heath's own very middle-of-the-road position on immigration entrenched him far more deeply in his own party, partly against its own will. There was other salvage work to be done after Powell, on the East of Suez question. In August 1968 Heath was in Australia, proclaiming British interests and intentions in a tone that won cool admiration from the no-nonsense Australians. 'I would like the people of Britain to be judged on their merit,' he said; and equally Britain must look at Australia as a business proposition. 'We intend to work from a cool calculation of where British interests really lie. As a result of this cool calculation I have come to the conclusion that the stability of South-East Asia is for us, as for you, a vital interest.'[1]

His argument presaged the arguments about Simonstown: 'Look at the hundreds of millions of dollars invested in Singapore and Malaysia and here – and look at the amount of investment which comes into our country and our balance of payments. Then look at the small amount we pay to keep forces in those areas.'

He also regretted, in April 1969, the Labour Government's

[1] *The Times*, 15 August 1968.

decision to withdraw from the Persian Gulf – as he put it, to 'abandon' the Gulf. It would be a Conservative policy to stay if the powers in the area so wished.

One can well imagine that, given Palmerston's Empire to cradle, his lullaby would not have been so different from that which filled the heads of Englishmen with sweet imaginings, and seduced so much loyalty from the parts of the Empire itself a century before.

Or, as it was put more crisply by a former colleague, 'He's basically very Right wing about these things. He's a Tory – very Right wing abroad and rather liberal at home – a traditional type, like Disraeli. He is often compared to Peel, merely because Peel had an awkward manner I think, but Peel was also rather stiff at home, and he's much more liberal than Peel ever was. Disraeli was the reformer at home and the Imperator abroad and that's the way Ted sees himself now, and the way I see him.'

That is the view from approximately the centre of the Conservative Party. From a step or two to the Right or the Left Heath is recognizably the same figure: but the perspective of the background, of his motives, shifts according to the position of the viewer. To me, at least, he is naturally to the Right of his party on every issue until the case is proven, to him and then by him, as being better solved otherwise.

13

Sailing for Victory

Heath's personal life and development was, thankfully, a good deal less traumatic than his political life during the years in Opposition. Of course the two cannot be totally separated but his moments of sober despondency seem invariably to have been caused by political set-backs. Whatever his personal problems, there were apparently none he could not cope with fairly easily: and no doubt one reason for this was the lack of need for an extroverted emotional and sexual life. By confining his deepest affections to his father, brother and friends, Heath had successfully avoided giving unnecessary hostages to fortune. If he did not have the comforts of family life, he did not have the demands of a family either; and since his need for the company of women had never been very great, he was not putting himself under a strain by depriving himself of an ingredient essential to his own view of personal happiness. Instead, he was able to concentrate nearly all his requirements of life in the political sphere.

Of course, there were those who hoped to see romance bloom in his life. Among them was his father, who had once said, 'He's married to politics', but privately, as a man who was now very happily married for the third time, could not quite understand the self-containment of a son who had chosen a different life. The newspapers too would have liked to find a match for him; when Heath spent a week in Switzerland working for Brown, Shipley early in 1965, before he was leader, the *Evening Standard* hastily noted that Mrs June Osborn was in Zermatt with her son Christopher.[1] Mrs Osborn was the widow of

[1] *Evening Standard*, 7 January 1965.

Franz Osborn, the pianist; music, as so often with his friends, was common ground where he could happily tread.

He realized that being a bachelor was a political disadvantage, and a less honest man might have concluded that to marry for convenience would further his political career, whatever unhappiness it might inflict on a partner chosen for such reasons. However, after the shock of the sudden ending of his friendship with Kay Raven he never again formed a relationship that looked even remotely, to the most hopeful friend, like leading to romance. But he felt that criticism of his knowledge of life based on the fact that he was not, and never had been, married was somewhat irrelevant – 'after all, bachelors have to live,' he somewhat plaintively told a Radio Four interviewer. In answer to a direct question about whether he would have liked to find a wife he said, 'Yes, I . . . yes. But it hasn't worked out that way.' And in a rare moment of revealed sensitivity he said, 'I think sometimes the thing which hurts most is when there is a great deal of criticism of myself which I know is going to upset them.' ('Them' being his family.)

Of course, not every bachelor has the chance of marriage; but there is evidence that, over the years, there were at least two women who might have received Edward Heath's suit kindly.

Perhaps the most perceptive comment on his single state comes from an older man who watched him very carefully and concluded, 'If he'd married and it hadn't gone well it would have been terrible for him.' This is most true; his critical perfectionist qualities and his natural romanticism would have been hard enough to meet; but, not met, his sense of duty and his pride might have driven him onto the rocks of long-lasting misery. It is a reasonably safe conclusion that he is far happier single than he would have been in most marriages. However, a *perfectly* happy, if in other respects ordinary, marriage would have given him various satisfactions – that of exercising unselfishness and tolerance, for instance – that he has not often known.

Like most people, he has grown more exacting with the passage of time. One friend comments sharply, 'He couldn't marry a widow. It would have to be someone far better than anyone had ever had before.'

A hard task indeed.

Even being one of his family or friends can sometimes be hard enough. 'His father and I agree that no one can be as hurtful as he is at times,' says a friend who is fond of him, but outside that inner ring to which one would expect the ability to hurt to be confined.

He is, as his step-mother says, better at showing his affection from a distance. She has known what it is to walk into her sitting-room and find it full of orchids sent from Hong Kong. 'He thinks nothing of telephoning his father from Australia,' says James Prior. He can be profoundly moved by religious ceremonies: the rending of the curtains at midnight at Easter in San Marco left him transfixed. Off guard, he sometimes reveals glimpses of what a Cabinet friend terms 'a sentimentality in himself that he can't abide in others'.

But the moments of admitted though most profound affection are few, just as the declarations of his anxiety are few. It is by their experience, not by his words, that those close to him know him. 'I can tell from just looking at him when he's hurt,' says his father, and his brother has only to listen to a syllable or two of him on television to know, from his voice, if he is tired or worried – yet having something of the same shyness with words, neither father nor brother can define the physical changes they instinctively discern.

Another ardent admirer of him on television is Maggie May, the family beagle, mother amongst others of Sydney, Hobart and Co., who knows him the instant he appears on the screen and watches riveted. When Heath arrives home he will sometimes just snatch Maggie May under his arm and rush upstairs with her, pouring out a sudden affection never seen once by some who have worked with him for over twenty years – one of the latter told me you could never imagine Heath playing with children or dogs, yet, privately he does both.

In his own room he seems to find a blend of security and peace, knowing the family is there even if he can't, at the moment, or, usually, ever, tell them what is troubling him. The next morning he will lie in bed undisturbed, sleeping a worry off, until he thumps on the floor to signal that he is awake, and then Mary takes him up a cup of tea. Such moments have become scarcer with the availability of Chequers, where he loves to entertain, and also with the strict security precautions and office requisites that accompany his present office.

At Chequers, which he uses far more than previous Conservative Prime Ministers who had their own country houses, he has been able to expand a side of his nature that had been concertinaed in early years. He has lavished new decor on several rooms, and through wide open windows the fresh air pours in, and the music pours out. He is now, in the words of one of the most exacting of critics, a 'superlative host' – at least when he is giving his mind to the occasion.

He has also learned to place the same importance and nearly the same trust in his true friendships that he once reserved only for his family. Friends and colleagues admit they would not like to go to him with news of a peccadillo, or get drunk with him, but say that whenever someone he is fond of is in any real trouble he is passionately anxious to alleviate it in whatever way he can. Illness and physical disability seem to release some emotional energy in him: one man remembers him looking down with a smile of total radiance at a beautiful woman in a wheelchair, and he spent half an hour at Chequers after lunch one day over Christmas 1970 talking to one of his Cabinet Minister's cousins who was dying of cancer, and was fervently interested in politics. This might seem at first no less than normal humanity, but remembering Heath's own memories of his mother's illness, his squeamishness, and that he is as thrifty with time as with money, it can be construed as true kindness: certainly those who were present all thought it so.

The old tendency to tease persists under normal circumstances, however. At the Broadstairs carol service which he has conducted since 1935, it is now the custom to have a celebrity to take the collection, which goes to charity. For his first Christmas as Prime Minister he chose Susan Hampshire. Each year the guest tries to get a bigger collection; but when the slip of paper giving the takings was handed to Heath this particular year, he pulled a long face. Miss Hampshire blushed a deep pink. One of the congregation said, 'When the service was over he announced that the collection was some thirty-five pounds bigger than it had been previously – but he'd given her a miserable fifteen minutes.'

He even felt he could display his sense of humour in public. 'He'd watch his tongue on the way up, although he'd always made jokes about people in private,' said one behind-the-scenes spectator.

Now, at Downing Street, visitors and applicants for jobs sometimes

find themselves facing a wit so unexpected – and sometimes so un-
answerable – that they occasionally feel, as one man complained to
one of Heath's secretaries afterwards, 'He spent the whole time laugh-
ing at me.' The laughter is not, however, always cutting, it may
sometimes be beneficent. A graphologist once remarked brilliantly
of Heath, 'When he laughs he's blushing.' This is often true: but his
laughter is also used to screen dismay, to play for time, or simply
meditate.

One might reasonably expect a man so terse and often tough with
others to have a reasonable resistance to criticism of himself: yet,
like many a highly critical man, Heath can himself be easily hurt by
even a distant, or glancing, shot. Reading a profile of himself one
day, he came across a phrase which upset him considerably. 'It says
I have no close friends,' he told Madron. 'They don't know about
us.' The unfortunate irony of this was that until that moment,
Seligman himself says he had no idea that he was regarded as a very
close friend.

In fact, because his affection is implicit and not overt, because he
receives confidences but does not give them, because he gives help
more easily than he receives it, because he is embarrassed by displays
of affection, or almost any emotions other than the cold passions of
anger and righteous indignation (although he enjoys sentiment from
a distance), Heath does not really have friends who one could call
extremely close. He has, instead, very good friends: friends who
understand him better than he knows, and perhaps would like, but
always remain slightly puzzled by some things in his nature; friends
who are prepared to give most of the warmth, at least in the early
stages of the relationship; friends who have been around for a long
time and with whom trust has been consolidated by time rather than
forged by sudden understanding.

Heath responds to people very often with a slightly modified
version of their behaviour to him; therefore anyone who shows
genuine care for him has the chance of receiving slow, careful
friendship back; but for anyone who has the slightest animosity or
coldness there is a Siberian reception. This puts at a disadvantage
anyone who, like himself, finds it hard to make the first outgoing
moves in a relationship. One person who describes himself as
'somewhat reticent and private, but usually I can go 70 per cent of

the way in making the moves' admits that with Heath he finds it difficult to do more than 30 per cent – therefore, while he admires him greatly, and has known him for many years, he has never felt close to him. And Heath himself is sometimes felt, by those with the sensitivity to hear the unsaid, only just to hold himself back from the brink of a confidence, or an appeal. A friend who has often sat listening to music with him says, 'Quite often I've known that he was wondering whether to tell me something: and then he's just got up and changed the record.'

If this involves some conflict, it must also mean fewer regrets: politicians have more to fear from revealing themselves than almost anyone, and evidently Heath's love of privacy is involved with some ingrained, if theoretical, suspicion of others, together with the occasional self-doubts that everyone suffers from time to time. It does not mean, on the other hand, that he is lonely: lonelier far to say a thing, and find no one understands it, and worst of all to be understood too well, and betrayed. But, while introverted, Heath is not greatly introspective. When normally healthy and busy he is not lonely at all; but occasionally he is, and knows that he is. When that is the case, he finds it hard to admit it.

For this is a man whose emotional force has been concentrated by his denial of many of its natural outlets, even the indirect one of talking about it. He seems not to have grasped the truth that an emotional, like a physical, muscle may become almost spastically unreliable if, instead of being exercised and controlled through use, it is hopefully ignored.

Therefore he may be gripped by sudden, erratic, shyness or anger, or some other unexpected emotion. This volatility, which is quite at odds with his consistency of purpose, combines with his slowness in making the approaches and means that his best relationships are confined to personalities of one particular type – calm, honest, reliable, extroverted.

An astute observer has summed it up: 'Ideally you must love him and talk fairly straight.'

It was during the years in Opposition that Heath really developed a new interest which has allowed him greater social freedom than any other, because its social demands were so minimal: sailing.

'He had been looking round for a hobby for some time,' remembers

Mr Pye – an extraordinarily revealing remark, again showing his concern with the shape of his life and desire to maintain a balance in it. No doubt he was very conscious even at the time of the colossal demands made by high office and the virtues of being, as Churchill liked to be, stretched in the opposite direction.

After his fairly disastrous start with Madron in Villefranche in 1965, when they nearly went on the rocks, he said that he was going to sail back in Broadstairs. 'I didn't think he would . . . but two or three years later there he was, an expert, and by '69 a leading yachtsman,' says his friend, slightly bemused by him as usual.

Heath was already a member of the Broadstairs Sailing Club, but had never taken an active part in its activities. Now, under the tuition of another member, Gordon Knight, he had his first lessons at sea in a solid type of boat, one of the local sixteen-foot Foreland Class. The next year, in 1967, he bought a Snipe, and, Knight remembers, 'sailed with reasonable success – he was quite good'. Then, in 1968, he did something that Madron considered quite mad.

'He bought a Fireball, a thing that young people race in and do gymnastics in – not a grown man's boat,' recalls Seligman. 'I tried to talk him out of the idea of a Fireball, but he was very hurt and said that he was a real sailor now.'

Gordon Knight approved his pupil's choice. The Fireball, which cost something over two hundred and fifty pounds, he describes as the equivalent of a Lotus Elan on water. And he comments, 'He was a very quick learner. I wouldn't say that he's athletic – he applies his mind more than his body, but that's more important in sailing. He enjoyed the tactical side; yet he was patient in light airs and didn't appear to be frustrated.

'I didn't have to repeat anything at all – each time out was a continuation, not a repetition. From the first, even when the first time out it was blowing quite hard and he didn't know how to distribute his weight to the best advantage, he showed no apprehension at all – he seemed all aglow with it and oblivious to the dangers. That's a very good sign and impressed me, most people are afraid at first. He has a rather shy and gentle nature but he's extremely tough in some respects, morally and physically.

'You need guts and intelligence for racing – you don't have to be a great athlete. I think it was also a help to be with less complicated people – he's completely relaxed with people that he knows, and has made a great number of real friends.'

Madron Seligman saw it as the same triumph of character over environment to which he should have grown used, but always continued to surprise him.

'At the beginning I don't think he had a natural feel for it – just determination. But now he has a feel for the waves and the wind. It was typical of him to go ahead despite people being sceptical about his abilities.'

Heath acquired his first racing cruiser, *Morning Cloud I*, in 1969, and in the spring of 1971 *Morning Cloud II* was launched. The price of the new yacht – £22,000 – caused much speculation. 'People forget that you can buy yachts on hire purchase just as you can motor cars,' says one of his friends. Heath himself claims he spent his savings on the purchase: one would guess that he did not spend them all.[1]

In Shadow Cabinet meetings, colleagues would see Heath studying a tiny square of paper just as they were halfway through an intricate argument: some of them wondered if Heath was keeping his own check on their information, but one of them says, 'I always knew what he was looking at – it was the times of the tides at Ramsgate.'

A frequent complaint was: 'When he says "We" you don't know whether he's talking about *Morning Cloud* or the Cabinet.' But the parts of his life were kept in watertight compartments, away from each other.

And his famous victory in the tough Australian race from Sydney to Hobart in 1969 had its own value in political terms, when it came to dealing with the sceptics. 'Ted was a week late joining the crew because Parliament sat late. Before he arrived they'd entered three races, and been placed, but they hadn't had a win. As soon as he got there they won the hardest race of the lot,' was the parable a friend heard one Conservative telling others. 'The man's got something.'

Anthony Churchill, navigator of the Heath plus Five team which sailed the first *Morning Cloud* to victory in that race, gave an excellent analysis of four months' preparation for the race, and the days spent speeding over 670 sea miles, in *Yachting World Annual*. It contains a

---

[1] Interview with Heath, *World in Action*, 3 August 1971.

fascinating account of how Heath applies himself to a problem, and his interaction with a team.

In advance, it looked as if *Morning Cloud* stood little chance. One of the crew wrote, 'We have to recognize that *Morning Cloud* is at the lower end of waterline length of boats competing, and will stand a chance only if the proportion of light airs is large enough and if it is the boat best equipped to take advantage of this situation . . .'

She was one of sixty-nine competitors, and, if this were not daunting enough, no yacht except an Australian or a New Zealander had ever won since the first contest in 1945.

Yet, at this twenty-fourth attempt since then, and her own first try, *Morning Cloud* set up three records, and achieved outstandingly the aim 'to take our ocean racing out of the doldrums'.

Australia involved entirely different conditions for the British team: dramatic changes of wind forces and direction, steeper seas – 'yachts can fall off waves with a terrifying succession of thuds, and broken masts are commonplace' – and killer sharks.

Breakfast meetings in Albany and late-night phone calls from August on saw the emergence of a detailed plan, which in some respects sounds primitive. They decided to dispense with cutter gear, usually considered an essential rig for the Australian coast, because none of the six was used to it, 'and our feeling was that we would need helmsmen, not crew, in the 670 mile race.' Instead of having a thermometer fitted through the hull to detect the helpful warm current, as many Australian yachts do, they decided to trail a bucket overboard occasionally with the thermometer in it.

Navigation could not be from the land – during the day there would be heat haze, at night the lights would not be powerful enough to be seen offshore. Beacons and current readings could prove unreliable. So they must steer by the stars.

The biggest equipment problem of all was their sail area; and Churchill says, 'Many memos were sent to Ted Heath and there were almost resignations from the crew during the following debates.' Having decided on the area, new sails were purchased, and *Morning Cloud* was ready to go down under.

There were no tides to contend with, only currents. The famous southerly current, which could be located by its temperature (higher than the surrounding seas) fascinated them – 'if we could get into this current and nobody else did then we had a potential one to three knots on our side for the first half of the race', after which the current turns east and would be no further use.

But hours of discussion with veterans of the race suggested more and more that the current might provide a wild-goose chase. 'After strong southerly winds it changes direction and flows northwards instead of south. When running south, it sometimes runs strongly for five miles from the shore and sometimes fifty miles from the shore and there are weird counter-currents. Even if, by chance, you find the current, it may disappear after a mile and re-appear elsewhere many miles away.

'We decided to place little reliance on this will-o'-the-wisp . . .'

But while not *relying* on luck, Heath and his team did not eliminate the help the current might give them in advance; they would not forsake it, it would have to forsake them . . . till they knew, they would make alternative plans.

On the day of the race, there was a northerly wind which gave them two alternatives – to sail close to the shore, or to sail offshore on a fast reach. From thirty miles out they would be in a commanding position to sail fast no matter where the wind was. And it took them across the hundred fathom mark, which was where they would locate the current if it was there. Out came the thermometer in its bucket of water. 'It didn't go up so we shrugged our shoulders and forgot the current.'

Now those yachts which had made a decision to stay near the shore fell upon the windless conditions they had feared most, including the two giant yachts, *Crusade* and *Apollo*. So, with three hundred miles to go, the contest now lay between *Morning Cloud* and the medium-sized yachts. Heath and his crew were determined to get to leeward of the rest, and to keep physically ahead in these still fairly early stages.

From now on judgment and luck went hand in hand. The weather forecasts mentioned depressions, with westerly winds following, which could have been dangerous; but by sailing for a point between their chief rivals and the turning mark, *Morning Cloud* might place herself so that the direction of the wind did not matter.

Churchill concluded, 'Our manoeuvre worked: all but the biggest *Thunderbolt* were behind us . . . for a day we had gale-force winds on the nose. That ended *Thunderbolt*'s chances. It was now near the end of a long race and the plans to have a crew packed with helmsmen had worked. Their helming was exact, and the yacht kept moving fast. The proof was in the fact that we had kept ahead of the one tonners, and indeed finished ahead of every man jack of them.

'That was the concrete reason for our victory, though preparing for the conditions down in Australia was a major help'.

Heath himself, who is a good helmsman as well as skipper and always takes the helm at the beginning and end of a race, saw a deeper pattern in his victory: to him, in retrospect, it was virtually inevitable. 'We have shown', he told another yachting writer, 'that planning and preparation pay.'[1] And in a more euphoric give-away to David Coleman on *Sportsnight with Coleman* he told television viewers, 'Well, it's certainly true we used our grey matter such as we've got and we certainly exploited the rules as far as we could, but we kept within the rules.'

He could not have made victory happen without the northerly wind. But he had avoided dealing with new and tricky equipment, taking on extra crew, or expecting too much from the unpredictable southerly current. Instead he had backed simple, well tried methods, a specialist crew he knew well, and, after taking advice from all of them, his own judgment.

There was no doubt who was the skipper: a debonair observer of Heath's relations with his crew (which tend perhaps to be better than with most people since each man knows what he is expecting from the other, and usually gets it) remarks, 'They can say what they like to him, and bloody this and that, as long as they say Sir at the end.'

It is from another member of Broadstairs Sailing Club, a young man called Robin Page, that one of the zaniest and most endearing stories ever told about Heath comes. They had gone fishing together one day in the late '60s. 'He had a Russian coming to see him, and he wanted to provide a typically English fish dinner – Whitstable oysters and Dover sole. He said he was going to try and catch the sole. I said, "You'll never do it," and he said "Yes, I will, yes, I will." In the end he caught a codling. It was typical of the man.'

[1] Profile by Graham Soames in *Yachts & Yachting*, 3 August 1971.

In this relaxed and private way, Heath thus began, in his fifties to lose the loneliness of his boyhood. This was the chief incidental benefit he gained from sailing – the main end always being in this as in politics, 'to win', the order given to all his children by Joseph Kennedy, father of the late President, whom Heath admired. 'There is the exhilaration of a contest', he says, 'and sailing also has its emotional moments.'

Heath's new persona as the bachelor yachtsman was also enormously helpful in terms of his public image. Though he did not take up sailing in order to balance his public picture, neither would he have taken up any interest that might have damaged him in the public eye. Certainly his concern with his public was a valid interest, and in 1967 it was partly for the public that he dieted strenuously enough to lose about a stone, and changed his spectacles for contact lenses – which of course he could not wear at sea in high winds.

He would not pretend to an interest in any aristocratic pursuit in order to win support from the snob side of the party. 'He thinks the leisured classes are too stupid for words,' says one former close colleague. Among his hates are the party games he found he was expected to play if he accepted a weekend invitation to a house-party – he seldom did – and horse-racing, which he found as pointless as the cross-country running he had endured at school. When, however, he killed a stag with his first shot at his first attempt on Lord Margadale's estate in Islay, he found an exciting new interest. In other words, he is simple enough at the sporting level, as well as many others, to be like other men; to enjoy what he does well, and to dislike what he does badly. But, having a natural tendency to intolerance and a scathing tongue, he pours unnecessary scorn on the latter.

Thus, in spite of his undoubted good intentions for others, he has become increasingly a self-centred man: and, what is more, with a feeling of complete justification in this belief that he knows what is best not only for himself but for others. Just how good his friends are – which in turn reflects the true basic value they find in the man, whatever difficulties there are – emerges from the following conversation between a husband and wife whose fondness and admiration for Heath have grown over the past fifteen years or so. Their determina-

tion not to seek anything extraneous from the friendship means they
have asked to remain anonymous.

He: 'We became closer because he could rely on me. And he is
the most wholly reliable man I've ever met in my life. He has
relatively few close friends, but they are the most reliable
people I know.'

She: 'What about punctuality?'

He: 'I can rely on him to be late!'

She: 'I have never known a man get his own way so much, in the
most maddening fashion. I remember once when he invited
me to Glyndebourne, about four weeks before the performance. I said no, I couldn't go. Then two days before the
performance he rang up to tell me the arrangements. I
reminded him that I'd said I couldn't manage it, but he told
me what time I'd be picked up, and I found myself paddling
off to Glyndebourne like a sheep . . . and I was furious.'

The assurance that he knows what is best for other people springs,
presumably, from Heath's own very certain sense of values, and his
feeling of familiarity with the scales of morality. This pervades even
his senses: *Fidelio* is his favourite opera, he says, because it represents
the triumph of good over evil. It is also, of course, a most romantic
choice in every sense; and this romantic streak also underlies his love
of Strauss, particularly *Der Rosenkavalier*, and of Mahler.

Fidelio can be interpreted as the defeat of political injustice; and in
the character of Leonora herself, the highest human qualities are
seen. Beethoven seems to have been inspired by an ethical force to
compose some of his most spiritually, as well as sensuously, moving
music in *Fidelio*. It is a combination irresistible to Heath, who would
like to find such truth and beauty everywhere, and in his attempts to
do so reveals a self that is almost primitively demanding.

Those closest to him were subjected to the greatest demands.

'Sometimes I felt he'd forgotten I had a family,' said John
MacGregor, formerly the head of his private office, who now works
for Hill, Samuel and Co. Ltd.

At first, he admitted, this sometimes annoyed him; although his
wife, who had herself worked for Heath, was very understanding
about him being called away late at night and at weekends. But one

day something brought a new revelation to him. He had told Heath about a personal worry, and gone home on Friday night. On the Saturday evening or, less probably the Sunday (he is not sure which), the telephone rang, and he thought, 'another weekend gone'. But instead of a summons to duty, Heath simply told him of various friends he had contacted, and telephone calls he had made, during the day, on MacGregor's behalf. 'He had spent half the weekend quietly doing this for me,' he realized.

As he got to know his leader better his admiration for him increased, until, having left him, he could say 'I've never had such a stimulating three and a half years. He changed the *scale* of my thinking. He is what I would like to be.'

Others are only aware of the outward manners and manifestations of Heath, and apparently unconscious of any directing ethos in him. This, and straightforward snobbishness as well as aesthetic withdrawal from him, continued to be tremendous drawbacks during the 1970 campaign.

One traditionally Tory lady said, 'When I see him bustling down the street carrying Elgar, I think "How can the office of British Prime Minister fall into the hands of a man who walks like that!" '. Accordingly, she voted Liberal.

(She was far from unique in her reaction, if not in her expression of it, which is in itself a comment on the political life of this country. A good many of those who seem to confuse the standards and needs of their own drawing rooms with those of No. 10 might remember the words Heath himself once underlined in an essay on Mahler's Fourth Symphony, '. . . the good taste which is ready to take offence at Mahler's sentimentality will be all the better for being shocked'.)

He was sensitive to such reactions. He knew he did not evoke the whole-hearted enthusiasm of the Magic Circle, upon which previous Conservative leaders had been able to rely almost automatically, still less on the extreme Right wing. The results of the opinion polls, which took on the appearance of unpopularity polls, were constantly drummed into him during the 1970 campaign.

So for all his outward composure the spectacle of Edward Heath sitting in the Drill Hall in Bexleyheath late on polling day on 18 June could have been interpreted as a sad one.

By midnight, however, the results were looking very good; an hour or so later the question was not so much who was going to win but how big the Conservatives' majority was going to be. A swift change of tone overcame the television commentators, and Heath wryly remarked, 'They've been telling me all the week I was going to lose, and now they're picking my bloody Cabinet for me!'

He gave a television interview, then there was an instant party in Reginald Pye's flat. Shortly before 3 a.m., the new Prime Minister left for London under police protection. Democracy had made him; yet, particularly at first, his predilections as a Prime Minister would continue to be what they had always been – oligarchic, rather than democratic.

14
The Trial

Edward Heath came to power with one tremendous advantage over almost every other Prime Minister this country has had in recent years: he was not greatly liked. He had never been used to being greatly liked, and, while he might have briefly enjoyed the sensation of popularity, it was not something he needed. In fact, having seen the fate of popular contemporaries, say Maudling and Wilson, and having studied the figure of the past, such as Lord Simon, of whom Macmillan wrote 'his tragedy was that he wanted to be liked', popularity might have made him very uneasy and suspicious. 'Men,' Macmillan continued, 'especially politicians, are like boys. They often reject those who seek their affections and look up to those who treat them with a certain negligence, and contempt.'[1]

This was not true of Heath. Rejection, as we have seen, had never produced this immature reaction in him. His analysis of the effect of the French rebuff to the British over the Common Market in 1963, with its consequent souring of public opinion towards the Community, shows clearly that, to him, coldness must bring coldness. It is, as he would say, a healthy reaction.

He could not, of course, have survived without the loyalty, respect and affection of a chosen few: what his family and one or two friends supplied in his private life, a tiny nucleus of his colleagues gave unstintingly to his political life.

Members of the Cabinet who had never previously been close to him found him a little unapproachable, and even suspicious. This

---

[1] *Winds of Change*, Macmillan, 1966.

may have been a consequence both of his feeling of isolation during the election and of his new position, just as when first made leader he had complained that he no longer knew whom to trust. Yet those who had gained his confidence over the years found him 'so trusting as to be amazing'. He could command the total loyalty of these few. One man, formerly a member of his own team and now earning a living elsewhere, still 'worships the ground he walks on', and carries on as an extra-mural adviser. William Whitelaw, Secretary of State for Northern Ireland who spent six years as his Chief Whip, is a man both bluff and delicate. He says, 'I think he also inspires curiously, and in a very odd way, much more respect and even in degree affection from his closest colleagues than it really is possible to imagine . . . The reason is that he doesn't seek to do so at all, and yet he does it without trying. It is a very great skill.'

It is more of a genius than a skill. It is also useful. To command the certain admiration of those capable of appreciating you, to care not for the rest, must produce a considerable liberation from the desire to curry favour.

There could be two views of the source of this admiration: some believe that Heath is a vacuum and that those who like him are merely filling it with their own good-will. Others, and I am among them, believe that there is a substantial if veiled element of good-will in Heath's own nature. These people believe that the hostility and anger he shows cannot be completely divorced from a mainspring of *agape*, of genuine care for the state of his fellow men. That this is more often directed at groups of people rather than individuals is not merely a reflection of his political training. It is a more natural mode of expressing concern from a moralist, from someone whose religion is still an interwoven part of normal life and from a man whose natural self-containment and self-centredness, combined with his belief, make him readily moved by injustice, less easily moved to pity. And if this is not a popular motive in a world more conscious of erotic and sentimental love than of the harder force of detached care, of *dutiful* love, it is still one that can play with tremendous force upon the central levers of human response. To care sublimely, even if that must mean detachedly, for others is not only Christian: it may well, according to Heath's own beliefs about the economics of affection, eventually awaken a corresponding response.

This is partly a civilized reaction, but it is also partly primitive – the healthiness of seeking where you will find. Some people respond more primitively to him as the strong man, the survivor, the leader of the pack. He has himself developed much that is primitive in his chosen nature, and has long perceived the necessity for self-dependence, for concentration of his resources, for displays of leadership. His opposition to the 1965 Finance Bill was a sophisticated version of the gorilla's display charge, showing that it would be unwise to challenge his leadership. Yet he has also retained some characteristics from his sensitive, more civilized nature, and from this comes his belief in the concentration of resources for the benefit of the weakest members of the community. The survival of the fittest and the weakest is guaranteed. It is the majority he fails adequately to consider: the vast mass of the others who find themselves suddenly, under this new form of Conservatism, adrift on what he would call their own mediocrity.

He neither fully understands nor greatly wants to understand the mind of the average intelligent worker. Still less could he comprehend the difficulties of the less articulate, with their 'presenting illnesses', their complaints sometimes completely unrelated to the genuine and desperate cause of their anxiety. But he is at once spiritually, culturally, and ideally at home in Strasbourg, with its mixed German and French ancestry, its faith in statesmanship, and its practical implementation of romantic political aspirations.

His own brand of realism could enable him to overcome short-term and tactical problems by imposing rigidly calculated solutions, overriding opposition with his mixture of obstinacy and obtuseness. He may also be able to envisage and create long-term opportunities for himself and for this country by applying his own rules and the results of his analysis in known territory (the past) to unknown territory (the future). Such projection does not seem intangible to him, but a more solid, safer, and faster craft, than wait-and-see.

Give him a simple problem, and he will provide a simple answer. Even the future, so mysterious to most of us, is easily charted by him: one can plan a straightforward journey there, in his view, simply *because* there are few landmarks.

But, if most people make the mistake of confusing and confounding the simple, they sometimes achieve a balance by going to the heart of a complex current issue: instinct, intuition, or the divine conjunction of two veering thoughts produces an answer.

This is not Edward Heath's forte. 'He is like a computer. Feed him with information and all you have to do is wait for the answer,' says one Cabinet colleague. It is a simile often applied to him. Heath, like the computer, can be over-burdened by disparate, ill-categorized, badly programmed pieces of information. It is at these moments, which fortunately for him occur infrequently in political life that finds Heath at his least sure and with least to contribute. He does not often give a wrong answer; nor does he usually prophesy the right one. Instead, there is a protracted silence: the great powerful machine tries in vain to match its material, and simply has to go on waiting until more facts are available. It is the subsequent silence that unnerves a public used to the clamour of alternatives and potential solutions.

It is strange that Heath, normally a man acutely conscious of danger as he showed by his premonitions in the 1930s, should have reacted so slowly to the incipient threat of Ireland. Even the computer, one feels, should have flashed notice of an emergency, if not provided a solution. Yet, according to some of those closest to him, he was not particularly attentive to the problem – likely to prove the most intractable not only of this administration but of future Governments – more than a year after he became Prime Minister, and two years after Wilson had moved troops into Ulster. 'There are times', said a colleague before Heath even thought of concentrating on Ireland, 'when I imagine him saying to Hell with Northern Ireland – it's about time they sorted it out. But then where does adherence to the Constitution, to the Crown, come in? It's back to the problem underlying Rhodesia . . .'

Ulster, of course, had acted out of turn, and at first Heath treated it rather like static on the line of his important telecommunications – the implementation of his manifesto.

He also had a natural reluctance to interfere in the domain of Reginald Maudling, his Home Secretary. Maudling's equable temperament was a great advantage to the party after he lost the leadership stakes in 1965, and his ability to continue in his relationship with the Prime Minister without any obvious animosity appearing between the two was a great help to the party, but perhaps no great immediate help to Northern Ireland. 'It was great credit to Reggie – in any case there would only have been embarrassment from public confrontations with the leader – and Ted has gone out of his way to avoid giving cause for a confrontation', remarked a senior official. Maudling's refusal to flap as the pressures increased in the province also evoked a genuine admiration from Heath, who was prepared to hold back from intervention as long as he thought this might eventually benefit the province.

But, as deaths and damage multiplied after the killing of the first British soldier on 5 February 1971, and still more after 9 August when Mr Faulkner authorized internment of suspects under the Special Powers Act, the practical Prime Minister was forced to consider it for what it was: potential civil war. Patrick Cosgrave, who was then working in the Conservative Research Department, analysed the situation in the summer of 1971 on Radio Eireann. Mr Lynch, he said, would be making a great mistake if he assumed either that Heath 'would, like Lloyd George half a century ago, be prepared to do some deal about the North, or that he felt involved in some kind of trap, some kind of morass that he couldn't get out of. Not at all. He is liberated by responsibility. He feels and acts upon a simple sense of obligation to the Protestant majority in Ulster who want to continue their allegiance to the Crown and in his support of those people he is rocklike, immovable.' Cosgrave continued, 'I think it is true to say that the present policy of the Government – of suppressing the I.R.A. come what may–not just has the support of the Tory Party in Parliament, but has it to such an extent that any deviation, any concession, any move to gratify, let us say Mr John Hume, would produce an instant Tory revolt large enough to imperil the life of the Government . . .'

Heath, however, as was to become apparent on another issue, but was already clear from his own past, is not a man to desire or cling to office for its own sake: to him, power, largely though not exclusively, equals responsibility. Therefore, while Heath like many of his followers reacted strongly against the sustained and savage campaign of violence that battered the heart of Ulster throughout the winter of 1971–72 and while he did feel a personal animosity against the leaders of the I.R.A., with their dual challenge to his own deputed authority and to the Crown, there was another side to the argument that formed more slowly in his mind. The reunification of Ireland was a solution not disparaged by all his colleagues: more important, it began to have his own inner ear, because he began to focus on his own duty to find a route towards what could eventually turn into a solution. It was not fear that delayed him, nor, after some weeks, anger, but the need to see a sufficiently plain formula worked out and the main opposition parties in Northern Ireland somehow diverted from their fierce refusal to discuss such a formula until internment had ended.

John Locke, who published *Civil Government* in 1960 and who impressed Heath at Oxford, once wrote: 'I would be quiet and I would be safe, but if I cannot enjoy them together the last must certainly be had at any rate.'[1] I told the Prime Minister – in the context of the Common Market, before he publicly made this an issue for resignation – that I felt he would react in the opposite way from Locke, and he agreed. On Ireland, as well, he would like to give priority to peace of mind and the peace of the people, not the life of the present Government.

But as months passed and initiatives remained untaken, the crisis corroded, delay meant more deaths, and the silence of the man who had failed to take the situation by the throat seemed more and more punishable since it inevitably lengthened the period before the tenants called a truce.

After the Londonderry shootings, lack of deep concern, or of concentration, was no longer a cause of his delay. The situation was increasingly pushing itself to the forefront of his mind, and delicate feelings about the propriety of taking over from Maudling were sunk beneath new problems. The Cabinet itself, and even the inner group of six who were concentrating particularly on Northern Ireland, were divided in their sympathies, and this was the main brake on action. Lord Carrington saw the eventual reunification of the island as a final possibility, and suggested interim measures that could lead to it: his was the most progressive stand in the inner group. Sir Alec Douglas-Home, the Foreign Secretary, argued strongly against this line, and William Whitelaw, who was to assume responsibility for the province, was also doubtful about it at first. Reginald Maudling

---

[1] *Two Tracts on Government*, by John Locke, edited by Philip Abrams, C.U.P., 1967.

and Anthony Barber seemed to occupy a half-way house on the issue.

Heath had first to be convinced himself, and then to carry first this inner group and then the whole Cabinet with his decision – this last necessity was the hardest of all. Great impatience with some aspects of the problem did not detract, in the final analysis, from his growing concern with the injustices of the situation, which affected most sections of the population indirectly, but were certainly causing more suffering among the particularly under-privileged Catholic population. Stormont's neglect of this problem for fifty years, and the Northern Ireland Government's refusal to face, realistically, the urgent need for reforms in this deteriorating situation, suggested to him a head-in-the-clouds attitude that must prove unproductive.

Such promises of reform as were made, and were intended to strengthen the voice of the Catholic minority in the affairs of the North, were finally seen as being used to disguise, not cure, the wounds of the minority.

This realization was calculated to arouse Heath's great indignation for three reasons. As a man with an acute sense of justice, he does dislike discrimination, and he does believe essentially in political freedom. Second, the stupidity of those Protestants who were increasing the dangers to themselves by failing to come to terms with the situation, but advocating sterner and more repressive measures still, would act as a minor irritant.

Third, he could relate the situation in Northern Ireland closely to his own position in the Conservative Party. He had had to contend with an intractable and extreme Right wing himself, and he had agonized but often stayed with his conscience. For him, moral courage had paid political dividends. He was therefore quick to realize that in Northern Ireland the scales had tipped the other way: that the increased Catholic part of the Stormont hierarchy was to consist of 'castle Catholics', privileged themselves and unrepresentative of those with the great grievances. He was convinced that Brian Faulkner, the Prime Minister of Northern Ireland, was being pushed further and further to the Right by Mr William Craig, leader of the Right-wing Protestant Vanguard movement. This was the position he had been nudged some way into himself over Rhodesia, but had resisted on capital punishment. He has also moved Left, not Right, since he gained office. 'I don't think anyone can show the Right wing had very much influence on our policies'[1] he said, proudly and with some truth, in May 1972.

After one final round of talks with Faulkner, whose outcome seems to have been calculated in advance, he acted on Thursday, 23 March 1972, to announce the Government's intention of imposing direct rule from Westminster in Northern Ireland. He also announced a start on the phasing out of internment, and regular plebiscites that should take the border 'out of the day-to-day political scene'.[2]

This was a telling phrase, revealing yet again Heath's desire to make lasting political decisions, and to avoid the temporary and transient.

This decisive action, long delayed but complete and sudden in announcement, was more radical than had been expected in both Southern and Northern Ireland alike, and certainly showed that in some nine months Edward Heath had evolved sufficiently to reverse the expectations of Right-wing elements at Westminster and among the Conservative Party in this country.

Stormont was gone, for the time being at least: what would eventually replace it? Many interim measures may be found, but reunification remains a final possibility and, for many, the main hope. It is a potent factor in Heath's own thinking, but a very distant possibility for all that.

Asked about reunification three weeks before the election, he replied, 'My attitude is very clear indeed – that this can only come about if the people of Northern Ireland wish it.'[3] This was the undertaking given by Attlee in section 1 of the Ireland Act, 1949, and reaffirmed successively by Churchill, Macmillan, Eden and Wilson. But, if Heath increasingly feels it would be right for the people of Northern Ireland to wish it, he is certainly a leader who would endeavour to make them wish it, in order to make the change constitutionally. The question of course is: How would he implant this wish, when the prospect of changing from being a majority in the North to a minority in a united Ireland seems to the Northern Protestants to be a death-wish?

Time may give its natural help here, if both sides of the border are

---

[1] Interview with the author at Chequers.
[2] *Hansard*, vol. 833, col. 1859.
[3] Mr Heath answering questions on B.B.C. Forum, 27 May 1970.

integrated under a higher umbrella inside the Common Market. This could give a greater sense of purpose to both communities and show the practical benefits of unity. It would provide the culmination of Heath's early view that Europe must eventually 'stop its civil wars and unite'.[1] Presumably this applies just as much, or more, to Ireland as to the rest of Europe, to which he was specifically referring.

Fate twisted and turned on the linked question of Ulster and the Common Market. At one moment it seemed that Heath might have seriously jeopardized his chances of carrying through the European Communities Bill, since the imposition of direct rule might lose him the votes of the Ulster Unionists whose votes could prove crucial at the third reading – there was only a majority of eight on the second reading in February 1972. 'It shows the courage of the man that he refused to be deterred by that,' said another member of the Cabinet. 'Mind you, I think he's relying on us to manhandle the Ulster Unionists through the lobby on the night of the vote!' In April, however, the resignation of Mr Roy Jenkins as deputy leader of the Labour Party, and the swift following of some of his friends from Labour's Front Bench, greatly reduced the danger to the Bill.

If the most serious problem, both in terms of lives and of political difficulty, that Heath had to face during his first two years in office was Ireland, it was seldom the one that was uppermost in his mind. The difficulties of the situation itself often enabled him to shelve it temporarily; it was an unpleasant fact of life that could probably not yet be changed and must therefore be endured with as little brooding as possible. This may not have been a creative attitude to the Irish problem, but, in relation to his other plans, it had its healthy side.

A new Prime Minister embarks on office rather as a couple embark on matrimony. Within a year the bliss, the shock, the round-the-clock demands, the power, and the responsibility, have had a chance to make themselves felt: within a year, usually, congeniality is proved, or divorce is in the air. Edward Heath was like a most happy bridegroom, all of whose desires had been aroused and then assuaged by the same delightful companion. In his second year of office, though the crises were worse, one felt he was settling down to a Darby

[1] Edward Heath interviewed on German television by Herr von Trosche, 9 March 1971.

and Joan relationship with government. Someone who has worked closely with five Conservative Prime Ministers counts him, unequivocally, the happiest of the lot in his job.

This might seem an inevitable consequence of achieving his ambition; but, really, it was not.

When Neville Chamberlain, a man of outwardly similar temperament, succeeded Baldwin, J. C. C. Davidson composed a memorandum to him. It was never sent, but under its title 'Things to Remember' were collected a number of observations that may have been true of political life in the 1930s, that one would in fact expect to be true of political life now, but for which Heath has in some cases shown a disregard that appears almost reckless.

The memo noted in its first six points:[1]

1. That it is essential to have the friendship of someone outside the Cabinet whose loyalty and discretion is beyond question . . . a confidant from whom no secrets are hid.

2. The Prime Minister is the loneliest man in England (subject to 1 above). He can only receive confidences from his Cabinet colleagues – it is seldom wise to lay bare all that is in his own mind to them.

3. . . . A Prime Minister . . . must avoid detail.

4. The Prime Minister, like the conjuror, has to see that a variety of problems of differing gravity and/or importance are kept moving towards decision, if not solution . . .

5. The Prime Minister must cease to look at questions with the eye of an advocate. He must be the judge before whom the case is argued by the Cabinet Ministers themselves. He must remember too that the best advocate is not necessarily right.

6. The Prime Minister must display greater tolerance than anyone else . . .

Point number 10 added, 'Lloyd George once said that there can be no friendship between the leading half dozen in the Cabinet . . .', which was almost certainly truer of his own Cabinet than Heath's.

[1] For full text of 'Things to Remember', see *Memoirs of a Conservative*, J. C. C. Davidson's Memoirs and Papers, 1910–1937, by Robert Rhodes James, Weidenfeld & Nicolson.

While Heath has made a point of keeping his non-political friends, even though he has less free time to spend with them or even to telephone them, there is certainly among them no confidant from whom no secrets are hid. Even Madron Seligman, who supplied support at Heath's moment of personal crisis over the abolition of resale price maintenance, says he is no longer consulted at such moments. Friends of the Prime Minister now are just that. There are compensations. One man, being delivered to Downing Street, was asked by the taxi-driver to declare himself: friend or colleague. 'Friend,' he replied. 'I never took a friend of Wilson's there,' replied the cabbie. 'I hear it's all right to be a friend of Heath's, but not to work with him – he wants his own way all the time.'

There was certainly no obvious need for a hostess at Downing Street or Chequers, since Heath himself entertained energetically enough for two. He was increasingly a gracious host, who took particular delight in musical occasions such as giving a party for Sir William Walton's 70th birthday, and inviting Yehudi Menuhin to play at a private concert. The high baronial panelled hall where he ('we' as he always terms it) has the concerts, holds up to 120 guests. He delights in selecting exactly the right recording – it was Wagner for me – to demonstrate his stereo equipment. Photographs and a model of *Morning Cloud* add his own signature to two of the newly- and prettily-decorated sitting-rooms. In one glass case stands his fine collection of Jacobean glass. This, one feels, is genuinely his *home*. Years of concentrating on work alone had given way to a gargantuan gregariousness: this overflow was one of the side effects of having achieved the beginning of his aims. Some who were constantly invited to his luncheon parties, dinners, and celebrations even began to feel a little breathless at trying to cope simultaneously with their own busy working, family, and social lives. But for Heath this rich new social life, as well as his sailing, seemed only to increase his energy for the next day's Cabinet.

As for loneliness, Heath is plainly less lonely as Prime Minister than he previously sometimes felt, or more importantly perhaps for a man of his pride, felt he looked. He is fulfilled in his job now, partly no doubt because of its outward and visible manifestations, but far more because of its inner rewards. The use of power can be heady even to the non-initiated; to someone who had practised the art for so long, and who intends to do so much with it, there is the tremendous and profound excitement of shaping the future now – what Heath sitting in an easy chair upstairs in Downing Street, and considering the importance of concentrating on issues that really matter in politics, suddenly bursts out and calls in his extraordinarily over-simple way, but in a voice suffused with emotion, 'Think Big'.

Because of the need for this, he does find it easy to avoid detail and to delegate, unlike other Prime Ministers (Eden for instance). Yet for his first six months in office he insisted on phrasing his own answers to Prime Minister's questions without the help of a 'style' man.

On the fourth point, the necessity of conjuring, Heath showed sometimes exhilarated, sometimes unwilling compliance with the laws of the political jungle, the need for physical display and *trompe l'œil*. But on the whole this does not come easily to him, and seems to come less easily now than before; he really is looking for solutions and not decisions.

However, what man is wise enough always to arrive at the solution without some intermediary decisions to throw into relief the final possibility? It is a dangerous course particularly for one who has not entirely ceased looking at things with the eye of an advocate. Only a clear and logical mind, integrity, and a real desire to see justice done have held back the potential praefect and censor in him.

Tolerance, we now see, is something a Prime Minister need not necessarily have, although if he does not have it he has to maintain the difficult balance just mentioned. 'Peter Carrington (now Chairman of the Party) is the only member of the Cabinet I've not seen him have a row with,' says another of its members. Heath seldom interferes once he has delegated, but when mistakes are made the price must be paid – so far more often in terms of mortification than in loss of office. The reputation for ruthlessness has made its continual application unnecessary; and in any case Heath probably has a more paternal feeling for members of his Cabinet, particularly when they are under fire, than for any other group. It is a different story when they are under fire from him. The term 'bully' has been applied to him by a former member of his team, and it is true that he does tend to bully people who do not stand up to him in arguments.

Nobody is allowed to smoke in Cabinet meetings. Heath himself never acquired the habit, and perhaps feels he is doing the others a favour – particularly the heavy smokers like Geoffrey Rippon – by safeguarding their health for two or three hours at a time. The reason given for the no-smoking order is that he sometimes works or gives interviews in the cabinet room, downstairs in Downing Street, when the Cabinet is not sitting, and does not see why he should have his comfort interfered with. (Field Marshal Montgomery frequently made the same rule at his briefings.) It followed from his personal belief that the Government initiated its campaign about the hazards of smoking with the warning now printed on each packet.

Many of the minor legislative reforms made early under his administration could, in slightly changed circumstances, have reflected a personal interest: but while, like any normal man, his interest is more quickly, and more deeply stirred, where he can identify, many other small reforms showed that stringent sense of justice that guides him in impersonal matters – and that usually gives balance to the rest.

There was the pension for widows aged between forty and fifty (which might have fitted his step-mother's case until she remarried); there was the overdue pension *as of right* for the over-eighties, which could have applied to someone of his father's age but with less providence and luck. 'I have a fixed income and I've never lived up to it,' William Heath declares: it comes now from the rent paid for his joinery equipment. Another injustice put right – and here Heath could hardly have been more disinterested, since it is hard to think of a single working wife among his friends – was the provision for the working wife to pay her own tax separately if her husband was willing to accept the single man's allowance.

On the debit side were the decisions to withdraw free school milk from children aged seven to eleven – the indignation stirred up was disproportionate, but an instinctive response to the meanness and aggression – and the rather absurd, as well as backward-looking, decision to undertake an expensive task of charging for entry to museums.

Heath enjoys doing his sums, and his feeling of administering the country's benefits more advantageously. However, sincerity is not the same as justice, and concentration of resources on the weakest in employment was lacking from the 1972 Budget. The lowest paid with large families stood to gain little from the tax changes, and Mr Roy Jenkins, still then the Shadow Chancellor, pointed out that 'the element of justice in the budget is short-term and the injustice is long-term'.[1]

Plans to establish eventually a form of negative income tax provided the greatest gleam of light for those with the lowest resources. But priorities in 1972 were markedly different, most noticeably in respect of the separate demands of inflation and of unemployment, from what they had been during the early months of the Government's life.

Some of these early changes, including the pension for the over-eighties, had emerged from the Selsdon Park weekend, which took place at the end of January 1970, and of which Heath afterwards said excitedly 'This last weekend was a terrific weekend, a tremendous weekend . . . I've never had the same experience as we've had this weekend, of working together solidly for this period, thinking alike and then being able to say there's a manifesto which we can put before the people . . .'

He is in fact a man to whom the *habit* of working with people is profoundly important. The weekend was a turning-point in his political maturity, according to one of those who had often felt critical of him but now felt that he was exchanging the insistence on 'new' policy for responsible policy. Power was close at hand; and such is the power of power that it can transform into better as well as worse. Heath was now emerging in a new dimension, one that would make one former Conservative minister admit a year later 'I voted for Reggie, and I told Ted. He didn't say much – I don't think he was surprised. But I think now I made the wrong decision. He has emerged as by far the strongest person in the Conservative Party.'

Tax reform, industrial relations, selectivity in the social services, and law and order were other issues for discussion at Selsdon. Not surprisingly, many of the conclusions were recognizable as tributaries of what twenty years before had been a reforming mainstream, as seen in the One Nation document. The decision to concentrate welfare on the neediest reflected the One Nation declaration. 'Our

---

[1] *Hansard*, vol. 833, col. 1525, 22 March 1972.

economic position does not, and will not for many years, allow us to carry out all the schemes that can be justified on social grounds alone, nor even to implement in full the social legislation that has been passed since 1944. Therefore Conservative policy insists on administrative efficiency in the social services, on the clear recognition of priorities . . .'

On taxation, One Nation had deduced 'the social well-being of the nation has already been endangered by the redistribution of wealth': the 1970 manifesto would seek to redress this with more definite proposals.

Interestingly, before there were any thoughts of the Common Market, One Nation had declared 'We believe that one of the most uneconomic ways in which the strong can help the weak is through the food subsidies.'

While the reform of industrial relations was not specifically envisaged until 1965, some hint of it could be divined in the One Nation declaration 'the health and life of the nation are endangered as soon as the rights of individuals come to be regarded as more important than the duties, or even as their prior condition . . .'

When describing the giant step forward in 1950, the *Guardian* said 'the Conservatives have never in their history produced so enlightened a statement on social policy – from full employment and education to the social services'. It would not be succeeded by another giant step. As far as most home principles were concerned, the spot had been marked. What the Heath Government would attempt to do would be to build the spot, digging the foundations deep. The main movement would be in foreign policy, to Europe.

Heath's single aim was like a star to him when he came into office. It was the restoration of Britain to her former health, and a world role commensurate with – though quite different in formation from – the one she had played in the golden years of the Victorian empire. The concept was romantic, the methods were not. Such restoration depended on bending the economy back to a straight line before society was undermined, shocking big business out of its lethargy, bad management, and reliance on the public purse, and having a strong voice in Europe. Hence it was fair to call him radical rather than progressive in method.

The three main strands of his policy were closely intertwined in his mind: going into Europe would itself, he thought, provide a much needed shake-up for Britain's industry, ultimately benefiting the economy, as well as providing her with her future outlet for leadership. Europe, besides, was something he would always be remembered by, and it was not an end but a beginning.

He had not changed his mind since March 1967 when he said that 'fundamentally the most important task facing Britain today is to ensure that not only in the short term but in the long term her balance of payments is in surplus'.[1]

Behind this simple financial statement lay the motive of what one of his friends calls his 'touch of Gaullism – la Gloire de la France'. It was no accident, that, planning la Gloire de l'Angleterre, he noted that 'national feeling in France, perhaps more than in any other country has laid at the root of French achievements, collective and individual'.[2] As an ardent patriot, it was something that made unequivocal sense to him, and that he thought should be seen with equal clarity by all those whose lives he was about to touch, directly or indirectly.

Since he himself is open to little inner conflict, it was others who were most aware of the danger he faced as a man not easily given to communication: a danger increased by the death of Iain Macleod. He himself was hardly aware of the contradiction implicit in his statement on taking office 'to govern is to serve'. To him, this made perfect sense – in applying to the country the cure he knew to be right for it, he was indeed administering to its future greatness.

In any literal sense, of course, he would have repudiated it entirely. To the new Prime Minister, leadership meant what it said, and he was unequivocal a year later in agreeing that it was far better to be Prime Minister than another member of the Cabinet.

How did he see himself in relation to the view of a Prime Minister as *primus inter pares*? One thing his colleagues did not like, he replied, was the 'wishy-washy'. 'The lead has got to come from somewhere.' There was no doubting where. He is most recognizably the throne behind the power. How, I asked, could he live with a decision like the then expected shut-down of so much of U.C.S., which he had

[1] *Old World, New Horizons*, by Edward Heath, O.U.P., 1970.
[2] Ibid.

called 'heart-breaking'. He replied: 'Most decisions are collective decisions, thrashed out at a long series of meetings. After working together closely, sometimes for nearly twenty years, people come to a collective decision. That is what makes it a tolerable process.'

I did press him on how he might behave if he found himself in a minority within his own Cabinet, but he pointed out that this was hypothetically unlikely – 'you come together as colleagues because broadly speaking you've got the same views' (the fate of Powell went unmentioned and historically unprecedented). 'I can't think of any British Prime Minister who's been in that position – not even Lloyd George.' Then he could not resist a mention, elegaic in tone, and strikingly unlike his usual public style, of Wilson's isolation by his colleagues after he retreated from his proposed industrial relations reforms *In Place of Strife*, and 'one by one they abandoned him'.

It was true that the Cabinet was united on most policies when the Conservatives first came into office in 1970, as one would expect of a party newly reinstated. Some two years later different and sometimes opposing points of view had been and sometimes still were held on the issues that had defied the logical cure laid down for them in Opposition, and prescribed over the first eighteen months. These differences, both from each other and from previous policy, emerged slowly, however, and were as far as possible disguised in a Government that was determined to increase its credibility by keeping its word.

It was this determination that produced the biggest furore, in the first seven months of the new Government, when Macmillan's Simonstown agreement came home to roost. When Sir Alec Douglas-Home said that the new Government would be standing by the agreement which entailed supplying arms to South Africa should these be ordered, anti-racialist and liberal opinion was outraged. Heath, considered a genuine hard-liner on this issue by those closest to him but thought by some others to be acting exclusively out of determination to show a united front, announced in his first speech to the Commons, 'We entered the Simonstown agreement and the Government intend to give effect to its purpose.' Personal impetus was lent to his attitude when President Kaunda of Zambia was invited to Chequers and an explosive argument vitiated hopes of future agreement between them.

When it became plain that the issue could dominate the Prime Ministers' Conference in Singapore in January 1971, informed opinion on most sides, with the exception of the far Right, urged him to reconsider, and to draw back while there was still time. Heath, however, had decided to use the issue for his own ends as far as possible: to vindicate both his country's and his own freedom from unwelcome pressure and advice. The confrontation, when it came, did not reveal inspired leadership. But it showed that the Prime Minister possessed some characteristics that are reputedly present in most Englishmen and certainly hold a high place among his own particular characteristics: obstinacy, a hatred of 'being diddled', and what he calls a 'typically British, pragmatic approach'.[1]

Heath walked out of the conference in the early hours of 22 January 1971. The immediate cause of this action was President Obote, who had compared the compromise proposal to set up a study group to consider the problem of the sale of arms to South Africa with Chamberlain's return from Munich, promising peace.

One enormous annoyance to Heath was the African delegates' overt emotionalism; and, as a studied as well as natural moralist himself, he particularly objected to their way of agreeing with a proposal in private and subsequently denouncing it in public. The threats to his own and to Britain's authority fuelled him with precisely the anger he needed to carry him across the border from cold, righteous indignation to genuine fury – which was incidentally far more acceptable.

On close inspection, the concrete cause of contention boiled down to fewer than a dozen Wasp helicopters. 'Were Eleven Wasps the Real Dispute?' queried *The Times* incredulously. Of course they were not; for while defending a principle, Heath had also been indulging in a display of logical elusiveness, giving his Prime Ministerial confrères the uneasy feeling, caught in a brilliant phrase by Roy Lewis of *The Times*, that they were 'jousting with the robot'.

They were not the only ones who found him elusive.

A colleague commented, 'He played it much longer and in a way much more subtly than I would have thought . . . he allowed the thing to drag on till a great deal of the steam had gone out of it. The

1 *Old World, New Horizons*, by Edward Heath, O.U.P., 1970.

Right wing was unable to accuse him of ratting on our commitment; at the same time he has still left his options open as to what we should supply and what we shouldn't supply. He *has* separated theory and practice.'

While Heath's anger at the Prime Ministers' Conference was genuine, the amount of anger he showed was doubtless deliberate – just as it is when he furiously upbraids a colleague in a way that makes every spectator thankful he has not provoked the storm. But that Heath can control the outward manifestations of anger to a great extent is shown by his very different behaviour when he is angry in his family circle, and merely walks to the bottom of the garden.

Since his display of this emotion has become much more obvious over the past three years, it is interesting to see how he answered a question of Robin Day's when he was still in Opposition. 'Is the real Ted Heath', asked Day, 'a man more capable of anger, of passion, of emotion, than might appear from the press or the television?'

'Well,' replied Heath, 'this after all is putting a value on particular qualities which most people wouldn't regard as being essential to leadership . . . Is it essential to be angry, is it essential to be emotional, to be a good leader? I would say no. I would think that those are things which warp judgment, and it is judgment which people want in a leader, they want to have confidence in his judgment and to know that he's going to lead them aright.'[1]

This indicates that it was fear of public distrust of his emotionalism that made him hide it as much as he did: and no doubt he agreed with such potential distrust, and feared his own emotionalism too.

Hence, no doubt, his strict rationing of the amount of anger, still more of other emotions, which he allows himself to exhibit, the impression of coldness he gives to those outside a small circle. The statement he made, that anger and emotionalism warp judgment, which can often be true, remains of great interest. To what extent has it warped his judgment, since he came to power?

Since his mind was firmly made up on most of the immediate major issues – the great exception being Ulster – before he arrived in Downing Street, it has probably been a source of extra inner power rather than of sudden divergences from his own basic positions. He never seems to make up his mind entirely in anger, or at

[1] B.B.C. Panorama, 25 June 1969.

least seldom acted upon the decision taken in anger unless and until cold deliberation had reinforced its validity.

Even so it was perhaps inevitable that, as the Gulliver of the team surviving after twenty months in office, he should have provoked the personal hostility, bitterness and anger of many trade unionists, and particularly of the miners, during the first confrontation that saw him pegged to the ground in Lilliput.

The bitterness of the clash with the miners was a foregone conclusion to many impartial spectators of the industrial scene long before it became a reality. In February 1970, Michael Charlton asked whether his proposals for anti-strike legislation was not likely to lead to 'head-on collisions and confrontation' with the unions, and how he could hope to avoid Wilson's fate. Heath replied with an innocence that was only in small part a bluff, so strong was his belief in the power of the British constitution, and his own obedience to duty, '. . . he hadn't got an electoral mandate to do it . . . We shall put it forward as our policy, and it will be there, the electorate will vote on it. Now when it's implemented I do not believe for one moment that the trade union leaders, let alone the trade union members, are going to challenge the verdict of the electorate in this democracy with a democratically elected Parliament in which a government is carrying through the policy in which it went to the electorate.'[1]

His own belief in hierarchy was so strong that he could not imagine it challenged: let alone challenged in England. Another reason for his certainty lay in the desire of large sections of the electorate to see the power of the Unions pruned. Questions put in a sample survey to 604 working-class voters, including 178 Conservatives, in six urban constituencies in the late 1960s produced the answer: that more than half of the total number interviewed said they thought the unions had too much power.[2]

The transformation of the extraordinarily complicated Bill into an almost equally complicated Act took precedence in Heath's timetable, while more acutely urgent issues hung fire. It was not quite a case of 'wretches hang that jurymen may dine', but it was effected with a tactlessness that offended many who thought the reforms

---

[1] Edward Heath interviewed on Panorama, 2 February 1970.
[2] *Studies in British Politics*, edited by Richard Rose, Macmillan, 1969.

necessary. How effective the Act will actually turn out to be remains moot. It was based on a document originally drafted by Conservative lawyers, but Lord Wilberforce pointed out in respect of the clauses dealing with collective bargaining that collective agreements 'are not simple – that they are of a diverse and often sophisticated kind and not really suitable to be brought into the ordinary legal process'. The Appeal Court's over-ruling of one of the first judgments made by the Industrial Relations Court proved a difficulty. Nor were there signs that the Act would improve labour relations or lessen industrial unrest.

The actual troubles that were getting perhaps less attention than they deserved while Government and departments were busy considering the Industrial Relations Bill – one would have expected a realistic Prime Minister to have allowed for more *ad hoc* insertions in his programme – included two major crises, the bankrupting of Rolls-Royce and the liquidation of Upper Clyde Shipbuilders.

Both running into severe difficulties in November 1970, when the new Prime Minister had had only five months of acclimatization to adjust himself from the theories of shaking up industry and weeding out bad management to the practical necessity of retaining the country's most potentially valuable, if imperfect, technology and trade.

Rolls-Royce was Britain's fourteenth largest company in terms of man-power, with 80,000 employees. Its prestige was still greater, but Heath has never been one to worship graven images, and it is easy to imagine the contempt that must have accompanied disillusionment when the discovery was made that the fixed price contract Rolls had entered into for the RB-211 engine for the American Lockheed Air-bus meant a loss. The Government offered £42 million in aid in November 1970, but when, two months later, the financial gap had widened to some £150 million the decision was made to put in the official receiver, and later to salvage by nationalization the offending but nevertheless most valuable part of the company – the aero-engine section, plus those parts responsible for the marine and industrial gas turbine engines.

For a Government that had been proceeding with its plan to hive off the profitable parts of nationalized industry to have to undertake a rescue of an unprofitable concern by nationalization was sport indeed for its ideological enemies. In fact the snug fit of the two component parts of this newly shaped policy made good sense: the pity was that the solution was not imposed sooner.

Heath anyway seized upon it as a salutary lesson, and made the 'bitter shock' the subject of his speech to Young Conservatives in Eastbourne on 7 February (1970). Illusions of prosperity came in for the biggest stick in his speech; after those trailed the guilt of a compulsory wage freeze (Labour's) and the still spiralling inflation.

The interim help that had been forthcoming for Rolls – even though it was not enough to turn the tide – was withheld from Upper Clyde Shipbuilders because the Government did not, during the four months from November 1970 to March 1971 guarantee credits essential for the daily inflow of cash in the yards.

The rundown over more than twenty years, from the point when just after the war, Britain was producing half the world's shipping, had not been halted by infusions of public money under the Labour Government; once again losses on fixed price contracts were a major disaster. But there were figures to suggest that the slide had levelled out, and that recovery might be within grasp. Three ships were delivered in 1968, seven in 1969, twelve in 1971, and the projection for 1971 was fifteen. The Government itself held 48 per cent of the shares in the company; yet, seven long months after the first signs of desperation, the company went into liquidation. Scotland's unemployment was already double that of the national average: by February 1972 the figure on Clydebank was 12·1 per cent, or more than one man in eight out of work.

Someone as dedicated as Heath to the principle of standing on your own feet might well have viewed the work-in at the Clydebank yard, which was still going strong eight months after the original total shut-down was announced, as a resourceful and independent gesture. Heath lacked the perspective to take this point of view. 'They were using plant and equipment owned by somebody else to hinder the modern development of the yard, on which their livelihood depended,' he said when I suggested they had been upholding the right to work. 'They damaged the reputation of the Clyde.'[1] Even after his initial anger at having his authority flouted had subsided, he remained a reluctant compromiser with compromise. The

[1] Interview with the author, May 1972.

allowance for a new company providing 2,500 jobs was almost certainly an attempt to undercut the work-in; the decision, at the beginning of 1972, to suspend redundancies until the end of February showed a cooler assessment of the situation: but in both national and regional terms, and in terms of individual families, the situation remained tragic, and both the decision itself, and still more its timing, questionable.

The Government's final, long-awaited, and surprising decision to inject £35 million into three of the U.C.S. yards (and later to infuse more money to help private enterprise, American buyers, to save the fourth, the Clydebank yard itself) was one of the most courageous decisions and admissions combined made by the Prime Minister. It was a confession that the wrong arguments had been listened to.

The new complex, as envisaged, should salvage at least 4,000 jobs, Mr Davies, Secretary of State for Trade and Industry, was at pains to impress upon his audience. A new note of concern had crept in with the implied apology.

Perhaps delegation was partly to blame for the interim misjudgment of the situation: but undoubtedly Mr Heath's initial belief in shock therapy was another factor. The courage of eventually coming to a decision in accordance with the facts, some of which had been available and more of which should have been available at the time of the proposed complete liquidation, cannot put right the orders cancelled meanwhile, nor the hardship and anxiety suffered.

In the interim, however, Heath had displayed a manner in his handling of these crises, particularly the second, that disturbed even his most loyal followers. They saw them as a halt in his greater receptivity as Prime Minister. 'There's a greater willingness to question what he's said and done, and yet more confidence in his general line and ability to push it through. He's been able to do the hard things and show why,' said one; then added, 'but he can get carried away by annoyance at the incompetence – then there's a hard-faced image. U.C.S. was not handled right. It was surprising because he does care about people.'

It could be argued that lame ducks need the divine gift of new wings, not sympathy, and Heath certainly would have regarded as two-faced any display of the liberalism he terms simply 'wet' unless, as happened eventually, it was accompanied by help in cash.

So, for a time, Prime Minister and workers began to divide as they had not done for nearly half a century, retreating behind the Rightness of the Causes.

Inflation, the unseen enemy that Heath had named as his prime target when he came into office, had played a triple role throughout this period, the first twenty months of his administration.

Inflation had been at its greatest for many years during his first year in office, and was undoubtedly fanned by decimalization. Food prices in some cases influenced by world shortages caught up to a large extent with many of those specifics that had been cited as more expensive in the Common Market, and this incidentally reduced popular fear of entry on these domestic budgetary grounds. (It was, nevertheless, to Heath's credit that, meeting his then Minister of Agriculture, currently Joint Deputy Chairman of the Party, after he had added to the current furore by suggesting that housewives had not really expected to see prices cut 'at a stroke' – a remark of Heath's taken out of context in most arguments anyway – the Prime Minister merely remarked, 'Oh God, I was hoping to avoid you.')

In his second year of Government, inflation remained high, but the underlying anxiety it brought with it had a counter-balancing effect: it enhanced the fear of unemployment which was already considerable, since the basic figure had reached, after nineteen months of Heath's administration, a notifiable one million. It was the highest figure on record since the fuel crisis of 1947. Whether rising unemployment was, as the Prime Minister himself insisted, a product of inflation, or whether it was independent of this, it certainly began to play upon the desire to keep jobs.

This in turn slowly damped down the hot-blooded strike. Strikes had increased to new peaks in 1970 and climbed still higher in the first quarter of 1971, when the number of days lost through strikes was the highest since 1926.

But it also meant that any large strike was likely to have been calculated in cold blood, after hard examination of all the possible consequences, and was therefore less likely to be eroded by Government delay.

Was the procrastination on the miners' case in fact deliberately planned, as an attempt to take the steam out of the rank and file, and leave the leadership suspended without support, or was it merely the result of what could still, in a Prime Minister with less than two years operation of supreme power, be termed understandable in terms of inexperience?

It is an administration that has, according to Heath's own preference, always liked to have all the facts and to think carefully before acting. The faults springing from delay have varied in gravity, but cannot be compared with the hypotheses springing from actions untaken.

In this case it seems motives became a little less than clear, and inexperience was largely to blame in that the confusion was not recognized as such. In the event the fault proved pardonable only in that it stopped short of complete national disaster, although Heath may not for long forgive himself – or some of his colleagues – for arriving unprepared at the confrontation.

In a sense his very clarity of mind was responsible. His vision of the country's malaise and the cure he had ready-mixed, as he told Terry Coleman two weeks before he came to power, 'the key to everything is the creation of more national wealth',[1] was bound to conflict at some stage with the belief that he uttered in the next breath – the Salvation Army's tenet that 'you can't cast out the devil on an empty belly'.[2] In his mind these were parallel lines, meeting only at infinity. In fact they met in February 1972.

The declaration of a state of emergency, the plunging of the nation into darkness and cold after five weeks of knowing the miners' demands and refusing to meet them, was a declaration of the Government's last card. It failed to win, and thus it was to a great extent the economy that had been gambled with, and been lost.

Heath was not alone to blame for the crisis, but his was the major responsibility. For one thing, during the early stages of negotiation with the miners, he delegated too much. The killing of thirteen people in Londonderry on 30 January 1972, had finally focused the Prime Minister's complete attention on the problem of Northern Ireland, where it should have been earlier, and taken it away from the immediate danger at hand. The second vote on the Common Market seized another slice of his concentration. However, when restrictions on the use of electricity were announced on 11 February,

---

[1] Interview with Terry Coleman in the *Guardian*, 9 June 1970.
[2] Ibid.

Mr Heath himself warned that millions of people would be put out of work, and some jobs would be permanently at risk. At this point, therefore, he was completely cognizant of the enormous issues involved: yet no attempt was made to stem the loss of the nation's life-blood until after the results of the Wilberforce inquiry were announced on 18 February and by then the situation in most generating stations had deteriorated to such an extent that it took weeks for them, and industry, to recover. It was a gigantic miscalculation, and the consequences both direct and (by example) indirect could have been, could yet be, disastrous.

The recommendation of Wilberforce to give the miners increases of more than 20 per cent, when the target ceiling was only about 8 per cent, was an immediate undisguised defeat for Government policy. Some idea of the proportions of the problem is given by a comparison with the 'Guiding Light' policy of ten years before. In 1962 it was hoped to peg increases to a $2-2\frac{1}{2}$ per cent scale. The strikers' most powerful weapons had been first their economic strength, second, public sympathy, and third the force of their claim to be a special case, which was in fact argued on emotional as well as factual grounds – some miners' wages had actually gone down in recent years, and highly paid men were sharing their wages with those less fortunate.

Robert Carr, the Leader of the House of Commons, then the Secretary of State for Employment, who had been at pains to point out that the miners had been under considerably less duress than they would have been under a statutory incomes policy, was now at pains to keep the Government from a repetition of such pressures by pointing out that their case was 'wholly exceptional'. If so, wondered logical minds, should not the exception have been admitted in time, at a considerable saving to the nation; and in spite of all Mr Carr's protestations that this would have been impossible, why should it have been?

The virtual certainty that the miners would have accepted a lower offer had it come soon enough than they finally got under Wilberforce, and that therefore hundreds of millions of pounds had been squandered from the national kitty, was a bad enough result. Another and more far-reaching consequence of the strike was the realization, which had never till then been fully faced, that a group of essential workers could not be outflanked. Apart from the unprecedented style of picketing that was involved – and that, ironically, might have been considered actionable two weeks later under newly emergent sections of the Industrial Relations Act – there was the basic and irrefutable fact that other people could not work the mines, that a paratrooper could not use a pick without some extensive training, that for some coalface tasks, fifteen years was a usual apprenticeship – and that these facts had either not been discovered, or had not been taken into account.

It is specious to argue the Prime Minister calculated that such a stranglehold strike would never win public toleration again, and that therefore every day he delayed was a day to his future credit. If anything, he lent power to those very elements inclined to the use of violence which he chastised in his low-keyed speech a few days later. He had miscalculated not only about the outcome of the strike, but, worse, about its possible long-term effects: in this way, his righteous indignation, his fight for non-inflationary wage settlements, his industrial crusade, had fuelled precisely those forces that might seek to destroy the social fabric he was struggling to restore. St George had mistaken the tail of the dragon for its head.

Some salt must have been added to his own wound by his knowledge that few credited him with the least sympathy for the miners themselves, and this he not only had but was proud of having. Some months before, a young man of twenty-six was recommended for the job of Chairman of a New Town Development by Peter Walker. 'Has your chap left school yet?' he scathingly inquired of his Minister.

The day for the young man's interview duly arrived, and he spent more than twenty minutes answering the Prime Minister's questions in Downing Street. At the end of that time, Heath took him upstairs and showed him a painting he bought some years ago. It shows a miner drinking in a Durham bar. 'Are you going to be able to see that that man's children and grandchildren have a better quality of life than he did?' he demanded. Then, his mind made up, he concluded, 'You'd better get on with it.'

But, as so often, his aim was long term. His short-term plan demanded patience and self-sacrifice, the lessons in living learned from his own parents. Thus by projecting his ambitions so far ahead, from the miner himself to his children and grandchildren, Heath had missed a golden opportunity for immediate magnanimity.

The defeat stung sharply. But if his smile was a little stiffer for a few days, he was not a deeply defeated man, nor one who would linger on the spot. This defeat only sharpened his determination to halt one cause of inflation by refusing high wage claims; and this policy may turn out to be the most expensive or the most viable for many years.

Only two months after the miners' strike had hit the economy so hard, another strike of equal potential danger was threatened by the railway unions. They wanted a 14 per cent increase, refused the 11 per cent offered by British Railways, and even when an independent referee, Mr Alex Jarratt (who had been the first secretary of the Prices and Incomes Board set up under the previous Labour Government) suggested a settlement of $12\frac{1}{2}$ per cent, this was rejected.

It was Heath's chance – politically unwelcome, but not perhaps without some personal zest for such a competitive man – for a major confrontation between the Government and the Unions, and his first opportunity to try out the powers of the new Industrial Relations Court when Mr Maurice Macmillan, the Secretary of State for Employment, sought and the Court ordered a cooling off period and then a ballot, in which the railwaymen voted in favour of further strike action. It was moment of chagrin; British Rail's 13 per cent compromise was further proof of an untenable labour and wages policy.

He is a politician who has always played for high stakes: as Prime Minister he is playing almost deliberately for higher stakes still – it is understandable, in this context, that he has found the difficulties of his first two years in office stimulating more than worrying, although he says with a fleeting smile, 'we don't create problems in order to solve them'.[1]

Because of this he sometimes alarms his colleagues by his extreme temperament which is only just moderated by his caution.

'I think he has complete and total belief in the value of determination. I think the election victory did this for him – he believes that if you go on fighting in a most determined way you will win through in the end, despite what all the critics say,' deduced one of these. 'He may even believe this to a dangerous degree.'

[1] Interview with the author, May 1972.

'Don't lose your nerve, he will always say, and he believes if you stand firm and carry on you will win through.'

The same careful observer, and staunch supporter, of his leader, however, believed that at the end of his first year of office he had modified his view slightly on the two crucial and interdependent areas. 'One is the right or wisdom of unfettered private enterprise ... I think he would now accept there is great value in having basically a working understanding between the C.B.I. and the T.U.C. and the Government ... the idea of standing on your own feet he believes in, but he's modified it. When the occasion shows that it's going to lead to great social difficulties he would obviously modify his views on that.'

This change, obvious to one of his most intimate colleagues – who was in fact largely responsible for it – only a year after he came to power, was not glimpsed by some of the most influential men in the party machine, or the most perceptive press and television commentators, until another six months had elapsed. This was largely because when Heath does change his viewpoint he likes to do so privately, behind a screen on which he continues publicly to project his old image. Then, suddenly, having prepared his new ground completely, he emerges with, hopefully, no gaps in his new armour. This was how Northern Ireland was handled; and it was to be the same with his changing priorities in handling unemployment and the economy.

Until late in 1971 he was easily recognizable in the phrase, well-tongued among parliamentarians and party officials alike, 'the toughest politician I've ever known'. Part of this reputation was due to his psychological inaccessibility, and this part would remain intact in many eyes – those of the people who, however hard they tried, could not come to grips with his intangible mainspring. Another part of his reputation depended on his care for people in general rather than people in particular, and on his belief, as one man put it, that 'he believes things are more important than people'. It was here that some began to have perceptions of a change, not in his avowed purpose and aims, but in his order of priorities for those aims, after he had been in office for some eighteen months.

The first evidence of this was scattered: in the nationalization of part of Rolls-Royce and still more in the decision to salvage part of U.C.S. in the hope that it might prove profitable but knowing that it probably would not, in a grant for Harland and Wolff which, noted a friend, 'would never have come under the most strident days of free market economy', in greater willingness to talk to the Unions. 'Where there is an industry which can be viable, Government is justified in helping it,' said the Prime Minister, and recalled a precedent in the Conservatives' £19m. aid for the reconstructing of the cotton industry in the late 1950s. 'One would rather have the widest area of agreement,' he said in May 1972, and cited this attitude in the regions and an annual review of pensions as two examples of accord.

Then, with the Budget in 1972, came a bunched rephrasing of policy. Anthony Barber, the Chancellor of the Exchequer, revealed the kernel central to all policy changes and reversals when he said 'the upward trend in unemployment was partly the result of very slow growth in 1970'.[1] Only a year before, investment grants and the Industrial Reorganization Corporation had been abolished, as part of the Government's belief in a free market. But now, in 1972, Mr Barber said it was their purpose to 're-establish the regional differentials', even to give 'development areas a more clear-cut preference than any previous system', and to extend grants to plant and machinery, as well as allowing for free depreciation.

Faced with the implication of consensus politics, Mr Heath was at pains to emphasize the differences from Labour's similar methods: 'These are not universal grants but are concentrated in the development areas. This is different from Labour. And' (seeing my smiles) 'the differences are important. In the context of going into Europe, regional policy will fit in perfectly.'

Samuel Brittan commented in the *Financial Times* 'one cannot help but mention that all the Chancellor's regional incentives were such as to make capital intensive projects particularly profitable in regions where labour is surplus.'[2]

Particularly remarkable to those who remembered Heath's stern attitude to Labour's devaluation in 1967 was Mr Barber's statement that 'it is neither necessary nor desirable to distort domestic economies to an unacceptable extent in order to maintain unrealistic exchange rates.'[3]

---

[1] *Hansard*, vol. 833, col. 1346 ff, 21 March 1972.
[2] *Financial Times*, 22 March 1972.
[3] *Hansard*, vol. 833, col. 1345, 21 March 1972.

In other words, devaluation would not be abjured if unemployment made it seem desirable: for devaluation would, by making British goods cheaper, increase exports, increase demand and growth, and should therefore bring down the number of those without work. The decision to float the pound was the interim solution to these internal pressures.

Thus the Prime Minister's first priority of 'getting on top of inflation' had apparently given way to 'getting on top of unemployment', partly perhaps because of an improved though still volatile balance-of-payments position. But forecasts about unemployment continued to be gloomy[1] again. Heath had procrastinated far too long. Compared with the tenor of discussion and decisions at Selsdon Park just over two years previously, when finances, cutting taxes, and controlling the Unions had taken precedence and shown the sharp edge of policy, this budget showed a greater concern with people, with the availability of work, perhaps on moral and humane as well no doubt as purely political grounds.

A few believed the new emphasis meant that Heath had never truly believed in the demands and risks of a free market. Others, particularly those who had gone through the gruelling procedure of influencing him towards his new attitudes, were a little wary of how far he might take his new determination. The change was even camouflaged by those who feared either that the party would lose credibility as the result of such changes, or that it would antagonize (that constant danger) its own Right wing, or that, worst of all, Heath would once more find himself labelled weak, as he had been over Rhodesia and as some in the Cabinet had feared he might in making his Northern Ireland initiatives.

Therefore colleagues were guarded in describing the change. 'It's true that he cares about unemployment more, but this is only as the figures have risen,' said one of them. 'I think for him 700,000 unemployed is a tolerable figure in a shakeout period, but one million is totally unacceptable. The turning point was about last October (1971) when he could see that the July measures were not bringing down unemployment. By that time some people had convinced him – and had convinced a lot of other people too – that the process of

---

[1] Forecast by the Institute of Social and Economic Research, published June 1972, predicted 750,000 out of work in January 1973.

weeding out, of displacement, was going to go on very much longer. And by October he decided that this was quite intolerable. The number of times I've heard him say, "We've just got to get on top of this unemployment", and not in terms of politics, because it's advisable, but emotionally, because he feels the figure is utterly wrong.' He himself said, 'Unemployment is always important. It is a waste of people's lives, damaging and demoralizing to any individual.' For a man who would always rather err on the side of sounding harder than he is – though he is often clever enough to use ambivalence as a matador uses his cape – this was a forthright condemnation.[1]

Meanwhile, the Government had acted against unemployment by bringing forward public investment schemes, roads, schools and hospitals. These were carefully timed to use up resources in the short term while there was spare capacity. By 1973 the private sector should need those resources itself to keep up its growth.

The logic of drawing a line between an endurable 700,000 out of work, but an unbearable one million, sounds strange: but it fits the usual pattern of the recurring battle between pragmatism and principle in Heath. There comes on many issues a point when, suddenly, he has to halt, where compromise is no longer acceptable, where conscience must have its own way even if it points a finger out of office. In this case it is unlikely to do that, although the desire to maintain the image of impenetrable toughness in the eyes of the Unions and his own Right wing alike show, indirectly, his vulnerability in changing.

In his constancy towards Europe, however, there was a great emotional advantage: the successful outcome of the negotiations in 1971 under Geoffrey Rippon, the Minister for Europe, owed an uncharted amount to Heath's own patience, persistence, and underlying warmth in the 1960–63 negotiations. And, whatever else he does, taking Britain into Europe is likely to be this Prime Minister's greatest achievement. Here his insight is deep, his sympathies genuine, his ambition creative. Just after the 1966 election, the *Sunday Times* pointed out in a leader that the loser had one advantage: 'We shall not get into Europe merely by canny politics and hard bargaining: we may get in if we possess a common enthusiasm and a

[1] Interview with the author May 1972.

common belief in Europe. This is something Mr Heath understands and that Mr Wilson so far does not.'

This was right. But love was not left to find its way unguided even between the pragmatic, efficient and far-sighted compatibilities of Mr Heath and M. Pompidou with their shared view of a more influential Europe. The omens for the meeting between Heath and Pompidou had been good since, less than three weeks after President de Gaulle's veto in 1963, Pompidou, then Prime Minister of France, had privately told people, 'In the end, at the end, Britain must be in. The normal role of Britain is to be a part of Europe because it is so closely linked by history and geography. But this will mean, undoubtedly, a great historical change for Britain.'[1] Success was due to the warmth of the thing and the fact that the difficulties were wished out of the way,' says one of his Cabinet colleagues – true enough since Commonwealth sugar, New Zealand butter and fisheries were all left on trust – 'but everything that could be was carefully planned and carefully sewn up. The meeting with Pompidou was the turning point. He came back certain that we could make it, and like a good general having found a gap in the enemy he would have liked to pour through.'

The Prime Minister was restrained from immediate action by his more cautious colleagues. That he gave in to a Cabinet whose view on the best time for preparing the country and taking a vote opposed his own, showed that he had far greater trust in them all than he had when he won the election almost single-handed. Yet such was his personal involvement in Europe that he would not even speak to a member in the House who did not support him on the Common Market.

Europe, he believes, after it has given its original therapeutic shock of competition to this country, will be our salvation and give Britain back her place in the world.

Similarly, becoming Prime Minister has given him the place he always felt should be his in the world. Outwardly he has, as friends put it, 'matured and flowered'. Inwardly, he will always strive for perfection, to the bewilderment of a great number of his fellow men, but, seldom, one would guess, particularly in the presence of more powerful opposition on both sides of the House, to their eventual detriment.

[1] *International Herald Tribune*, 19 May 1962, quoted by C. L. Sulzberger.

His own eyes are fixed on the future, which may be as well, since he is a man truly appreciated by very few of his contemporaries. The moments must be sweet for him when someone like Georg Solti, who had just received his K.B.E. from the hands of the Prime Minister at Covent Garden turned to a companion and said 'Anyway, what a wonderful country, what a marvellous country, where the Prime Minister – the Prime Minister! – turns to me and says "That chord – was it D sharp or D sharp minor?" '

Others may regret that Edward Heath, a man who, if he had followed a slightly different path might have known enormous contentment, has only known happiness. He does not.

One can trace the outline of the future. Once, when he was asked about Glyndebourne's function, he replied that they should not be governed by policy derived from a questionnaire of what the people want: instead, they 'ought to get on with their original job of giving us superlative Mozart performances'.

That is his perfectionist, narrow, but brave view of Government.

Index